Chasing Bandits

Chasing Bandits
America's Long War on Terror
Michael E. Neagle

The University of North Carolina Press CHAPEL HILL

© 2025 Michael E. Neagle
All rights reserved
Manufactured in the United States of America
Set in Merope by Rebecca Evans

Material in chapter 2 previously appeared as "A Bandit Worth Hunting: Pancho Villa and America's War on Terror in Mexico, 1916-1917," *Terrorism and Political Violence* 33, no. 7 (2021): 1492–1510.

Library of Congress Cataloging-in-Publication Data
Names: Neagle, Michael E. author
Title: Chasing bandits : America's long war on terror / Michael E. Neagle.
Description: Chapel Hill : The University of North Carolina Press, [2025] | Includes bibliographical references and index.
Identifiers: LCCN 2025029655 | ISBN 9781469691039 cloth alk. paper | ISBN 9781469691046 paperback alk. paper | ISBN 9781469684741 epub | ISBN 9781469691053 pdf
Subjects: LCSH: Aguinaldo, Emilio, 1869-1964 | Villa, Pancho, 1878-1923 | Sandino, Augusto César, 1895-1934 | Guevara, Che, 1928-1967 | Escobar, Pablo | Bin Laden, Osama, 1957-2011 | Unlawful combatants—Government policy—United States—Case studies | Non-state actors (International relations)—Government policy—United States—Case studies | Terrorism—Prevention—Government policy—United States—Case studies | United States—History, Military—20th century—Case studies | BISAC: HISTORY / United States / General | POLITICAL SCIENCE / Terrorism
Classification: LCC E745 .N43 2025
LC record available at https://lccn.loc.gov/2025029655

For product safety concerns under the European Union's General Product Safety Regulation (EU GPSR), please contact gpsr@mare-nostrum.co.uk or write to the University of North Carolina Press and Mare Nostrum Group B.V., Mauritskade 21D, 1091 GC Amsterdam, The Netherlands.

For Olivia and Ethan

Contents

List of Illustrations ix
Acknowledgments xi

Introduction 1

CHAPTER ONE
A Savage War 9
Emilio Aguinaldo in the Philippines

CHAPTER TWO
Hunting the Outlaw 33
Pancho Villa in Mexico

CHAPTER THREE
A Plain Bandit 55
Augusto Sandino in Nicaragua

CHAPTER FOUR
The Elusive Guerrilla 77
Che Guevara in Bolivia

CHAPTER FIVE
Dawn of Narcoterror 102
Pablo Escobar in Colombia

CHAPTER SIX
The Terrorist Apotheosis 127
Osama bin Laden in Afghanistan

Conclusion 151

Notes 159
Bibliography 181
Index 193

Illustrations

FIGURES

Puck magazine cover, 1899   17

Water cure in the Philippines, undated   22

Pancho Villa, 1911   37

Washington Evening Star political cartoon, 1916   43

Augusto Sandino, 1928   62

US Marines with Sandinista flag, 1932   73

Che Guevara, 1960   84

Body of Che Guevara, 1967   97

Pablo Escobar, 1988   106

Body of Pablo Escobar, 1993   122

Osama bin Laden, 1998   135

Bin Laden's compound in Abbottabad, Pakistan, 2011   146

MAPS

The Philippines   8

Northern Mexico   34

Western Nicaragua   56

Bolivia   89

Colombia   108

Afghanistan and Pakistan   126

Acknowledgments

My inspiration for this project came from early iterations of an undergraduate course I teach at Nichols College about the global war on terror. This conflict has resonated with many of my students, some of whom have been active participants in combat. I thought it important to develop a class that considered the deeper roots of the campaign to better explain how we got to this point—and why the fight endures. Thus, I have written this book with such students in mind.

A few, in particular, bear mention. Benjamin Davidson and Michaela Gamache served as helpful research assistants at a time when this book was getting off the ground. Their deep dives into relevant newspaper articles for chapters 1 and 2 helped me sharpen my rhetorical analysis, not only for those sections, but for the remainder of the book as well. Tom Cunningham, Chad Fischer, and Liam Meagher also provided validation for this project with their questions and curiosity during many sessions of my weekly student hours.

Faculty and administrative support at Nichols has been a great gift. Hans Despain was my strongest cheerleader and advocate throughout this endeavor as he has been throughout my tenure at the college. Boyd Brown, my terrorism studies program collaborator, was a great sounding board in helping me work through a variety of ideas. Paul Lambert and Emily Thomas have provided a friendly and encouraging cohort of historians that I do not take for granted. Nor do I overlook kind and supportive colleagues like Karol Gil-Vasquez, Prajjwal Panday, Jim Deys, Kellie Deys, Serkan Demirkilic, and Julio Elias, who checked in with me often and cheered each milestone of the project. I'm also grateful to Dan Borgia, Nick Barnes, Maureen Butler, Andrea Becker, and Alex Smith for their administrative help. At the Conant Library, Rosalba Onofrio, Carrie Grimshaw, and Sarah Strom patiently filled my (numerous) interlibrary loan requests. College trustee Robert "Kuppy" Kuppenheimer deserves special mention for his generous financial support to Nichols faculty over the years that enabled me to go to archives and conferences.

This book was strengthened tremendously by conversations and correspondence with some exceptionally sharp and generous people. Chief among them is Dominic DeBrincat. Any writer would be lucky to have a reader half as diligent, patient, and constructive, much less one who peppers his incisive suggestions with hilarious memes and images. Typically, I brace myself for any reader feedback I get, fearing the worst. Not with Dom. I'm also lucky to still have access to the sage advice of Frank Costigliola. My graduate mentor when I was at the University of Connecticut still cheerfully answers the call whenever I need him, as I often did while I was working on this book. Likewise, there were many people across the community of historians who lent me their insights on specific chapters or broader aspects of this project. They include Caitlin Carenen, Omar Dphrepaulezz, Joseph Gonzalez, Antonio Hernández-Matos, John Kincheloe, Alan McPherson, Aaron O'Connell, Chad Reid, Joe Stieb, Catherine Thompson, and Thomas Westerman. I'm also grateful for questions and suggestions from audience members at various professional conferences where I presented pieces of my work, particularly at the New England Historical Association (NEHA), Society for Historians of American Foreign Relations (SHAFR), Historians of the Twentieth Century United States (HOTCUS), and the Northeast Popular Culture Association (NEPCA).

At the University of North Carolina Press, Debbie Gershenowitz continues to be my publishing champion. This is the second time we have worked together on a book. Her enthusiasm for this project, especially when it was just a half-baked idea after I finished my first book, was a great source of validation that I had something worth pursuing. The team around her has been extraordinarily helpful, including her assistant, Alexis Dumain, as well as the publisher's two anonymous reviewers who provided thoughtful and trenchant feedback. Similarly, I had the benefit of comments from two other anonymous reviewers at *Terrorism and Political Violence* for a version of chapter 2 that appeared as an article in that journal.

Sadly, a couple of important people to my project are no longer here to see its completion. The idea for chapter 4 came from a carpooling conversation I enjoyed with colleague and fellow suburban Connecticut resident Mark Naigles. (Over the years, he patiently redirected many a student email incorrectly sent to him because our last names sound so similar.) Also, my mother-in-law, Margaret Silverman, who frequently—but never impatiently—checked in on my progress with the book. I think it would have made a nice addition to her ever-present Kindle.

Once again, my family has been the deepest source of support and encouragement throughout this process. My words of appreciation here barely capture the immense gratitude I have for them. They are my life's greatest blessing. My parents, Thomas and Elda Neagle, and brother, Robert, have been generous in so many ways — lending an ear, offering advice, promoting my work, and consistently ensuring that I'm well-fed. (Robert doesn't cook, but he's quick to pick up a check.) I could not ask for a more understanding partner than my wife, Susan. She graciously accepted my many research, writing, and conference trips while dutifully holding the fort at home. That includes our most recent addition, Rex. I was on sabbatical when we rescued him as a two-month-old puppy. He kept me on task, though, as I was able to write chapters 4 and 5 in between his frequent snoozes. My children, Olivia and Ethan, don't take naps anymore. If they did, perhaps I would have finished this book sooner. But watching them grow, learn, and develop into their own individuals has been a worthwhile investment of time and energy. To them, I dedicate this book with my love and admiration.

Chasing Bandits

Introduction

The world had never seen anything quite like it before.

The September 11, 2001, attack on the United States was the deadliest terrorist operation of all time, killing nearly 3,000 people. Much of the violence and destruction was captured on live television and would be replayed over and over for all to see. Although nationals of more than eighty countries died that day, the mission was aimed primarily against Americans. The nation was left stunned, saddened, fearful, and angry.

In response, President George W. Bush called for a "global war on terror," ostensibly to punish the planners—suspected to be part of Osama bin Laden's al-Qaeda network based in Afghanistan—and to prevent anything like 9/11 from happening again. "This will be a different type of war than we're used to. . . . This is a different type of enemy than we're used to," Bush warned.[1]

But the world had seen the United States engage in such wars and pursue such enemies before. Many times.

Since the turn of the twentieth century, the United States has been involved in a variety of operations to hunt down the same kinds of foreign foes as it has in the global war on terror (GWOT). Before the chase for bin Laden in Afghanistan, there were grueling military campaigns in the Philippines, Mexico, and Nicaragua, as well as covert missions in Bolivia and Colombia. In these cases, the enemies were nonstate actors, meaning they did not formally represent the countries from which they hailed or fought. These adversaries often operated in the shadows, employed a small cadre of loyal fighters, and nursed diverse grievances against US policy that compelled them to threaten or perpetrate violence in the name of their respective causes.

Their challenges to US interests and security earned them Americans' wrath within a framework that has maintained a remarkable consistency over time. The words used to describe them provide clear illustrations of this continuity. In the past, the danger was often couched in the language of "bandit," "savage," or "guerrilla." In the present, the term used most frequently is "terrorist." Although there are certainly important distinctions among these terms, such meanings in popular discourse have been essentially the same.

The terms connote criminality, incivility, and illegitimacy of both cause and means. A brief chronology reveals this constancy.

In the early twentieth century, combatants who engaged in unlawful violence—that is, not sanctioned by a state or respecting international conventions of warfare—were typically called "bandits." Historian Eric Hobsbawm's classic work on banditry describes them as "men outside the range of law and authority... violent and armed, [who] impose their will by extortion, robbery or otherwise on their victims." Hobsbawm's assessment emphasized social banditry—outlaws who confronted rural elites by fighting for justice or liberation and emerged as local heroes within peasant societies. Among contemporary American audiences, however, the term "bandit" was thoroughly pejorative. Rather than fighting for justice or liberation, the emphasis was on criminality and illegitimacy. There is little evidence in the historical record of US officials attributing any honor or nobility when using the term "bandit."[2]

Similarly, Americans of this era also commonly referred to irregular fighters from abroad as "savages." The term called to mind US settler clashes with American Indians waged over centuries. In the early twentieth-century context, the term was loaded with racial implications. The combatants in question were nonwhite peoples that many white Americans widely considered to be less developed than those of European descent. Such peoples generally came from tropical areas that were simply too hot and inhospitable to political, economic, and social improvement—or so the stereotype went. Climatic conditions had stunted their development. They lacked self-control or a grasp of modern sensibilities. It was out of primitive instinct, then, that they fought using objectionable tactics like sneak attacks, targeting civilians, and mutilating corpses.[3]

By midcentury, another term was becoming more commonly used to address such unscrupulous methods and fighters: "guerrilla." The term originated during the early nineteenth-century Spanish insurgency against French emperor Napoleon Bonaparte. But its hit-and-run methods had been used well before that conflict and continue to be employed around the globe by smaller, weaker forces against stronger militaries. Thus groups in authority have viewed this type of warfare with contempt. Moreover, critics dismissed such fighters as "professional revolutionaries" to suggest they were not true believers of a cause or were puppets of more sophisticated masters. During the Cold War era, many American observers presumed that the Soviet Union was pulling the strings behind these forces.[4]

By the mid-1970s, the term "terrorist" grew into vogue to describe such actors. The concept has been around for millennia but was first labeled as such during the French Revolution. Following the 1972 murder of Israeli Olympic team members at the hands of Palestinian militants in Munich, Germany, politicians and scholars began using "terrorist" more frequently. Scholars have long debated a precise definition. Yet in almost all considerations, the use or threat of unlawful violence to achieve a political or social objective is at its core. Above all, terrorism is a tactic—a means to an end; it's not an ideology or a worldview. It is also a subjective term applied to different actors depending on one's sympathies but almost always used derogatively. The term's application suggests that the kind of violence wrought by practitioners is outside acceptable moral bounds. Terrorism is widely considered an illegal and uncivil form of warfare. Those who engage in such practices, then, forfeit any claims to legitimacy.[5]

This book is less concerned about whether the individuals considered here should be labeled "bandits" or "terrorists." I take it as a given that many Americans in their time presumed they were. Rather, I explore how and why they were framed that way as well as the broader consequences of that depiction. To that end, I maintain that these pejorative descriptions have had two distinct utilities: one, to rally popular and political support in the United States by intimating cultural distinctions that suggested or reinforced a sense of American superiority, and two, to justify incursions abroad that provided the United States with more influence in places of strategic interest.

For those reasons, the examples I consider take place during the age of American empire. Although a compelling case can be made that the United States has been an empire since independence, historians generally agree that it has been one since the Spanish-American War of 1898. At that point, the United States secured extracontinental territory (Philippines, Puerto Rico, Guam, Hawai'i) and began exerting more influence in global affairs. Contemporary proponents of this expansion cited a variety of justifications. Some had commercial incentives to preserve an open door to markets and resources abroad that would be good for American businesses and sustain a consistently robust US economy. Others were inspired by a sense of racial, ethnic, and cultural superiority over nonwhite peoples considered to be less sophisticated or civilized. There also was an unmistakable missionary zeal to spread American customs in the belief that by making "them" more like "us," peace, order, and stability around the world would follow. To that end, protecting pliant governments that supported US interests served as another rationale to exert power abroad.[6]

In Latin America, these elements were all acutely evident. Not coincidentally, four of the case studies considered here are set in the region. By virtue of its proximity to the United States, Latin America was where US policymakers and power brokers honed various imperialistic approaches over the years—territorial, political, commercial, cultural—before doing likewise elsewhere around the world. American military power often supported this framework. In the early twentieth century, presidential administrations frequently sent troops to protect US interests, particularly in Central America and the Caribbean. But when such ventures grew more unpopular at home and abroad, covert missions or military aid to local allies became more common, especially during the Cold War era.[7]

This broadening US presence created repeated conflicts with those who resisted American influence. As the stories in this book show, these challengers had different motivations: win independence, exact revenge, achieve sovereignty, inspire liberation, enjoy entrepreneurial freedom, ensure cultural and religious purity. Their commonality, though, was that they all engaged in irregular warfare. They used these tactics not necessarily because of some ideological or cultural deficiency but rather to account for overwhelming US military superiority, especially in terms of technology. Yet US leaders faced strategic dilemmas about how to fight effectively against such unconventional foes whose approaches neutralized American advantages. The result, in the cases considered here, was that US engagements bent or broke established rules of war at times. If the enemy was using unlawful or unscrupulous methods to fight, then US combatants often felt justified doing likewise.

Popular rhetoric implicitly supported these rationalizations by suggesting that those who were not considered to be fully civilized men should not be treated as such. Americans portrayed these foes in dehumanizing terms, particularly as animals, insects, or specters. They were described as primitives, considered less developed because of their racial or ethnic background or less masculine by dint of their methods or behaviors. Moreover, these kinds of depictions, reinforced through terms like "bandit" or "terrorist," purposefully ignored these men's grievances—regardless of validity—and stymied national reflection about the costs and consequences of American expansion abroad.

This book tells the fascinating story of these pursuits. I explain the threats and challenges these enemies presented, describe the tactics employed to find them, analyze the rhetoric used to rally support against them, and consider the pursuits' broader consequences to the United States and the places where these foes were hunted. The missions were often costly endeavors in terms of lives and treasure and usually ended paradoxically. In places where the chases failed, the United States' larger objective was nonetheless achieved, whereas successful hunts rarely stymied the wider conflict.

Each target seized the imaginations of ordinary Americans in their day. Although there are certainly other examples of infamous twentieth-century international terrorists, such as Carlos the Jackal or Abu Nidal, they did not take direct aim at the United States to the same extent as the individuals I spotlight. This book also does not consider foreign enemies like Adolf Hitler, Joseph Stalin, or Saddam Hussein because they were heads of state. US tensions with those rivals produced conflicts on a different scale from the ones I consider here.

Given that the formal GWOT began more than two decades ago, ample time has passed in which to consider it historically. This broader perspective reveals that the hunt for bin Laden—the centerpiece of the GWOT—was not unique in US history. The American pursuit of similar men during the age of empire bears remarkable comparisons. As I explore with students, the fundamental question in the study of history is to assess change or continuity over time. This is not to suggest that these comparisons with past situations are exact; indeed, I subscribe to the aphorism often attributed to author Mark Twain that history does not repeat itself, but it often rhymes. Nevertheless, examining historical actors' language, attitudes, and tactics provides an illuminating window into past perceptions while exposing a crucial connective tissue across these seemingly disparate threats and conflicts. Such considerations offer a way to think about the GWOT as more than just a modern, Middle East–centric conflict.

Chapter 1 examines the US campaign against Emilio Aguinaldo in the Philippines beginning in 1899. Aguinaldo had briefly been an ally against Spain but turned on the Americans when the United States annexed his native land from the defeated Spanish rather than granting it independence. He then directed a decentralized rebellion from the Philippine hinterlands. Reports of Aguinaldo-led insurgents committing atrocities by killing prisoners and desecrating bodies compelled American politicians and the press to call Aguinaldo savage and uncivilized. Yet Americans, likewise, were accused of their own brutalities such as razing villages suspected of aiding rebels and using the "water cure," a tactic that later drew comparisons to twenty-first-century waterboarding. When the resistance expanded to the Moro Province in the southern Philippines, US forces were confronted by a Muslim-majority population that was commonly framed as barbaric and degenerate for its customs and fighting style.

In March 1916, a militia led by Francisco "Pancho" Villa raided the US-Mexican border town of Columbus, New Mexico, and killed eighteen Americans. It was one of the deadliest attacks by a private foreign party on US soil until September 11, 2001. News of the raid sparked outrage across the United States. Americans commonly referred to Villa as a bandit, a savage, an outlaw, and, even more dehumanizingly, a dog that had to be put down or an insect that must be exterminated. The military expedition to find Villa, which is the subject of chapter 2, brought the United States and Mexico to the brink of war. Goading the United States into a potentially destructive conflict was precisely the result that Villa had hoped to achieve as a way to get revenge against his former American allies and his rival Mexican revolutionary leaders.[8]

Augusto Sandino's rebellion against the US military presence in Nicaragua is addressed in chapter 3. Eager to keep peace between rival political factions in its Central American "backyard," the United States stationed marines in the country from 1927 to 1933 much to Sandino's chagrin. He viewed the American presence as a violation of Nicaraguan sovereignty. Sandino's campaign engaged in hit-and-run guerrilla tactics and occasionally mutilated the bodies of fallen US forces and their local allies. President Herbert Hoover called the elusive Sandino "a plain bandit," which became a commonly used term that positioned Sandino and his men as outside the bounds of legitimate resistance. It also suggested that the US response to that resistance did not have to abide by legitimate methods. To that point, Americans did not consider captured Sandinistas as "prisoners of war" and thus entitled to protections of international law—a legal argument that the Bush administration would make about detainees in the twenty-first-century GWOT.

Ernesto "Che" Guevara was one of the most famous men in the world when in 1965 he vanished from public view. A native Argentine, he had served in Cuba's revolutionary government before resigning to foment wars of liberation elsewhere in the world against US imperialism. US officials' Cold War–era anticommunist concerns about Guevara's influence is the basis for chapter 4. To undercut Guevara's platform, American observers used the term "guerrilla" as an epithet to suggest the illegitimacy, illegality, and lack of sophistication of his preferred approach to revolution. Some Americans referred to Guevara as a "professional revolutionary" to imply he didn't really believe in his cause and was fighting only for personal glory. At the same time, US officials recognized that Guevara was charismatic and eloquent, characteristics that could seduce people into accepting his anticapitalist ideology. This fear led to covert US efforts in the Congo and Bolivia to find Guevara.

Not all challengers to American empire were true revolutionaries. Colombia's Pablo Escobar, as covered in chapter 5, is a case in point. In the 1980s, he was one of the world's wealthiest men thanks to his role in the Medellín drug cartel. To protect his lucrative enterprise, he unleashed a wave of violence against the Colombian state. Yet he publicly portrayed himself as a businessman and a patriotic defender of the poor while framing his biggest fear—extradition to the United States—as an issue that undermined Colombian sovereignty. From Americans' perspective, Escobar became the face of the long-running "war on drugs." US officials referred to him as a "narcoterrorist" who threatened national security. This concern inspired a covert campaign of advisers from the Drug Enforcement Administration (DEA), Central Intelligence Agency (CIA), and Special Forces, as well as hundreds of millions of dollars of weapons, surveillance equipment and aid money to the Colombian government, to search for him.

Perhaps no foreign actor generated more animosity from Americans than Osama bin Laden, the subject of chapter 6. A wealthy and devoutly religious man, he eschewed a life of privilege to wage holy war against the United States at the turn of the twenty-first century. Bin Laden's aim was to transform the Middle East into an Islamist utopia and rid the region of America's secular and overbearing influence. To that end, he financed and organized a variety of attacks on the United States, culminating in 9/11. The public discourse about bin Laden drew from many of the same tropes addressed in other chapters—illegitimate, uncivil, inhuman—and framed him as a terrorist *par excellence*. To snuff out the threat of bin Laden and others of his ilk, Bush launched the GWOT. In this broad campaign over nearly a quarter century, the United States has conducted counterterrorism operations in more than eighty countries, including sustained military engagements in Afghanistan and Iraq, at an enormous cost in terms of lives and money.[9]

The narratives in this book purposely focus on threats to the United States from abroad. By no means have they been the only terrorist threats confronting the country. Indeed, domestic terror threats in the United States have been legion—from the Ku Klux Klan and anarchists in the late nineteenth and early twentieth centuries to Theodore Kaczynski (a.k.a., the Unabomber) and Timothy McVeigh in the 1990s, to right-wing white nationalists in the present. Yet terrorist or bandit threats from abroad provided unique challenges and opportunities for the burgeoning American empire. It is this intersection of terrorism and empire that I explore in this book.

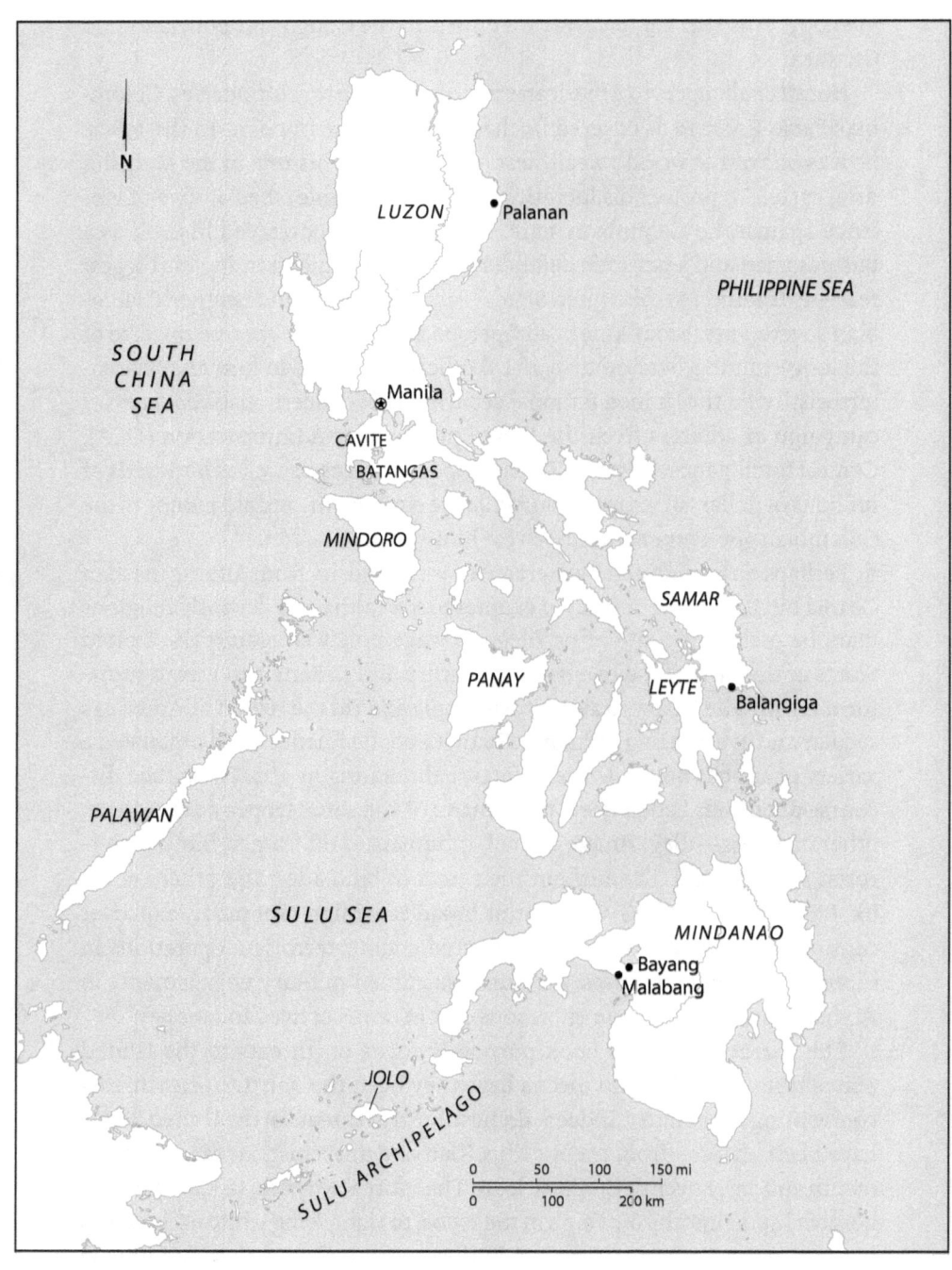

The Philippines

CHAPTER ONE

A Savage War
Emilio Aguinaldo in the Philippines

It was quiet when day broke on September 28, 1901. The men of Company C, Ninth Regiment of the US Infantry, were literally half a world away from home at their camp in Balangiga on the island of Samar in the Philippines, the newest colony of the United States. They were just settling in for breakfast before they were to begin their mission for the day. Nothing dangerous or glamorous. The troops were merely to do some sanitation duty and oversee an oath-taking ceremony among the townspeople. It looked to be an easy day.

It would be anything but.

As some of the men waited in the mess line around 6:45 a.m., a local police chief grabbed a rifle out of a soldier's hands. At that moment, church bells rang and hundreds of Filipinos—perhaps as many as 450—stormed out of the church and nearby jungle wielding bolos, a type of machete common in the Philippines. The attackers began hacking at the unarmed and unprepared US soldiers, killing many where they stood while seizing rifles and ammunition. It took an hour for Company C to get their bearings, grab their weapons, and repel the assailants. Not content to wait for a potential second wave, the surviving Americans escaped town via canoes. When they could catch their breath and take stock of what had happened, the shock began to settle in. Of the seventy-five men in Company C, forty-eight were killed or missing, with another twenty-one wounded. It was the military's worst defeat since Custer's Last Stand at Little Big Horn twenty-five years earlier.[1]

As sudden as the attack was to the Americans, it was not impulsive for the Filipinos. For the past two-and-a-half years, Filipino insurgents had been engaged in a small-scale, decentralized revolt against the US presence. Although the rebellion had slowed considerably by September 1901, the animosity was still palpable on Samar, the third largest of the Philippine islands. The insurgency had bred deepening resentment on both sides. In Balangiga, Company C had done little to win Filipino hearts and minds since arrival. The men often got into skirmishes with the locals, seized or destroyed food suspected of being earmarked for rebels, and harassed townswomen. The *insurrectos* saw an opportunity to strike. Some had come to town under the guise of sanitation workers. Others had entered the church disguised as women. Working with the police chief and a local priest, a plan was set in motion to get revenge on the unsuspecting Americans.

After news of the Balangiga massacre reached US military leaders in the Philippine capital of Manila, revenge was on American minds too. In October, General Jacob H. Smith arrived in Samar looking for vengeance on the insurgents and anyone who may have supported them. Smith was a Civil War veteran with the well-earned nickname "Hell-Roaring Jake" for ordering the execution of captured guerrillas. He sent out Maj. Littleton "Tony" Waller with orders to make Samar a "howling wilderness" by killing anyone over the age of ten carrying arms. "I wish you to kill and burn," Hell-Roaring Jake said. "The more you kill and the more you burn the better you will please me." Between October and December 1901, US forces killed or captured more than 759 *insurrectos* and destroyed 1,662 houses and 226 boats. During the campaign, Waller, who may have been suffering from delirium because of a fever, ordered the executions of eleven Filipino guides on the grounds they were holding out food from famished American troops. Reports of their activities led to public scrutiny of Waller and Smith, who were court-martialed. The repercussions, though, were miniscule. Waller was acquitted for the murder of the guides; Smith, a forty-one-year veteran of the military, was forced into retirement.[2]

The attack at Balangiga and the ensuing reprisal reflected a broader pattern that took place during the oft-forgotten Philippine-American War at the turn of the twentieth century. Shortly after the United States assumed sovereignty over the Philippines, Emilio Aguinaldo spearheaded an insurgency that began on the main island of Luzon before spreading throughout the archipelago. The rebellion drew American ire, not only for its audacity in challenging the United States, but more so for *how* rebels conducted themselves. Sneak attacks. Booby traps. Assassinations. Tortures and desecrations. American military men, politicians, and reporters considered these to be acts of savagery beyond the pale of civilized warfare. They derided Aguinaldo—and later the Muslim Moros of the southern Philippines—as criminals for the manner of their resistance. According to such logic, *insurrectos'* actions disqualified them from claiming political independence, which was supposed to be reserved for disciplined, responsible, law-abiding peoples. Moreover, insurgents' tactics justified brutal acts of retaliation and intimidation otherwise considered uncivilized or unethical. In the US attempt to put down these rebellions, soldiers often bent or broke recently established rules of engagement, creating a framework that would be used in future combat.

AS THE NINETEENTH CENTURY drew to a close, the United States sought "great power" status. Although politicians often liked to point out how a United States grounded in freedom, benevolence, and opportunity was different from European empires, in practice they followed many of the same templates. This approach was most notably evident in the seizure of colonies. Following war with Spain in 1898, the United States obtained the last vestiges of the Spanish empire—Puerto Rico, Guam, and the Philippines, along with a protectorate over Cuba. Acquisition of territory certainly was not new in American history. But what distinguished these additions was both their geographic distance from the heart of the United States and the absence of clamoring to make them full-fledged states. Instead, their value lay in their utility to project American power and—at least in the case of the Philippines—to use them as a stepping stone to potentially lucrative markets in Asia.

Moreover, the US presence in the Philippines presented an opportunity for Americans to take up the "white man's burden," as British poet Rudyard Kipling famously put it, and teach a backward people (read: nonwhite) how to be civilized. Politicians in the United States commonly presumed that racial inferiorities and centuries of Spanish domination left Filipinos unfit and unprepared for self-government. It would be irresponsible for the United States *not* to stay. President William McKinley presented the case in a February 1899 speech in Boston. In justifying US sovereignty in the Philippines, he imagined it would produce "a people redeemed from savage indolence and habits, devoted to the arts of peace, in touch with the commerce of trade of all nations, enjoying the blessings of freedom, of civil and religious liberty, of education, and of homes ... in the pathway of the world's best civilization."[3]

Setting aside the merits of such rationalizations, this mission would be no easy task. First, there was the problem of distance. The Philippine islands sit roughly 7,000 miles from the US West Coast. Getting men and materials there presented considerable supply chain problems (made somewhat easier by two other recent US acquisitions, Hawai'i and American Samoa). Additionally, the archipelago is made up of more than 7,500 islands covering some 115,000 square miles. A wide variety of ethnicities lived in the islands, many of which did not recognize much commonality with others as "Filipinos." With more than 100 languages spoken, the mere act of communication was a challenge.[4]

THE UNITED STATES was not the first great power faced with such issues in the Philippines. Spain had been managing these challenges since the sixteenth century, when it first staked its colonial claim to the Philippines' largest island, Luzon. This island was the stronghold of Spanish authority on the archipelago for nearly three centuries; its hold elsewhere—particularly in the south—was more tenuous because of the remoteness of many islands and the diversity of peoples.

By the 1890s, Filipino elites tired of Spanish dominion. In August 1896, an insurgent group known as the Katipunan began an armed rebellion. The rebels, led by thirty-two-year-old Andrés Bonifacio, enjoyed some initial success, rallying support and minor victories in the province of Cavite, south of Manila. But infighting among Katipunan factions stymied any prospect of triumph. In May 1897, Bonifacio lost a power struggle for leadership when he was arrested, tried, and executed by supporters of his rival, Emilio Aguinaldo, who would become the face of the revolution.[5]

Born in March 1869 of Tagalog (the Philippines' second-largest ethnic group) and Chinese ancestry, Aguinaldo came from a moderately well-to-do family in Cavite. As described by one contemporary American biographer, "Aguinaldo is short. His skin is dark. His head is large but well poised on a rather slight body. His hair is the shiny black of the Tagalog, and is combed pompadour, enhancing his height somewhat." He had some formal schooling but dropped out of a Manila prep school in his early teens. Aguinaldo joined the Katipunan during its nascent underground stages in the early 1890s and quickly rose up the ranks. Despite no formal military training, he was known in the group as *"generalissimo."* His strengths were twofold: a penchant to escape death or capture, and his abilities as a coalition-builder. Indeed, he proved to be a key link among urban elites (known as *ilustrados*), fighters, and local politicians, to the extent that he was widely accepted among Filipinos as the revolutionary leader after he disposed of Bonifacio.[6]

The rebels in Fall 1897 declared the Philippine Republic with Aguinaldo as president, but the rebellion stalled. The Spanish were eager to set this uprising aside while fighting a larger one in Cuba, its other major colony. In December, Aguinaldo signed the Pact of Biak-na-Bato, in which he agreed to cease hostilities and go into exile in Hong Kong in exchange for amnesty and 800,000 pesos. It would prove to be a temporary respite. Aguinaldo and his men did not receive all the agreed-upon money, which they used to justify their return. Aguinaldo then looked in early 1898 to align with a new ally that could help him achieve his ends: the United States.[7]

INDEED, AGUINALDO and the United States shared animosity toward the Spanish but for vastly different reasons. For Aguinaldo, it was on behalf of Filipino independence. For the United States, though, the Philippines was merely a sideshow; Cuba was the real target. United States policymakers and business leaders long had their eye on the jewel of the Spanish empire for commercial and geostrategic reasons. Cuba's War of Independence had generated a great deal of attention in the United States given the proximity of such a brutal conflict that claimed at least 200,000 lives. The McKinley administration placed the blame squarely on the Spanish government and threatened to step in to mediate—forcefully, if necessary. In April 1898, Congress supported McKinley's call for war and prepared to take on the reeling Spanish empire.

Following the axiom that "the enemy of my enemy is my friend," the United States and Aguinaldo's forces had ample reason to align. Looking to put pressure on one of Spain's weaknesses, the US military set its sights on the Philippines as the first point of attack. In February, a prescient Assistant Secretary of the Navy Theodore Roosevelt ordered Commodore George Dewey to anchor his fleet in Hong Kong, just 700 miles from Manila. Two months later, it would stage the first salvo in the war.

As fate would have it, Aguinaldo was in Hong Kong at the same time. He was seething over what he saw as Spanish treachery for the reneged money and the unfulfilled promised reforms for Filipino autonomy. Preparing for a seemingly inevitable war against Spain, US representatives met with Aguinaldo on at least two occasions. Aguinaldo later wrote that the Americans "urged me to return to the Philippines to renew hostilities against the Spaniards with the object of gaining our independence."[8]

On the morning of May 1, Dewey and his squadron of seven ships sailed into Manila Bay and decimated a comparably sized Spanish fleet. The lopsided body count reflected the totality of the US victory: 161 Spanish killed and another 210 wounded; just one American dead (of heat stroke) and nine injured. For the next two months, the US Navy established a blockade around Manila and thus a chokehold on Spanish control over the Philippines. While waiting for reinforcements, Dewey met with Aguinaldo on May 19 to discuss cooperation, the precise outlines of which remain in dispute. Aguinaldo claimed—writing in all capital letters for emphasis—that Dewey told him that "THE UNITED STATES WOULD UNQUESTIONABLY RECOGNIZE THE INDEPENDENCE OF THE PEOPLE OF THE PHILIPPINES." For his part, Dewey, in 1902 testimony to the US Senate, denied he made such assurances and maintained that he had never even heard of any desires for independence until the summer.[9]

Although Dewey did not consider himself to be in an alliance with Aguinaldo, he supported the Filipino's desire to fight the Spanish. Dewey figured such fighting would further erode enemy forces before US troops could arrive. To that end, he supplied Aguinaldo with guns and ammunition. The insurgents quickly went to work, pinning down Spanish forces around Manila during the summer. Aguinaldo proclaimed Philippine independence, including the formation of a government with an executive (himself), congress, and courts.

American reporting about Aguinaldo during the summer of 1898 shared a similar ambivalence about the Filipino leader and the merits of Philippine independence. On the one hand, outlets such as the *Minneapolis Journal* suggested the righteousness of Aguinaldo's cause, noting that he had been "betrayed by the Spaniards with promises of reform which were never kept and promises of pardon which were made to be broken." A correspondent for the *Philadelphia Inquirer* paid him the backhanded compliment of being the "smallest fighting machine in the world." On the other hand, the *Springfield (MA) Daily Republican* was deeply suspicious. Aguinaldo's acceptance of Spanish cash a year earlier made the newspaper skeptical about his true motivations, calling him "an ambitious, self-seeking, bribe-taking adventurer." Any people that would make someone like him a leader, it reasoned, were not ready to become an independent republic, and such a government "would prove as absurd as it would be weak and corrupt." Such contrasting reactions illustrated the different considerations that Americans had about Aguinaldo and the US presence in the Philippines. Supporters with legitimate anticolonial sympathies recognized Aguinaldo's usefulness in fighting Spain. Yet opponents and skeptics were wary of challenges to US interests and aligning with nonwhite partners.[10]

For its part, the teetering Spanish military was loath to surrender to rebels they looked down on. The United States was not keen on the idea, either, given the McKinley administration's indecisiveness about what to do with the archipelago after the war. Instead, US and Spanish forces agreed in August to stage a mock fight in Manila with a token exchange of gunfire after which the Spanish would surrender to the United States. Aguinaldo quickly sniffed out the conspiracy. Not only had the US military refused to let Filipino insurgents enter the capital city just as they were on the verge of victory, but Dewey also refused to meet with him or his men. Conditions would effectively remain in a holding pattern the rest of the year while US and Spanish representatives negotiated a formal end to the war. Yet it was clear that a new conflict was brewing between the United States and Aguinaldo's forces.[11]

EVEN IN THE BEST of circumstances, a military occupation of Manila was a difficult proposition. Given its tropical climate, residents and visitors had to cope with the perpetual heat, humidity, and rain. Moreover, the influx of refugees to the city after more than two years of fighting had boosted the city's population from 10,000 to an estimated 70,000. The local infrastructure struggled to handle the flood of people, especially when it came to sanitation. As a result, there were outbreaks of diseases, including typhus, malaria, and dengue.[12]

As it became clear that the United States would assume colonial control over the Philippines, tensions escalated between US forces and Filipino insurgents. For weeks, US troops and Filipinos traded insults—and, occasionally, gunfire. The boiling point came on February 4, 1899, as the US Senate prepared to vote on the Treaty of Paris that would formally end the war with Spain and make the Philippines a US colony. In the Manila suburb of Santa Mesa, members of the First Nebraska volunteers opened fire on perceived hostiles, killing three. Filipinos returned fire. Given the tinderbox of conditions, confusion, and competition for control, this shooting was the spark that set off the Philippine-American War.[13]

The following morning, the Battle of Manila began in earnest. At that point, forces loyal to Aguinaldo were at their peak, outnumbering the US Army in terms of combatants, weapons, and fighting experience. Yet they were unable to maintain their advantage. US forces smashed through Filipino lines along a sixteen-mile front. Undertaken much like a traditional battle with clearly delineated lines, the initial fighting proved to be the bloodiest of the war. The United States suffered 238 casualties, including forty-four killed in action. Estimates of Filipino casualties varied widely, maybe as many as 4,000, with some 700 to 1,000 killed in action. Soon after the battle, reports surfaced of US troops firing indiscriminately on civilians and prisoners. Aguinaldo wrote about the "ruffianly abuses which the American soldiers committed on innocent and defenseless people in Manila, shooting women and children simply because they were leaning out of windows; entering houses at midnight without the occupants' permission—forcing open trunks and wardrobes and stealing money, jewellery [sic] and all valuables they came across." At the same time, according to historian Brian Linn, "Americans accused their opponents of shooting at ambulances, litter bearers, Red Cross workers, and the wounded; of continuing to fire after raising a white flag; and of torturing a wounded doctor to death." Such perceptions and accusations of fighting dirty set the tenor of the war.[14]

In the first months of the conflict, it was important to Aguinaldo to fight as conventionally as possible. Filipino leadership was sensitive to claims—first by the Spanish, then by the Americans—that they were "uncivilized" and thus unfit for self-government. To disprove such characterizations and to demonstrate the legitimacy of their cause, they looked to prosecute the war according to US and European norms. This approach involved a clear hierarchy of command, taking and holding cities or territory, and portraying themselves as a genuine army rather than an insurgency.

But the conventional approach did not fare well. After Manila, US forces continued to rout the rebels, driving them from other key cities. Thomas Osborne of the First Tennessee Cavalry vividly recalled the destruction wrought from a US naval bombardment. He wrote to his sister that what he had witnessed "will never grow old to my memory. Every house in town was burned and I saw dead women, dead horses, dead men, dead dogs, dead cows and many burned people, and some with both legs shot off, others with one arm torn off and their carcasses lying partly in the fire and partly out." Similar scenes played out elsewhere in the archipelago, leading Aguinaldo to consider a drastic strategic shift.[15]

BY THE END OF 1899, Filipino rebels dropped their conventional battlefield approach and moved to a guerrilla campaign. Insurgent forces scattered into smaller, regional units, used hit-and-run tactics, and blended more effectively into the countryside to avoid detection. In later testimony to the US Senate, William Howard Taft, the future president who was the first US civilian governor of the Philippines, said that "without that system of terrorism the guerrilla campaign would have ended very quickly." Aguinaldo hoped to keep the war going long enough for it to become unpopular in the United States, where a loud anti-imperialist sentiment—voiced most prominently by the likes of author Mark Twain, industrialist Andrew Carnegie, and labor leader Samuel Gompers—advocated for getting out of the Philippines entirely. He figured that a bloody, costly, and lengthy war would sap Americans' will to fight and they would eventually leave.[16]

To that end, Aguinaldo's forces staged low-intensity strikes in small groups. Operating in decentralized cells, they seemed to be everywhere—and nowhere. According to Taft, "It was impossible to identify the guerrillas, who would dress like amigos at one time and then sneak out of the town . . . and become part of the insurgent force." They attacked vulnerable US patrols and supply wagons, cut telegraph wires, and took potshots into American-occupied towns before melting back into the countryside. The guerrillas set

Just weeks into the Filipino rebellion against the United States, in 1899, the popular humor magazine *Puck* depicted the firm hand of American might coming down on Emilio Aguinaldo, portrayed as a would-be dictator. Courtesy of the Library of Congress.

booby traps along trails to slow US troop movements. Although not responsible for a large loss of life, there were enough stories of the traps' deadly efficiency that made Americans think twice about every step they took. An unnamed American soldier told a reporter in 1902 about deep pits hidden in dense jungle trails with poisoned stakes at the bottom as well as spring-release spears with similar toxins. Another soldier wrote home: "While there is no enemy in sight... we are always on the lookout and we have slept in our shoes ever since we have landed."[17]

More than anything, US soldiers feared capture by insurgents. Stories abound of brutal treatment in captivity. For example, three Americans taken captive in November 1899 claimed to have been starved, slashed, and frequently subject to mock executions. Two of them managed to escape after six weeks to tell of their ordeal. American zoologist Dean Worcester, who spent eighteen years living in the Philippines and was part of two civilian commissions tasked with determining the US administration of the archipelago, reported even more macabre stories. One missing American was found crucified upside down and his "abdominal wall had been carefully opened so that his intestines might hang down his face." Another American prisoner "had been buried in the ground with only his head projecting. His mouth had been propped open with a stick, a trail of sugar laid to it through the forest, and a handful thrown into it. Millions of ants had done the rest."[18]

The more common targets of insurgents' ire, though, were other Filipinos who collaborated with or showed fealty to Americans. The effectiveness of American colonial government required such cooperation given the relatively few US officials present across the archipelago. According to Linn, "Many terrorist actions, especially the killing of collaborators, were not indiscriminate but rather directed against specific targets, carried out in front of numerous witnesses, and publicized heavily. By publicly assassinating an Army guide or a collaborating *presidente*, they not only removed a dangerous threat but deterred potential *americanistas*."[19]

The ways in which victims were killed compounded the terror. Some American sympathizers were said to have been burned alive. Others allegedly had their tongues cut out. In one instance, militia units in a remote area of northern Luzon hacked to death thirty *americanistas*. Records of such attacks were spotty, so there is no way to determine precisely how many supposed sympathizers were killed. But of recorded assassinations, roughly one-quarter were civic officials entrusted with administering order under the colonial government. While such attacks certainly disrupted US efforts to establish civil government, some locals fought back. In the village of Bucay in northern Luzon, guerrillas had targeted chiefs for kidnapping and murder. Linn wrote that "this terrorism, however, turned the town solidly against the guerrillas and soon armed villagers were accompanying the [American] soldiers on expeditions."[20]

NEWS OF THESE ATTACKS prompted visceral reactions from Americans at home. Newspapers, politicians, and military personnel in the United States called insurgent tactics uncivilized and criminal. The *Meriden (CT) Morning Record*, for example, opined that "there is no longer any pretense on the part of Aguinaldo and his followers of maintaining anything approaching civilized warfare. His armies are composed wholly of Tagal [sic] bandits." Likewise, Gen. Arthur MacArthur, who served as military governor of the Philippines in 1900–1901, claimed that as Aguinaldo's forces transitioned from conventional to guerrilla warfare "there was no insurgent force left to strike at." He declared that all further resistance from that point be labeled "banditry." Not only did the term suggest that opposition to US rule was criminal and thus subject to sanction, but it also connoted that the purported cause for which they were fighting—independence—was illegitimate.[21]

The kind of conflict that US troops were facing was not unique. Other contemporary colonial powers had faced similar warfare around the world, including the British in South Africa, the French in Tunisia, and the Spanish in Cuba. The United States had had its own encounters. Many US regiments stationed in the Philippines hailed from western states, which engaged in the Indian Wars of the late nineteenth century; by one estimate, more than 80 percent of the US generals who served in the Philippines up to 1902 had fought against American Indians. Some politicians drew deliberate comparisons to justify the righteousness of the American cause. Senator William Stewart compared Aguinaldo with "Tecumseh, Sitting Bull, Old Cochise or some other celebrated Indian warrior" for using guerrilla warfare. Likewise, Roosevelt argued that the United States must prevail in the Philippines as it had in the Indian Wars "so that one more fair spot of the world's surface shall have been snatched from the forces of darkness.... To turn over the islands to Aguinaldo and his followers [would bring] ... tyrannical oppression."[22]

Insurgents' tactics also fed into long-standing racial stereotypes. Coming during the era of Jim Crow segregation at home, the turn of the twentieth century was rife with pseudoscientific justifications of racial hierarchies that placed whites at the top with mixed races and nonwhites below. The common understanding among such adherents was that dark-skinned peoples were not intellectually developed enough to warrant their own sovereignty; leaving them to their own devices would thus be dangerous and irresponsible. Aguinaldo's reliance on guerrilla warfare reinforced this belief to US officials. Secretary of War Elihu Root, who was responsible for overseeing the pacification of the Philippines, wrote that "the war on the part of the Filipinos has been conducted with the barbarous cruelty common among uncivilized races." Historian Paul Kramer argues that Americans interpreted guerrilla tactics as "the inherent war of preference of 'lower races.'"[23]

White US soldiers trying to fit unfamiliar Filipinos into their conception of racial hierarchies often defaulted to a common epithet from back home—"nigger." Howard McFarland, a sergeant with Company B of the Forty-Third Infantry, minced no words in describing the opposition. "At the best, this is a very rich country; and we want it. My way of getting it would be to put a regiment into a skirmish line, and blow every nigger into a nigger heaven." He bragged that men from his company had "killed seventy-five nigger bolomen and ten of the nigger gunners.... When we find one that is not dead, we have bayonets." H. L. Wells, a newspaper correspondent in Manila, corroborated such stories, which illustrated a deep-seated contempt for the enemy. He wrote: "There is no question that our men do 'shoot niggers' somewhat in the sporting spirit, but that is because war and their environments have rubbed off the thin veneer of civilization.... Undoubtedly, they do not regard the shooting of Filipinos just as they would the shooting of white troops. This is partly because they are 'only niggers,' and partly because they despise them for their treacherous servility.... The soldiers feel that they are fighting with savages, not with soldiers."[24]

Not every US soldier agreed with such sentiments. Black troops in the Philippines understandably found the racist language demeaning and offensive. But there is little evidence it tempered white troops' rhetoric. One anonymous Black soldier wrote that white military men "talked with impunity of 'niggers' to our soldiers, never once thinking that they were talking to home 'niggers' and should they be brought to remember that at home this is the same vile epithet they hurl at us, they beg pardon and make some effeminate excuse about what the Filipino is called." As targets of similar invective, Black soldiers often expressed sympathy for what Filipinos endured. In a letter published by the Cleveland *Gazette*, Patrick Mason of the Twenty-Fourth Infantry wrote, "I feel sorry for these people and all that have come under the control of the United States. I don't believe they will be justly dealt by. The first thing in the morning is the 'Nigger' and the last thing at night is the 'Nigger.' You have no idea the way these people are treated by the Americans here." Sentiments like Mason's suggested that Black US soldiers possessed a deeper understanding of Filipino resistance to US rule than their white counterparts could comprehend.[25]

Beyond the epithets and condescension, Americans' belief in the criminality and savagery of the Filipino rebellion gave them license to pursue counterinsurgency with little adherence to their own standards of civilized warfare. Since the Civil War, the US military had been developing such rules. Francis Lieber in 1863 produced the most notable contribution to this effort. Enshrined as General Orders No. 100 but more popularly referred to as the Lieber Code, the directive consisted of 157 articles about how the US military should approach combat against a hostile army. It included statutes against torture, distinguished between soldiers and noncombatants, and protected prisoners from execution or assassination. Notably, however, there were exceptions for "war-rebels," who were considered illegitimate combatants because they were "without commission." Such fighters "shall be treated summarily as highway robbers or pirates." US soldiers widely considered Filipino rebels to be in this category and treated them accordingly.[26]

On an individual level, Filipinos suspected of guerrilla attacks—or aiding and abetting such attacks—were subject to torture. There were instances of prisoners being outright murdered following their capture. In other cases, torture was as much a means of punishment and vengeance as a method of interrogation. The most infamous form, if not the most common, was the "water cure." A prisoner would be held down on his back. A stick would be inserted in the mouth to hold it open and a pail of water poured in, sometimes multiple buckets, to instill the sensation of drowning or suffocation. The stomachs of victims were said to swell. Just as the victim passed out, they would either be rolled over to let the water out or—in more extreme cases—someone would punch or kick their stomach to revive them. The process would be repeated if no information was forthcoming.[27]

American defenders rationalized the tactic in a variety of ways. They blamed the initial use of the practice on Macabebe Scouts, Filipino allies who worked as fighters, informants, or interpreters for the US military. Others said that the victims had it coming. Worcester, for example, had no sympathy for those subjected to the torture because they "were themselves bloody murderers." Besides, he reasoned, the water cure seldom resulted in permanent injury. One officer, Maj. Edwin F. Glenn, admitted to the practice during a court martial on the grounds he was trying to shorten the war. His defense was mildly effective. Although found guilty, Glenn only drew a month's suspension and a $50 fine.[28]

The "water cure" was the most infamous form of torture committed by US forces and their allies. It was often justified because the prisoner was not considered to be a legitimate combatant entitled to safe-treatment protections under international law. Courtesy of the US National Archives and Records Administration.

On a collective level, suspected guerrillas or uncooperative civilians faced other reprisals. It was not uncommon for US soldiers to raze villages if it was believed they housed or supported insurgents or saboteurs. The destruction included burning houses and crops, as well as slaughtering livestock. Those not arrested might be sent to a concentration camp—in the literal sense of the term rather than systematic murder—to weed out *insurrectos* from civilians. It was a practice done by other contemporary great powers against anticolonial rebels. The results were often devastating. The most notorious example came in Batangas Province in southern Luzon. General J. Franklin Bell established so-called zones of protection to stymie locals' support of insurgents. These hastily arranged areas, however, were breeding grounds for disease, compounded by malnutrition and poor sanitation. An estimated 11,000 civilians died as a result.[29]

American officials defended these actions, most often by claiming that military personnel were just reacting to the conditions and people around them. "I think I know why these things have happened," Senator Henry Cabot Lodge said. "I think they have grown out of the conditions of warfare, of the war that was waged by the Filipinos themselves, a semicivilized people, with all the tendencies and characteristics of Asiatics, with the Asiatic indifference to life, with the Asiatic treachery and the Asiatic cruelty, all tinctured and increased by three hundred years of subjection to Spain." Secretary Root recognized that in some cases, US military personnel went too far. He cited forty-four cases of cruelty prosecuted in military courts that resulted in thirty-nine convictions. Nevertheless, he maintained that "the war in the Philippines has been conducted by the American Army with scrupulous regard for the rules of civilized warfare with careful and genuine consideration for the prisoner and the non-combatant, with self-restraint, and with humanity never surpassed."[30]

General Robert P. Hughes, however, exhibited much less regret. In March 1902 testimony to the US Senate, he admitted to ordering homes and villages razed according to a particular formula. If locals helped guerrillas, a few houses would be set ablaze. But if a detachment of insurgents was discovered there, then the entire village would be burned. His admission led to this exchange with Senator Joseph Rollins:

> ROLLINS: "But is [burning a village] within the ordinary rules of civilized warfare?"
> HUGHES: "These people are not civilized."
> ROLLINS: "Then I understand you to say it is not civilized warfare?"
> HUGHES: "No; I think it is not."

Hughes, though, insisted that the Filipinos brought such destruction upon themselves. Their tactics of treachery and terror had to be met in kind. "I went there supposing these people to be sufficiently civilized to follow the ordinary rules of civilized warfare," he said. "I became convinced, greatly to my sorrow, that they would not follow the rules of war."[31]

AS THE WAR CONTINUED INTO 1901, one man was conspicuously absent. While US forces and Macabebe Scouts hunted insurgents in northern Luzon, there seemed to be no trace of Emilio Aguinaldo. The wide dragnet through the Philippines had found nothing. The *Chicago Tribune* reported on March 1, 1901, that the United States had extended its search to Singapore and Hong Kong. Some frustrated US military officials openly speculated that he was dead.[32]

The report, though, may have been subterfuge. By that point, the US military had its best lead on Aguinaldo's location and was devising a plan to capture him. In February, an Aguinaldo courier surrendered, carrying with him documents that pointed to the insurgent leader's hideout in Palanan in

A Savage War

remote northeastern Luzon. The task of what to do with this information fell to Gen. Frederick Funston. Standing just five feet, four inches tall, the thirty-five-year-old Kansan had a big reputation as a risk-taker. He had fought on behalf of Cuban rebels as a volunteer well before US entry into that war and nearly died in combat. Early in the Philippine-American War, he led his men under fire across a dangerous river, an act for which he won the Medal of Honor. Now, he planned an even riskier mission.[33]

Funston's idea was to have Macabebe Scouts masquerade as the reinforcements Aguinaldo had requested, along with a handful of US soldiers—including himself—posing as POWs. Assisted by a Spanish mercenary named Lázaro Segovia, the team sailed roughly 100 miles south of their destination, then trekked through treacherous, insurgent-friendly terrain on the way to Aguinaldo's hideout.

They arrived at the camp on March 23, initially welcomed by Aguinaldo's personal security. After exchanging pleasantries, Segovia grew concerned that the insurgents were becoming suspicious. He gave the signal for Macabebes to open fire. Thinking it was just celebratory gunfire, a confused Aguinaldo yelled at everyone, "Stop that foolishness! Quit wasting ammunition!" By the time he realized what was really going on, it was too late. Segovia drew his weapon and opened fire on Aguinaldo's associates in the room. One account claims that Hilario Tal Placido, a Filipino who had once fought in the Philippine army but was part of the ruse, grabbed Aguinaldo and literally sat on him to hold him down. Aguinaldo, though, later insisted that he wanted to die but one of his associates subdued him and pleaded with him to stay alive. Regardless, Aguinaldo was an American prisoner.[34]

As word of Aguinaldo's capture reached the United States, reactions ranged from jubilation to skepticism about whether the violence would subside. "The reign of terror that was spread among the natives is coming to an end," the *Los Angeles Times* declared. Similarly, the *New York Tribune* celebrated apprehending a man it described as a "vain, deceitful, cruel, tyrannical adventurer who has betrayed all who have trusted him and who has sought to aggrandize himself by means of systemic murder and arson." Publicly, US military officers had mixed reactions. Commanding general of the United States Army Nelson Miles said, "In my opinion, this will tend to settle all the trouble in the Philippines. The capture of their leader is sure to dishearten Aguinaldo's followers, and although there may be more or less trouble for some time... I believe the backbone of the trouble is broken." General Elwell Otis, who had served as military governor of the Philippines before being replaced by MacArthur, was more circumspect. "The influence of Aguinaldo has been waning for some time," he said, "therefore the importance of the capture is not so great as might be supposed.... Aguinaldo was once looked upon by the Filipino people as a little god, but this sentiment has been lost almost completely."³⁵

Nevertheless, it was important for the US mission not to make Aguinaldo a martyr but rather to get him to renounce the rebellion and swear allegiance to the United States. To encourage Aguinaldo's acquiescence, the US military provided him with far more comforts than rank-and-file insurgents enjoyed. He was held under guard in an apartment close to MacArthur's Manila headquarters with access to an interpreter, a typewriter, and a secretary. He also was allowed visitation from family, including his wife and mother. Such respectful treatment quickly bore fruit. On April 2, Aguinaldo privately took an oath of allegiance to the United States. On April 19, he issued a public statement urging his supporters to end their insurrection and accept US sovereignty.³⁶

In the weeks that followed, the resistance became even more fragmented. Thousands of insurgents and their leaders were captured or surrendered, lured by promises of lenient terms or forgiveness. There were holdouts and pockets of resistance, though. The Balangiga Massacre of September 1901 certainly was evidence of that. Yet the violence generally tapered to such an extent that on July 4, 1902, President Theodore Roosevelt proclaimed that the war was over. He offered amnesty to insurgents who "committed many acts in violation of the laws of civilized warfare," ignorant of such standards though they may have been.³⁷

There was one notable exception to Roosevelt's proclamation — "the country inhabited by the Moro tribes." The US encounter with insurgents in the Philippines was not quite over yet.

THE TERM "BOONDOCKS" is common in today's American lexicon to refer to something situated far away. It was adapted from the Tagalog word *bundok*, which means "mountain" or "remote area." To Americans stationed in the Philippines, this word fit perfectly for the southern region of the archipelago, which consists of hundreds of islands, most notably Mindanao, the second-largest in the Philippines and greater than the size of Ireland.³⁸

During the Spanish colonial era, the region existed as an almost separate entity from the northern half of the islands. Its people long resisted foreign rule and enjoyed semiautonomy. The area was home to a wide array of ethnolinguistic peoples. Religion was the one thing many of them had in common. Unlike Luzon, which featured many Catholics because of more concentrated

A Savage War 25

Spanish influence, the people of the southern islands were mainly Muslims. Islam arrived in the area in the fifteenth century and served as a loose bond among the diverse people. When American officials arrived at the turn of the twentieth century, they tended to conflate these ethnicities together as "Moro," which was what the Spanish had called them.

Aware of this history, US officials were not eager to start a pacification campaign while the war against Aguinaldo's forces was ongoing. To that end, in August 1899 Gen. John C. Bates came to an arrangement with Muslim chiefs in the region. Under terms of the Bates Agreement, the United States declared sovereignty while pledging not to interfere with the authority of Muslim leaders or infringe on religious customs. Although there would later be some dispute about the extent to which Moros truly agreed to US claims of sovereignty given some subtle distinctions in translations of the text, the agreement maintained peace for a time.[39]

As the war with Aguinaldo and his supporters came to an end, though, attention shifted to the region the United States called the Moro Province. Officials aimed to bring civilization—according to American norms—to the roughly 300,000 people living in this territory. The mission included building roads and bridges, widening access to public health services, creating schools, and improving sanitation. For Gen. Leonard Wood, the first US military governor of the province, it also involved ushering cultural changes. Wood had gained fame as commander of Theodore Roosevelt's "Rough Riders" and later as military governor of Cuba. In his latter role, he looked to bring about progressive reforms to civilize "savage" peoples. He brought that same mentality to the Moro Province. Wood wanted to eliminate what he saw as backward customs, especially practices of polygamy and slavery, and sought to move Moros away from religious interpretations of justice—in which men faced amputation of an arm for conviction of theft or women subjected to stoning if guilty of adultery—and more toward American-style jurisprudence. To teach good financial governance, he imposed taxes to pay for infrastructure improvements and schools.[40]

These reforms provoked a Moro backlash. Many natives grew anxious that the United States was trying to force their conversion from Islam and change their way of life. The presence of an increasing number of armed non-Muslims was deeply unsettling. And paying taxes to the United States felt like tribute, which was something applied to a defeated people. As a result, many of them declared jihad—*fisabil*, as the locals called it—against the Americans.[41]

The first attacks on Americans began in March 1902 on Mindanao, mostly ambushes on vulnerable targets. To that point, US soldiers stationed in the area had moved about freely, with little fear. That sense of security ended abruptly. An eighteen-man detachment on the way to Lake Lanao was riding through a dense jungle trail when they were fired on without warning. In a panic, the men abandoned their horses and fled into the jungle; one American was killed. Days later, two soldiers in Malabang were jumped by six Moros. One American was hacked to death with a bolo, and the other escaped.

After two weeks of fruitless outreach to local chiefs, US forces staged a punitive expedition in search of the attackers. Led by two-time Medal of Honor winner Col. Frank D. Baldwin, the men of the Twenty-Seventh Infantry reached Bayang, which the *Chicago Tribune* described as "the most savage part of Mindanao." There, 470 Americans lay siege to a well-defended fort with roughly 600 warriors inside. Armed with superior firepower, the Americans prevailed with relatively light casualties (eight killed, forty-five wounded) compared with the Moros, who lost an estimated 200 to 400 fighters. Yet suggestions of Moro treachery pervaded in accounts of the battle. For example, some Moros were said to be hiding in tall grass outside the fort, where they lay in wait to attack members of the hospital corps attending to wounded Americans. The infantry's official report to the War Department noted that "some Moro wounded tried to stab soldiers trying to help them." Moreover, thirty-nine Moro prisoners escaped capture after a coordinated uprising. In the end, though, those who had staged the attacks that precipitated the Battle of Bayang were not caught, much less identified. But the US point of retribution and pacification had been made.[42]

THIS PATTERN OF ATTACKS and counterattacks continued in the Moro Province for the next few years. Moros would occasionally hit American camps or caravans with sniper fire, steal rifles, or cut telegraph lines. Americans would hold Muslim chiefs responsible, get little satisfaction through negotiation, and ultimately retaliate with expeditions against Moro strongholds. Exasperated by this cycle, President Roosevelt abrogated the Bates Agreement in March 1904, claiming that the Sultan of Sulu—who, in reality, had little authority over the disparate Muslim groups in Moro Province—failed to bring local resistance to heel and thereby undermined US administration of the colony. By that point, US officials already had moved to criminalize the insurgency. The Taft-led Philippine Commission in November 1902 passed the Brigandage Act that cast harsh punishments on bands of three or more who used force or violence. Those found guilty of violating the law faced at least twenty years in prison or even execution. Essentially, the law categorized further Filipino resistance to US rule as banditry.[43]

This classification reflected the dim view many US officials had of Moros. US military officers, in particular, commonly referred to Moros as "savages." Writing in the *Atlantic* in 1906, Col. Robert L. Bullard asserted that Moros had a "long tradition of piracy, lawlessness and savagery." He added that "Moros everywhere were thieves, robbers, pirates, and slave-takers, in a state of continual violence and wrong-doing toward one another and all men, so far as they dared." One anonymous lieutenant claimed that Moros had not evolved in twelve centuries. "He is still the same undersized brown devil who files his teeth, kills best with a knife, and knows that he goes with glory to Allah if he slays a single Christian." General Wood minced no words in explaining his view of the locals: "Moros are, in a way, religious and moral degenerates."[44]

At the same time, some officers had a grudging admiration for Moros' bravery and willingness to face death head-on. In contrast to Aguinaldo's forces in Luzon who relied almost exclusively on guerrilla warfare, Moros engaged in open combat when confronted. Maj. Hugh Scott submitted his own pseudoscientific explanation. "The Moro appears to have a nervous system differing from that of a white man, for he carries lead like a grizzly bear and keeps coming on after being shot again and again," he wrote. "One Moro of Jolo was shot through the body by seven army revolver bullets, yet kept coming on with enough vitality and force to shear off the leg of an engineer soldier, more smoothly than it could have been taken off by a surgeon." Superficially, such a depiction could be seen as complimentary of the Moros' toughness. Yet it also played into the "savage" stereotype by making them seem comparatively primitive than were presumably more civilized Americans.[45]

Such bravery bore considerable risks for American soldiers. Many Moro fighters refused to be captured and were willing to fight to the death. Their determination came from two sources. One was Moros' wide belief that Americans would not take prisoners. Reports from the fight in Luzon in which Americans killed prisoners—like Major Waller's excursion after Balangiga—certainly were a case in point. The second reason was the practice of *juramentado*, a ritual in which Moro fighters would prepare themselves for battles that were essentially suicide missions. As described by historian Michael Hawkins, these attackers "typically engaged in elaborate rituals prior to their assaults, including ritualistic cleansing, shaving, binding the body to prevent blood loss and prolong their attacks, donning symbolic clothing and magic amulets, reciting prayers, and polishing and sharpening weapons, which usually consisted of a kris and a barong." For Moros, death in battle against nonbelievers was venerated as a form of martyrdom. Americans, though, considered such behavior to be barbarous and irrational.[46]

AS A DECENTRALIZED and disparate group of people, Moros did not have a single leader who guided resistance against the United States or became the face of the insurgency as Aguinaldo had in Luzon. Nevertheless, two leaders stood out among the pockets of opposition in Moro Province. The first was Panglima Hassan, a subordinate of the sultan in the Sulu archipelago. Wood met with Hassan in August 1903 as he was settling into his role as provincial governor. The meeting proved to be a disaster. Hassan was put off by Wood's arrogance as well as the American's proposed reforms, particularly about slavery. The trigger came in October when a group of American map surveyors was ambushed when it strayed into territory controlled by a Hassan ally; two Americans were wounded and eight Moros killed. Wood's ire was raised further when he learned that Hassan seemed to be organizing a resistance. In November, Wood ordered Scott to begin an expedition to find and eliminate Hassan.[47]

In short order, US forces tracked him down. He was briefly captured but escaped when a band of sword-wielding insurgents rescued him. As he was fleeing, Hassan allegedly shot a pistol out of Scott's hand, costing the major two fingers. Wood personally led a campaign that lobbed sustained assaults on any areas where Hassan or his allies were suspected of hiding. Some 1,500 Moros—including women and children—were killed along the way. The following March, nearly 400 of Scott's men found Hassan and two associates hiding near the volcanic crater of Bud Bagsak. At dawn, the three men charged. Two were killed instantly. The third, despite being shot thirty-two times, kept crawling toward the Americans until he took a bullet to the head at point-blank range. It was Hassan.[48]

The second and perhaps the most notable Moro antagonist was Datu Ali, who claimed to be a descendent of the prophet Mohammad. His father had ruled Mindanao in the 1880s, and his father-in-law, Datu Piang, was well-connected with Chinese traders before the American invasion. Piang resolved to work with the United States, but two things compelled Ali to resist. The first was Wood's September 1903 antislavery proclamation that established punishments of up to twenty years in prison and fines of 10,000 pesos. Ali interpreted it as an infringement on Moro customs that could undermine his authority as a *datu*, or chief. The other was humiliation when US officials rescinded an invitation to lead a Moro delegation to the 1904 World's Fair in St. Louis. To pay for his travel and entourage of wives and slaves, he borrowed $10,000 from Piang, which he subsequently gambled away. An embarrassed and infuriated Ali resolved to fight back against the Americans, and his call attracted some 2,000 supporters to the Cotabato Valley in central Mindanao where they built up a fortress, or *cotta*. Wood initiated a campaign in March 1904 to snuff out the threat. His outnumbered—though far more potent— forces easily destroyed the *cotta*, but Ali escaped.[49]

For the next year and a half, Ali led a guerrilla campaign that harassed US forces and any Moros who dared cooperate with Americans. His deadliest strike came in May 1904, when roughly fifty men ambushed members of the Seventeenth Infantry traveling on a narrow, swampy path. Fifteen Americans were killed, some allegedly disemboweled or beheaded. Two US soldiers were captured, but to everyone's surprise, they were released unharmed along with a message requesting a truce. Wood balked at the idea, determined to capture a man he came to grudgingly admit was "by far the most capable Moro we have run into." Despite a $500 bounty for his capture, Ali seemed to vanish.[50]

The big break came in October 1905 when Captain Frank McCoy, Wood's aide, got a tip about Ali's whereabouts from a rival Moro leader who was upset that Ali had taken his wife. A detachment of 100 Americans from the Twenty-Second Infantry made the perilous journey through jungle-covered mountains over six days. When they arrived at Ali's residence and surrounded it, the Americans found him sitting on the porch chewing betel nut. The surprised Ali allegedly fired the first shot, killing one private, before he was hit in the chest by a bullet. Wounded, Ali tried to escape out the back door but met a hail of gunfire. In all, he was shot fifteen times. As the smoke cleared, Ali, his son, and ten followers were dead. Two Americans were killed in the raid. The *Washington Post* lauded the mission as more dangerous than Funston's to get Aguinaldo and celebrated the end of Ali's "band of outlaws and murderers with whom for several years he maintained a reign of terror."[51]

Although the most notorious Moro insurgent was dead, sporadic resistance in the province continued for years. Wood was determined to meet such opposition with a heavy hand. In Wood's two and a half years as provincial governor, US forces and their allies in the American-led Filipino constabulary had more than 100 engagements with Moro fighters. Thanks to their vastly superior firepower, US troops won the body count. Yet challenges to US control continued. The most infamous example came in March

1906 at Bud Dajo, a dormant volcanic crater where a group of Tausug Moros fortified themselves looking to preserve their Islamic cultural and political autonomy. Wood personally oversaw an assault that killed nearly 1,000 Moro men, women, and children.[52]

The last major battle took place in June 1913 on the island of Jolo. Moros led by Datu Amil resisted mandates to disarm. He and some 1,000 followers fled to Bud Bagsak, the extinct volcano that rises nearly 3,700 feet. Gen. John "Black Jack" Pershing—governor of the Moro Province who would go on to greater fame in Mexico and World War I—organized a group of 1,000 US troops and Moro Scouts to assault Amil's *cotta*. It took five days of fighting over steep terrain for the US-Filipino forces to secure the mountain. Pershing wrote that there was "probably no fiercer battle since [the] American occupation." Another American commander marveled at the ferocity and determination of Amil's forces, who were hopelessly outgunned yet threw "spears, bolos, rocks, cooking utensils, and every conceivable object" in the fight. Although some Moros escaped, most were killed, perhaps as many as 500, including Datu Amil. By comparison, just three Americans, three Philippine Scouts, and nine allied Moro Scouts were killed.[53]

Four days after the battle, Pershing recommended moving all US forces out of Moro Province. He retained reservations about Moros' "savage characteristics" and bemoaned that they were "naturally suspicious and often deceitful . . . always treacherous and cruel in dealing with . . . enemies." Yet in presuming the region was sufficiently pacified, he preferred having local Moros take care of policing, assisted by US civilians who could help build a more modern society. Although occasional resistance and skirmishes would persist, the United States essentially declared victory and sent forces home.[54]

IN ITS ATTEMPT TO PACIFY the Philippines and hunt down insurgents who resisted its authority, the United States sent more than 126,000 soldiers to the archipelago. Of those, more than 4,200 died. The toll was far worse for Filipinos. Absent precise contemporary records, historians generally estimate at least 200,000—mostly civilians—lost their lives, not merely from the violence but by accompanying disease and starvation that stemmed from the fighting.[55]

Given the brutality of the conflict and the terrible cost of the war, the US-Philippine union was quite remarkable. It was an uneasy, unequal alliance, to be sure, but it endured, even through the Japanese invasion during World War II. Aside from that brief interregnum, the Philippines remained a US territory until July 4, 1946, when it was granted independence.

One of the notable participants in the flag-raising ceremony was Emilio Aguinaldo, then seventy-seven years old. He was joined by another MacArthur: Douglas, the famed general and son of Aguinaldo's pursuer from nearly a half century earlier. By then, in the twilight of his life, time and the long-awaited attainment of independence had healed old wounds. He mostly remained in the background of colonial-era politics except for running for president of the commonwealth in 1935, when he lost to Manuel Quezon. Accused of collaborating with the Japanese during World War II, he was later acquitted as part of a general amnesty. In his 1957 memoir, Aguinaldo conceded that US sovereignty may have been best for the Philippines in the long run. Had the United States not kept control, he surmised, the archipelago may have been partitioned by other European powers, such as Great Britain or Germany. "While I regret the Philippine-American War, it was not our own making," he wrote. "Personally, I have not harbored any rancor nor resentment against America or the Americans."[56]

The feeling, apparently, was mutual. When Aguinaldo died from a stroke in February 1964 at the age of ninety-four, a variety of US dignitaries, including President Lyndon B. Johnson, issued tributes. Douglas MacArthur's, though, was most notable. "He was the very incarnation of the Filipino desire for liberty and freedom and his country owes him much," the retired general said. "He was a lifelong friend of mine and his death saddens me." Such sentiments demonstrated that—whether he intended to or not—Aguinaldo successfully rehabilitated his reputation among Americans. Although his zeal for independence never wavered, in renouncing violence and acquiescing to US authority, he reframed himself from the man once referred to as "that bandit Aguinaldo."[57]

AGUINALDO MAY HAVE BEEN the first foreign "bandit" that the United States faced in the imperial era, but there would be more to come. As the United States was learning how to manage its colonial possessions overseas at the dawn of the twentieth century, it also had to shore up its interests closer to home. Neighboring Mexico, with which the United States long had contentious relations, was in the midst of a revolution that threatened American commercial concerns. In the quest for allies, the United States seemed to have found one in famed outlaw Francisco "Pancho" Villa. But like the US alliance with Aguinaldo, the partnership with Villa was fleeting, ending in acrimony and bloodshed—this time on American soil.

CHAPTER TWO
Hunting the Outlaw
Pancho Villa in Mexico

Frank Tompkins and his soldiers were in a bad way.

The US major and about 100 members of the Thirteenth Cavalry were passing through the northern Mexican town of Parral on April 12, 1916. After weeks marching through the desert, they were looking forward to finding hot baths, cool drinks, and warm food. Instead, they received an icy reception from the townspeople and a garrison of roughly 500 Mexican soldiers. The local commanding officer, General Ismael Lozano, told Tompkins that he and his troops were not welcome but would lead them out of town to a place where they could camp. But as the Americans were being escorted, the locals began shooting sporadically at the rear of the column. Lozano denied any responsibility and sent the Americans on their way.

Tompkins smelled a trap. In the distance, he could see Mexican troops gathering in an apparent attempt to surround the cavalry. As Tompkins warned the Mexicans to back off, they opened fire, killing the sergeant next to him with a bullet through the eye. The Americans were able to fend off the initial assault and headed north in search of reinforcements. For the next three hours, Mexican forces continued their pursuit. In the retreat, Tompkins was shot in the shoulder but carried on. Ultimately, the outnumbered yet better skilled and equipped Thirteenth Cavalry reached safety at Santa Cruz de Villegas, roughly fifteen miles from where the attack began. That evening, Lozano sent a note to Tompkins pledging to withdraw his soldiers if the Americans agreed to leave. Tompkins likewise agreed to leave if Lozano withdrew his soldiers. As the dust settled, Tompkins counted three dead Americans, six wounded, and one missing; estimates suggest at least forty Mexicans were killed.[1]

Next to the loss of life, the great tragedy of the Battle of Parral was that the Thirteenth Cavalry were not supposed to be fighting Mexican soldiers in the first place. They were supposed to be looking for José Doroteo Arango Arámbula, the man better known to the world as Francisco "Pancho" Villa. One month earlier, Villa had led some 400 members of his private militia in an attack on the US-Mexican border town of Columbus, New Mexico. The

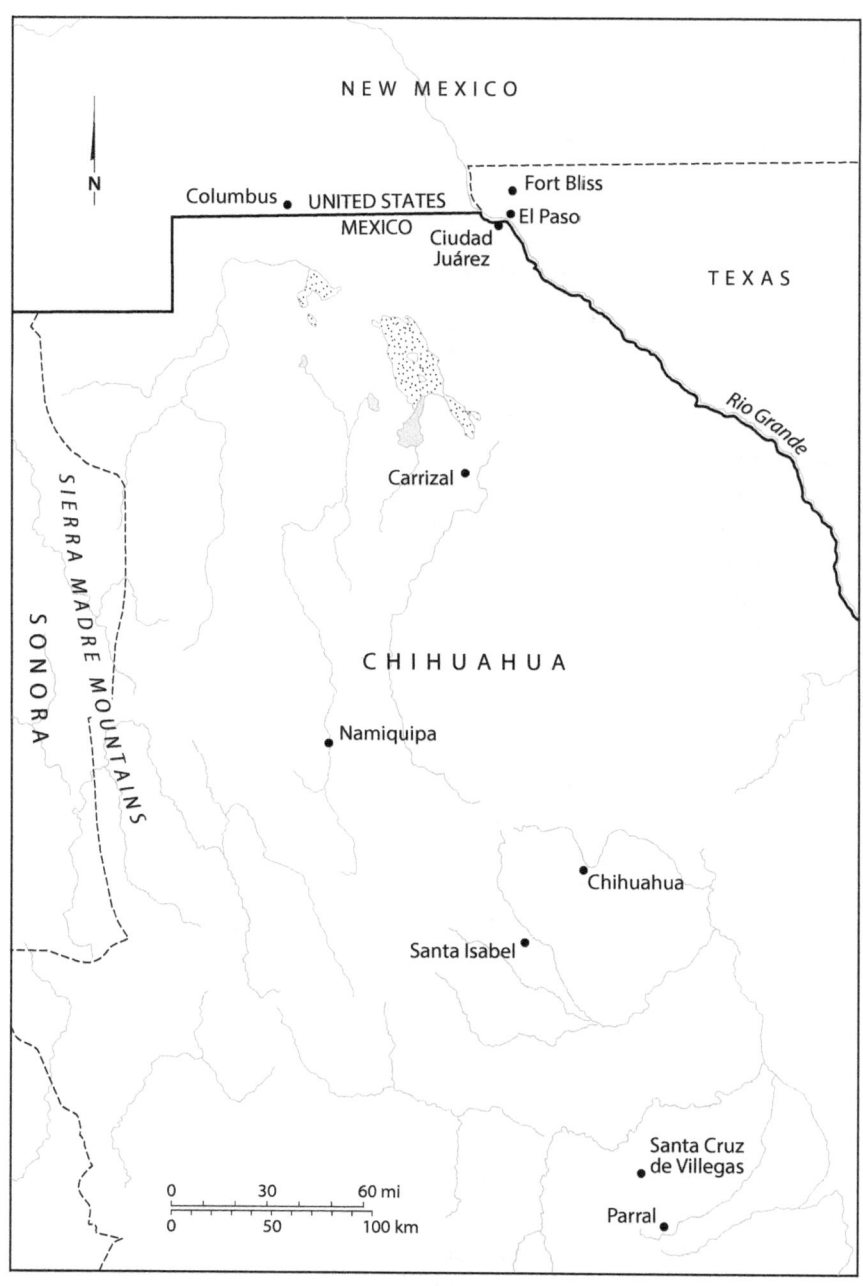

Northern Mexico

assault killed eighteen Americans in what would be one of the deadliest attacks by a private foreign party on US soil until September 11, 2001.

When news broke about what had happened in New Mexico, outrage swept the nation. The *El Paso Herald* called Villa a "professional murderer" and a "brutal assassin, thirsting for blood." From the media capital of the country, the *New York World* opined, "Nothing less than Villa's life can atone for the outrage at Columbus, N.M.... Every drop of American blood shed at Columbus is on his hands." In Humboldt, Iowa, hometown of one of the slain Americans, locals raised funds to go toward a reward for Villa's capture.[2]

The US mainland had not been attacked by a foreign foe since the War of 1812. In light of the extraordinary threat, there was a great deal of pressure on President Woodrow Wilson to do... something. Those who had criticized Wilson's reluctance to get the United States involved in World War I hoped Villa's attack would stir the president into a forceful response. "The alarm clock has gone off under the ear of the professional pacifist," the *Tacoma Times* wrote. "Maybe he'll get up in time for business." One of Wilson's chief political tormenters, Senator Henry Cabot Lodge, similarly piled on. "The recent killing of American men, the outraging of American women, and the invasion of American soil with its consequent national humiliation have happened because this Administration has not stood from the beginning for the protection of American rights," he said.[3]

Wilson, though, was hesitant to turn an attack by a private militia into an all-out war. According to his personal secretary, Joseph Tumulty, the president told him, "'*There won't be any war with Mexico if I can prevent it*,' no matter how loud the gentlemen on the hill yell for it and demand it." Wilson's anxieties stemmed not from pacificism; indeed, the president was one of the most ardent military interventionists in US history, sending troops to six Latin American nations during his administration, including Mexico just two years earlier. Rather, he had an eye on World War I. At least in Tumulty's retelling, Wilson worried that a US-Mexican war would divert attention and critical resources from a potential showdown with Germany.[4]

Despite the criticism, Wilson acted decisively. The day after the Columbus raid, the White House announced a Punitive Expedition consisting of an "adequate force"—that eventually would reach more than 7,000 soldiers—designed to capture Villa in Mexico "with scrupulous respect for the sovereignty of that republic." General Frederick Funston, famous for leading the capture of Emilio Aguinaldo fifteen years earlier, was tasked to oversee the operation with Gen. John "Black Jack" Pershing, another veteran of the war in the Philippines, chosen to command in the field. The Wilson administration, though, took great pains not to characterize the US military response as a war or an intervention. In a press statement later that month, the administration reiterated that "the expedition is simply a punitive measure aimed solely at the elimination of the bandits who raided Columbus and who infest an unprotected district along the border and use it as a base of operations against American lives and property." Wilson himself followed that up with a statement calling on the press not to portray the Punitive Expedition as an intervention.[5]

Yet a wider war is very nearly what happened, as Tompkins's experience can attest. The Battle of Parral was not an isolated incident. America's pursuit of Villa and its fight against banditry in Mexico nearly spun out of control and would bear remarkable hallmarks to a broader war on terror a century later.

LONG BEFORE HIS ATTACK on Columbus, Francisco "Pancho" Villa was already well-known in the United States and Mexico. Born in June 1878 in the Mexican state of Durango, Villa came from a family of sharecroppers and was the oldest of five siblings. When Villa was still a boy, his father died, leaving him essentially the head of the household. Further details of his early life, though, are shrouded in myth. One account claims that at sixteen years old, Villa shot and wounded the owner of the *hacienda* where his family lived and worked when the man made overtures to Villa's sister. Fearing arrest, Villa went on the run, changed his name, and became an outlaw. Other versions suggest Villa took up a life of crime to seek vengeance on the landed elites that dominated Mexico. Still others portrayed him as a cold-blooded killer. A 1913 *New York Times* profile of Villa helped burnish his legend internationally as a "bandit outlaw." The *Times* surmised that the "complete list of murders the responsibility for which directly or indirectly rests upon the shoulders of Villa has never been written. . . . Villa is not the kind of a man who kills for matters of simple honor. When he fights it is for reward, and the reward, if he can manage it, must be paid in gold."[6]

Villa established his international reputation at a time when Mexico was in turmoil. For nearly thirty-five years, the country had been under the thumb of Porfirio Díaz, a man friendly to the interests of landed elites and foreign capital at the expense of the impoverished masses. But in 1911, widespread unrest finally compelled the longtime dictator to go into exile. Over the next few years, a variety of coalitions came together to vie for power, only to splinter and devolve into violence. Although the period known as the Mexican Revolution would produce significant and long-lasting political and economic reforms, at least 1 million people likely died as a result of the conflict.

The man born José Doroteo Arango Arámbula was more widely known to the world as Pancho Villa, shown here in 1911. Initially considered an ally to the United States during the Mexican Revolution, Villa later became public enemy number one for his actions after the alliance fizzled. Courtesy of the Library of Congress.

In this context, US-Mexican relations were fraught. They were still strained from the 1846–48 war in which Mexico surrendered more than half its territory for a paltry $15 million. In the following decades, American business leaders invested heavily in Mexico's mining, railroads, and oil. Díaz and other elites welcomed these infusions of capital, if not necessarily the US influence in Mexican political and economic affairs that came with it. Although hailed by US leaders like Theodore Roosevelt, who referred to Díaz as "the greatest statesman now living," the Mexican leader seemed to rue the arrangement. In a line often attributed to him, Díaz said, "Poor Mexico—so far from God, so close to the United States."[7]

Although the Mexican Revolution was primarily a domestic affair, the United States was not merely a bystander. American business and political leaders worried about the revolution's effects on US properties and investments. They quickly lost faith in Francisco Madero, who had replaced Díaz as president, for failing to provide sufficient order and stability. United States Ambassador to Mexico Henry Lane Wilson (no relation to Woodrow) helped organize a coup d'état that led to Madero's assassination in February 1913. General Victoriano Huerta then assumed control. But Woodrow Wilson, who began his presidential term the following month, decried the move. He was deeply offended by Huerta's unconstitutional seizure of power. This opposition led the Wilson administration to search for an ally who could set Mexico on a more righteous path while, more importantly, providing order, stability, and protection of foreign interests.

FOR A TIME, it seemed like Pancho Villa might fit the bill. He was part of a coalition called the Constitutionalists, a disparate group that rejected Huerta's dictatorial rule and proclaimed their own political legitimacy after Madero's fall. Villa had cobbled together his own militia and pledged allegiance to other revolutionaries, such as Emiliano Zapata and Venustiano Carranza, against Huerta.

In areas of northern Mexico that he controlled, Villa impressed US officials with his ability to maintain order while allowing American-owned businesses to operate unfettered. This approach seemed to be deliberate. Villa purposely steered clear of pressuring US properties while taking a hostile stance against other foreign-owned enterprises and landholdings. Villa most frequently targeted mining companies, one of the preeminent industries in northern Mexico. He often confiscated land and tribute from such businesses while calling for higher wages for local laborers that were his primary base of support. When unsatisfied, he threatened to kill or capture foreign nationals whose governments, in turn, would appeal to the US government to help win their safety. But he generally left US-owned companies alone. Villa exacted enough loot from Mexican landowners and other foreign nationals—Spaniards, primarily—that antagonizing the United States was simply unnecessary. Because he seemed so cooperative with their interests, US mining executives in Mexico and many US government officials concluded that Villa was a rational actor with whom they could peacefully coexist.[8]

Occasionally, Villa met with American military officers to discuss common cause. One of the first was in August 1914 in El Paso, Texas, where he was greeted by Pershing and members of the Thirteenth Cavalry, which would later be tasked with capturing Villa. On the drive to Pershing's home at nearby Fort Bliss, the local newspaper reported that throngs of onlookers "cheered heartily and shouts of 'Viva Villa' were frequent along the line of march." A year later, Villa went to El Paso again, this time to meet with Hugh

Scott, since promoted to general and army chief of staff following his service in the Philippines against the Moros. Having heard reports of Villa executing prisoners, Scott wanted to talk with him about acceptable forms of conduct in war that could help ensure continued US support. Villa seemed receptive to Scott's counsel. Their interaction led Scott to conclude that "if [Villa] continues on his course in insisting on constitutional government and putting his personal ambitions aside he will be considered as the 'Washington' of Mexico." Favorable comparison to the preeminent Founding Father was high praise, indeed, and suggested the possibility of Mexico someday becoming more like the United States if Villa could adhere to American mores.[9]

Although Scott's lofty aspirations for Villa were widely shared at the time, the bandit label still stuck. Private and public descriptions during the early days of the Mexican Revolution often referred to Villa as a "bandit-general" or even an "ex-bandit." The persistence of the term—modified though it may have been—showed that Villa could not quite escape his past. Moreover, such terminology revealed an uneasy American acceptance of him as an ally. No matter what he might do to support US interests in the Mexican Revolution, the stigma of criminality remained.[10]

Racial conceptions certainly affected Americans' ambivalence. Newspaper profiles and private correspondence often noted his mixed-race heritage, which did not play well in Jim Crow America. Writing a nationally syndicated profile in March 1914, E. Alexander Powell reported that Villa's "head is covered with black hair as crisp and curly as a negro's." Two months later, the *New York Times* interviewed ethnologist and archaeologist Frederick L. Monsen, who had traveled to Mexico and claimed to have met Villa. Monsen said, "I have never made up my mind whether he has any black blood in him or not. He is, of course, very largely of Indian blood." While the public speculated about Villa's ethnicity, the Wilson administration privately addressed the topic as well. Based on a briefing from a State Department agent in Mexico, Secretary of State William Jennings Bryan reported to Wilson in August 1914 that Villa was "a mixture of Spanish and Indian and that there may be some trace of African blood." He added that Villa was barely literate, a teetotaler, and did not gamble except at the cockfights he attended every Sunday. Bryan ultimately concluded that "we can have some influence with Villa." These depictions of Villa as racially inferior, poorly educated, and morally suspect cut two ways. On the one hand, it made many white Americans wary of associating with him. On the other hand, it led government officials and the American public to conclude that such an underdeveloped person could be malleable to US interests.[11]

Some US officials, however, were not convinced that they could or should accommodate someone like Villa. Gaston Schmutz, who served as a US consul in Mexico, did not buy the idea of Villa as a democratic champion given his violent tendencies. In a June 1915 letter to Washington, he wrote, "It is positively disgusting to read the expression of high moral ideals in General Villa's reply to President Wilson's note and to see the contemptible and hypocritical defrauding of the ignorant peon for his personal gain and greed and the tyrannical brutal oppression with which he treats all who are not willing to bow down servilely and obey his infamous and senseless decrees."[12]

Later that year, customs agent Zachary Cobb reported from El Paso with a similar concern: Villa had been stealing property in Mexico and selling it in the United States to help fund his side in the Mexican Revolution. Should such activity be allowed to continue, Cobb argued, it could produce more unlawful elements along the border. "I hope you may conclude to discontinue representations to Villa, or to any of the Villa chiefs, because of my belief that they do more harm, in the quasi-recognition and resulting encouragement of continued independent activities, than good in affording any actual protection," he stated. "It is earnestly to be hoped that you may find it consistent to break things off short here, taking the chance of Villa retaliating with possible increased depredations for a while, but in all probability causing his complete collapse." Such sentiments from on-the-ground US representatives like Schmutz and Cobb foreshadowed an impending US policy shift toward Villa. Closer proximity to Villa gave them a different appreciation of his activities than officials had in Washington. Eventually their arguments would come to be shared by the Wilson administration and the broader American public.[13]

UP TO THAT POINT, though, Villa had been quite useful to the United States. He had been receptive to US military outreach and respectful of US business interests. Equally important, he offered no criticism of the Wilson administration during the seven-month US occupation of the Mexican port city of Vera Cruz beginning in April 1914, a move that stoked anti-American sentiment across Mexico. At the time, Wilson privately lamented Villa's bad reputation in the US press. "Our own papers were prejudiced enough in all conscience against Villa and Carranza and everything that was happening in the north of Mexico," the president wrote, "but at last the light is dawning on them in spite of them and they are beginning to see things as they really are." Getting the popular press to portray Villa in a more flattering light would undoubtedly make Wilson's tough stance on Mexico—which included the use of US troops and withholding diplomatic recognition of the Huerta government—more palatable to the American public.[14]

At least one newspaper reflected Wilson's observation. The *Albuquerque Journal*, for example, refuted popular perceptions about Villa.

> To a majority of people the name of Pancho Villa calls up a vision of a rude, uncouth, scowling, low-browed villain, a bandit, a savage leader of savage men, their object loot and license. But that is not the real Villa. . . . In every respect he is a wonderful man, wonderful in the breadth of his natural abilities, wonderful in his development, wonderful in his sublime courage and self-confidence, wonderful in his firmness and stability of purpose, wonderful in his moderation and self-constraint, wonderful in his control of himself and of the elements out of which he has created the force with which he is resistlessly and relentlessly driving his way toward the goal of his ambition.

The explicit contrast between savagery and self-control reflected early twentieth-century conventions about barbarism and civilization. Popular racial conceptions of the time suggested nonwhite peoples represented the former and white Americans the latter. Notably, the *Albuquerque Journal* depicted Villa as having civilized traits usually attributed to whites.[15]

During this period of alliance, US officials often referred to Villa as "General Villa," connoting an elevated status and acceptability despite not having any formal military training. John Lind, who Wilson sent as an envoy to Mexico, referred to Villa as "an intrepid and resourceful general. He is the highest type of physical, moral and mental efficiency that the conditions and the environment could be reasonably expected to produce. . . . I believe him a true, virulent type of the most promising element of the Mexican population." Such platitudes—albeit steeped in conventional racist sentiment—were seldom uttered by US officials after March 1916.[16]

ASIDE FROM BEING just three miles from the US-Mexican border, the sleepy town of Columbus, New Mexico, was not all that remarkable. It had been established around the turn of the century as a railway station. One US military officer at the time noted that it "did not present an attractive appearance." Another writer remarked that the town was bleak, desolate, and "ugly." It had three hotels, two restaurants, a bank, a drugstore, and some general stores. Members of the Thirteenth Cavalry were stationed there. Most of the population were either just passing through or hadn't lived there very long.[17]

Villa's raid began in the predawn darkness of March 9, 1916. The attackers, though not in uniform, did not hide their affiliation. They shouted, "Viva Mexico!" and "Viva Villa!" as they laid waste to Columbus. Most accounts state that the attackers came in two waves, one going to the military post at nearby Camp Furlong, the other into the center of town. Villa's whereabouts during the attack remains a source of contention. Initial US government reports maintained that he was with the attackers on the front lines. But subsequent scholarly accounts cast doubt on that assertion. Witnesses interviewed after the fact placed Villa on both sides of the border during the raid.[18]

Regardless of their leader's precise location, the Villistas ransacked the town. They set fire to the grocery store and looted as they attacked. The worst of the civilian casualties took place at the Commercial Hotel, where five Americans were killed. One victim, a hotel guest named John Walton Walker, was said to have been dragged away from his wife, decapitated, and burned by Villa's men. The raiders also targeted homes, including the families of soldiers stationed at the nearby camp. In the confusion, many of the soldiers tried to hustle their families to safety before setting their sights on the Villistas. After three hours, the raiders were repelled across the border as US troops gave chase some five miles into Mexican territory. Most estimates suggest that as many as one hundred Mexicans were killed in the attack and during the ensuing retreat.[19]

Back in smoldering Columbus, residents remained on edge for days. Rumors persisted that Villa would come back to inflict more damage. "Feeling in Columbus ran high tonight," the *New York Times* reported the day after the raid. "It was feared that Villa's men might return and attempt to complete their work. Every one on the streets was armed, and the troops were patrolling the line and the main streets. Civilians were guarding the bank and other places of business." Other stories reported sightings of Villa's men north of the border again, perhaps on the way to other towns in New Mexico. Locals' palpable fear and desire for vengeance was initially directed at Mexican nationals living in town. According to one account, twelve Mexicans were killed over three nights after the raid. The town's *Columbus Courier* newspaper reported that "all Mexicans who were not personally known by American citizens were ordered to leave town, and every suspicious character was forced to leave, with instructions that they would be executed if they came back here. Those who returned are now numbered with the dead."[20]

Although the most famous example, the raid on Columbus was not the first time that Villa's men had targeted Americans. Two months earlier, on January 10, a few dozen Villistas stopped a passenger train near Santa Isabel,

This political cartoon by Clifford Berryman appeared in the *Washington Evening Star* in 1916, the day after the raid on Columbus, New Mexico. It depicts an angry Uncle Sam crossing the border into Mexico to pursue Pancho Villa, who has a smoking gun in hand. Courtesy of the US National Archives and Records Administration.

Mexico—roughly 250 miles south of El Paso. According to eyewitness testimony, the militia men climbed on board shouting "Viva Villa!" and "Death to the Gringos." They assured Mexican passengers that they would not harm their fellow countrymen and were instead targeting only Americans. They marched the American passengers off the train, stripped them of their clothes, and shot each of them—save for one, Thomas B. Holmes, who managed to escape and hide in some nearby bushes. Eighteen Americans, all of whom worked for a mining company in Mexico, were killed. Moreover, the Villistas were said to have mutilated the bodies of the deceased—bayoneting corpses, crushing genitals, and gauging eyes. Pershing called the murders "the crowning piece of barbarism."[21]

Although Villa was far from the scene, these were clearly his men following his directive. Historian Friedrich Katz has argued that even if Villa did not personally order the killing of the Americans at Santa Isabel, it was in keeping with his prior warnings against Americans in late-1915 when his relationship with the United States deteriorated as the Wilson administration pulled back its support. One of Villa's lieutenants, Pablo López, was the local leader who commanded the raid. He later confessed to the crime after his April 1916 capture by Mexican authorities loyal to Carranza, who fell out with Villa two years earlier. In a subsequent interview with the Associated Press while in captivity, López offered some explanation for the massacre. "The Santa Isabel affair partly satisfied my master's desire for revenge, but it did not succeed in satisfying his other wishes," López said. "So we marched on Columbus—we invaded American soil." López, who had taken part in the attack on Columbus, remained unbowed and unapologetic to the end. When he was executed by a Carrancista firing squad in June 1916, his last request was to remove any American witnesses. The anti-American vitriol he displayed in his final days was typical of hard-core Villistas. But it would come to be shared by many Mexicans over the next few months as the US pursuit of Villa and his men intensified.[22]

WITH THE SANTA ISABEL MASSACRE still fresh in Americans' minds, news of the Columbus raid brought swift and fierce condemnation of Villa. Many such reactions called for his immediate execution. Gen. Nelson Miles, a veteran of the Civil War and the War of 1898, told the *New York Times*, "Villa and his bandits should be exterminated and the quicker that he and his followers are lined up in front of a wall and shot the better off will be Mexico and the United States." Newspaper editorials echoed those sentiments. The *Olympia Daily Recorder* declared: "To get rid of Villa, it will be necessary to catch the ruffian by the throat and hold him up until he ceases to breathe. Cruel? Perhaps, but highly efficient, and about the only way to accomplish the desired result, which is to get rid of Mr. Villa once and for all." More than just public posturing, such language also permeated privately among US officials. Secretary of State Robert Lansing, for instance, noted that he wanted to pressure Carranza, now recognized as Mexico's president, to "do everything in his power to pursue, capture, and exterminate this lawless element." These reactions reflected the notion that Villa's attack was so heinous that it justified his immediate and, if need be, extrajudicial death.[23]

Some of the terminology used to describe Villa revealed a deep-seated anger that dehumanized Villa, degrading him to an insect or animal. The extermination rhetoric, like the kind used by Miles and Lansing, conjured images of pest control. To that point, one US official in Mexico noted that the state of Durango had been "infested" with Villistas. Such talk of infestation suggested that Villa's men be confronted immediately, lest they bring a plague of lawlessness that could spread. More than one observer equated Villa to a canine. George Carothers, a part-time US consul in Torreón who had a close relationship with Villa while he was still on good terms with the United States, said, "This is a different man than we knew. All the brutality of his nature has come to the front, and he should be killed like a dog." Drawing out the metaphor further, much like a dog, Villa had once been a reliable friend to the United States, but now that he was no longer useful and was deemed a threat after Santa Isabel and Columbus, he had to be put down.[24]

Such animalistic rhetoric further suggested the continuing danger Villa posed to the United States even after Columbus. Former president William Howard Taft noted, "The sooner Villa's fangs are drawn the better." And Pershing stated that "Villa is like a coyote, and you know how hard a coyote is to catch." Descriptions by US officials not only drew analogies to communicate to the American public the lingering threat that Villa posed but also implicitly delegitimized whatever grievances Villa may have held against the United States.[25]

SCHOLARS FOR YEARS have debated Villa's intentions. One theory, not widely shared, suggested that Villa attacked Columbus simply to loot and restock diminished supplies, including horses and guns. Another notion is that his attack was retribution against American merchant Sam Ravel for an arms deal gone wrong, in which Villa did not receive the munitions for which he had paid. This theory is given some credence because the Commercial Hotel in Columbus, site of the worst civilian casualties in the raid, was a Ravel property. There are also broader conspiracy theories that Villa's attack was supported by foreign agents. One idea is that US businesspeople, eager to instigate military intervention that might lead to the acquisition of Mexican territory, put Villa up to it. The other contention is that German authorities encouraged Villa to start a war against the United States, with the hope that a conflict would dampen the sale of US war matériel to Europe during a time when the United States remained neutral during World War I. None of the aforementioned ideas, however, is grounded in much tangible evidence.[26]

The more credible theory—which remains speculative because Villa never publicly addressed the Columbus attack—is that he was angered at the Wilson administration for withdrawing its support and was trying to instigate a wider war between the United States and Mexico. The seeds were sown in October 1915 when Wilson recognized Carranza, Villa's chief rival after the fall of Huerta, as Mexico's head of state. The US government subsequently placed an arms embargo against Villa and allowed Carrancista forces to pass through US territory on their way to a crucial victory over Villistas at Agua Prieta weeks later. According to Katz, three concerns drove Wilson's change of heart. First, Carranza appeared to have control over most of Mexico and seemed on his way to winning the war against Villa and his allies anyway. Second, Wilson wanted to have good relations with Mexico in the event that formal US intervention in World War I would be necessary. Third, Carranza had given assurances to US officials that he would bring about democratic reforms and protect US-owned property.[27]

This turn of events enraged Villa and set him on a path to conflict with the United States. In a screed published in a local newspaper a week after his defeat at Agua Prieta, he accused Carranza of making a secret pact with the United States that would have granted Mexico's northern neighbor undue influence in Mexican affairs. While he declared no animosity "against the real people of the United States of North America," Villa also stated that Wilson's withdrawal of support "freed me of the obligation to give guarantees to foreigners." On January 8, 1916, Villa wrote to his chief ally in southern Mexico, Emiliano Zapata, urging him to send troops north to fight the United States. "We decided not to fire a bullet more against Mexicans, our brothers," Villa wrote, "and to prepare and organize ourselves to attack the Americans in their own dens." Two days after Villa wrote this letter, the Santa Isabel massacre took place.[28]

Based on these sources, it appears that Villa's grand strategy was to attack the United States in the hopes of instigating a US military reprisal. Such an intervention would have two benefits to Villa. First, it would put Carranza in a quandary: either prevent the presence of US troops in Mexico and incur the wrath of the United States, or allow the US military to come in and risk appearing like an American patsy. This latter possibility would bring about a second benefit to Villa—becoming a symbol of national defiance against the gringos and uniting the disparate factions of the Mexican Revolution under his leadership.

Villa did not say much about it on the record, but a variety of secondhand accounts noted his deep animosity toward the United States. In his Associated Press interview before his execution, López said, "My master, Don Pancho Villa, continually was telling us that since the gringoes [sic] had given him the 'double cross,' he meant not only to get back at them, but to try to waken our country to the danger that was very close." Bunk Spencer, one of the American civilians Villa held hostage before the Columbus attack, later told newspapers that Villa rallied his troops by railing against the United States. "He told the men that 'gringos' were to blame for conditions in Mexico, and abused Americans with every profane word he knew because the Carranza soldiers were allowed to go through the United States to reach Agua Prieta, where Villa was defeated. He didn't talk very long but before he got through, the men were crying and swearing and shrieking. Several of them got down on the ground and beat the earth with their hands." Some of the Villistas captured at Columbus offered their perspective to US officials about Villa's state of mind. According to a report from Pershing, "Prisoners state Villa very bitter, vowing death to all Americans." To complicate matters, however, some prisoners stated that they did not realize they were in US territory and instead believed they were raiding a Mexican town controlled by Carrancistas. Such confusion suggests that if anti-Americanism inspired Villa's raid, the feeling may not have permeated among all his foot soldiers.[29]

Regardless of what Villa had told his men in advance about Columbus, clearly his fortunes sagged after Agua Prieta. He began lashing out at civilian targets—not just in the United States but in Mexico as well. For example, in the town of San Pedro de la Cueva following a small exchange of gunfire with villagers, Villa ordered all adult men to be rounded up and shot. More than sixty people were killed, including a priest whom Villa allegedly shot himself. Although Villa was said to have shown remorse afterward, the executions revealed his increasing desperation in late 1915 and early 1916. Such erratic behavior also discredits his reputation as a social bandit like the kind described by historian Eric Hobsbawm. Katz incisively observed, "As his popular support dwindled, Villa resorted more and more to terror."[30]

IF VILLA'S AIM in the Columbus raid was to goad a US military response to put Carranza in a difficult position and rally Mexican nationalist sentiment on his behalf, he succeeded. The day after the attack, the Wilson administration announced the Punitive Expedition with the "sole object of capturing Villa and preventing any further raids by his band." Additional orders stated that "the work of these troops will be regarded as finished as soon as

Villa band or bands are known to be broken up." The move had a great deal of support in the US Congress and newspaper editorials across the country. Pershing led the mission in the field. He had plenty of experience in such combat following his pursuit of Moros in the Philippines and his early-career involvement in the war against famed Apache chief Geronimo in the 1880s.[31]

From the start, the expedition was beset by challenges. The first problem was simply getting around the rugged terrain of the northern Mexican desert. The heat and scarcity of water added a significant degree of difficulty. Operating in unfamiliar and hostile Mexican territory taxed a supply chain that extended hundreds of miles. Playing cat and mouse with the US army on Villa's home turf gave Villa an advantage that Pershing recognized. "Villa is entirely familiar with every foot of [the Mexican province of] Chihuahua, and the Mexican people, through friendship or fear, have always kept him advised of our every movement," Pershing wrote to General Funston. "He carries little food, lives off the country, rides his mounts hard and replaces them with fresh stock taken wherever found. Thus, he has had the advantage since the end of the first twenty-four hours after the Columbus raid occurred."[32]

The expedition, then, depended heavily on local scouts. Many of them proved unreliable for a variety of reasons: support for Villa, fear of Villa, or hostility toward the US presence. In his memoirs, Pershing recalled Mexican guides taking American troops on circuitous routes as they pursued leads on Villa's location. Even the Carrancistas, who were ostensibly aligned with US forces against Villa, often sent the Americans on wild-goose chases. "Before a week had passed," Pershing wrote, "it was perfectly clear that we were being intentionally deceived." Tompkins, who had been stationed in Columbus when Villa attacked, recognized that even if the locals were not actively sabotaging efforts by Americans, they certainly were not rooting for them. "Several Mexicans said that they would consider it a national disgrace if the Americans should capture Villa," he wrote. Tompkins noted that he and his troops regularly encountered hostile villagers even before Parral. Eager to avoid a violent confrontation with civilians, the US contingent often retreated. In one instance when the locals were verbally harassing US troops, Tompkins yelled back, "Viva Villa!" His unexpected response drew laughs and diffused the tension.[33]

To nullify Villa's advantages, the expedition tried three tactics that bore distinctive parallels to the twenty-first-century global war on terror. The first was to use a relatively new innovation—airplanes—in the search for Villa. Yet even that technological advantage was mitigated by the elements. The

JN-3 biplanes had a ceiling of 10,000 feet, equal to some of the peaks in Chihuahua. High winds and driving sand also limited the aircrafts' usefulness in reconnaissance. Of the eight planes the expedition used, only two of them returned to the United States in one piece. The use of aerial vehicles in the search for enemies was similar to the US use of drones, or unmanned aerial vehicles (UAV), in the twenty-first century. But unlike drones' mixed record of success—finding and killing high-value targets but also causing many unintended civilian casualties—the use of airplanes in Mexico was rather ineffective. One notable distinction between the two is that because the aircraft were used exclusively for surveillance, no record exists of any airplane-related Villista or civilian casualties in Mexico.[34]

Pershing established a local constabulary as the second tactic. Such a force ideally would help identify allies and provide security. It's an approach that would come to be a feature of future US occupations from Nicaragua and the Dominican Republic in the 1920s to Afghanistan and Iraq in the twenty-first century. Pershing created one in the town of Namiquipa, deep in the heart of Chihuahua, to offer the locals protection from Villistas and to help in the search. In May 1916, Pershing reported that the detachment worked with US troops to find a weapons cache used by Villa's men. But it seems that this constabulary did not provide many more lasting, tangible benefits. According to Tompkins, "Guides and messengers were hard to get and very unreliable, as they feared retaliation by Villa for serving the Americans." Katz writes that one of the constabulary leaders, José María Espinosa, was targeted when he returned to Namiquipa in 1933, "ambushed and killed by men who had neither forgotten nor forgiven his role in 1916." Such reprisals were not unlike the many instances of translators, bureaucrats, police, and soldiers—as well as their families—being marked for death by local insurgents for cooperating with Americans in Iraq and Afghanistan.[35]

A third tactic that would come to be familiar in later years was a targeted assassination attempt. Frustrated at the inability to capture Villa, US officials recruited Japanese men living in Mexico to poison him by spiking his coffee. The men got close to Villa by posing as messengers from his wife and his brother and claiming they wanted to join his militia. In September 1916, the agents reported that they had administered the poison, but a suspicious Villa had given half his cup to an underling to drink first. When Villa drank his half, the spies' desired effect failed to materialize. One scholar has claimed that the attempt against Villa was "the first known American-sponsored assassination attempt." It certainly would not be the last.[36]

AMID THESE FAILURES, the hunt for Villa brought new ruptures to US-Mexican relations. Carranza considered the sustained presence of US troops a violation of Mexican sovereignty. Initially, though, he had a different take. The day after the Columbus attack, Carranza expressed support for the expedition to find and capture Villa on the condition that Mexican authorities be given similar rights to go into US territory should Villistas attack Carrancistas. Otherwise, Carranza warned, "my Government shall consider this act as an invasion of national territory." Secretary of State Lansing agreed to those terms. The scope of the ensuing Punitive Expedition, however, seemed to exceed Carranza's expectations. Throughout March and April 1916, he protested to the US government and tried to place limits on the expedition. He proposed that any border crossing would take place only in unpopulated areas, away from towns or bases, limited to no more than 1,000 men for five days. The Wilson administration rejected any such conditions, and Pershing likewise ignored them.[37]

Tensions escalated as the Punitive Expedition encountered Carranza's forces seemingly as often as it did Villa's. Two incidents brought the countries to the brink of war. The first was the Battle of Parral on April 12. Two months later, another skirmish between US and Carranza forces took place at Carrizal. In this clash, an estimated forty-five Mexican troops were killed as well as nine Americans; an additional twenty-three US troops were captured but later released. In between these clashes, Scott and Funston met with Mexican general Álvaro Obregón in El Paso to discuss the withdrawal of US troops. Although cordial in public, Funston privately fumed about Mexican treachery. He wrote to Pershing that there was "absolute proof of deliberate and premeditated intention on part of Carranza forces from the first to prevent [the] success [of] this expedition. Carranza's officers have stated openly that they would not allow Americans to capture Villa and as already stated in previous reports they have without doubt aided him to escape."[38]

This frustration led some military officers to consider occupying all of Chihuahua until Villa could be caught. Pershing put forth such a recommendation. Tompkins took the idea a step further and argued that the United States should have invaded all of Mexico. "That we failed to do so was a fatal error," he wrote years later in his memoir, "for our continued acceptance of Mexican abuse not only warranted Mexican contempt but weakened our prestige abroad." Even George S. Patton, who was a lieutenant in the expedition and would go on to win fame as a general during World War II, privately called for a wider occupation of Mexico. In a September 1916 letter to his father, Patton criticized Wilson's reluctance to widen the search for Villa, saying that the president "has not the soul of a louse nor the mind of a worm or the backbone of a jellyfish."[39]

Ultimately, Wilson rejected officers' calls to expand the mission. After Carrizal, US forces pulled back into northern Chihuahua, where they remained without much incident until early February 1917, by which point formal US entry into World War I was on the horizon. Secretary of War Newton Baker, who began his tenure on the day of the Columbus raid, reported the expedition a success. "Its objective, of course, was the capture of Villa, if that could be accomplished, but its real purpose was an extension of the power of the United States . . . as a means of controlling lawless aggressions of bandits and preventing attacks by them across the international frontier. This purpose is fully and finally accomplished." Likewise, Pershing asserted that the Punitive Expedition accomplished its most important objective despite Carranza's intransigence. "We had not captured Villa to be sure, as we had hoped to do, but when active pursuit stopped we had broken up and scattered his band, which was our original mission," he wrote.[40]

Although Baker and Pershing may have been guilty of a little apple-polishing given that Villa remained at large, the Punitive Expedition did have some success. Within the first three months of the mission, more than 400 of Villa's men had been killed, including Villa's second in command, Candelario Cervantes. US forces had also been very close to nabbing Villa himself in the town of Guerrero just three weeks into the expedition, when he was likely wounded.[41]

Moreover, two groups of Villistas were captured and tried in New Mexico courts for the murder of a man named Charles D. Miller during the Columbus raid. Among the first group, seven men in April 1916 were found guilty. Although no evidence showed they were directly involved in Miller's death, a jury convicted them by virtue of their participation in the attack. Six men were hanged, and one had a sentence commuted to life imprisonment. In the second group, which had been captured in Namiquipa, seventeen men in August 1917 pleaded guilty to second-degree murder and received sentences of up to eighty years in prison. Three years later, though, New Mexico's governor pardoned them all on the grounds that he considered them soldiers following orders and that the men thought they were fighting Carrancistas, not Americans.[42]

These "victories" came at an estimated cost of $340 million—both for the expedition itself and for the improvements in defenses at the border. According to the Department of War, twenty-six US servicemen were killed, another twenty-five were wounded, and one was missing. Among Mexicans, it estimated 200 soldiers were killed or wounded.[43]

SKIRMISHES WITH VILLISTAS flared on occasion over the next few years, by which point Villa had been largely neutralized in the ongoing Mexican Revolution. In June 1919, a cross-border exchange of gunfire resulted in some 1,600 US troops entering Mexico at Ciudad Juárez, where thirty-six Villistas were killed. American forces returned north within forty-eight hours. In Mexico, Villa's men continued to raid mines and occasionally captured US citizens. For example, three Americans were held briefly in October 1918 and released without incident. A year later, in December, Villa's men kidnapped American Frank Hugo, who managed a ranch in Coahuila. He was released after a few days on condition that he say nothing about where he was held or publicly disclose if he had paid the reported $10,000 ransom. "I was treated like one of the party and became really favorably impressed with Pancho Villa," Hugo told the *New York Times*. He continued, "Pancho Villa has traits I could not help admiring. When he talks to you he looks you squarely in the eyes and leaves no doubt in your mind but that he means business." Such comments suggested a subtle reconsideration of Villa's reputation among some Americans.[44]

Although American audiences often reflexively described Villa as a "bandit," the *New York Times* challenged that assumption in a June 1917 editorial a few months after the Punitive Expedition, questioning whether the "bandit" label truly applied to Villa. In a rather extraordinary article that undercut contemporary conventional wisdom, the newspaper argued, "Perhaps it would help somewhat if we ceased to apply Anglo-Saxon standards" on Villa and instead consider him within the broader context of the Mexican Revolution and Mexican society. The editorial continued, "He was a bandit because he did not have enough military strength to be called a rebel; now he has got it and is a bandit no longer. It was only in the legal sense that he was a bandit at all. There is not much use in wasting epithets and denunciation upon him. . . . A good way to begin is to cease hurling adjectives at Villa and observe him." The editorial reveals how Americans struggled to understand and come to terms with Villa. It recognized a significant cultural bias that prevented many Americans from comprehending any practical or pragmatic reasons for Villa's raid on Columbus. Instead of uncritically affixing a label on the enemy, the editorial argued, Americans might have been better off avoiding future attacks by seeking to understand the opponent on his own terms.[45]

Such reconsiderations, though, were uncommon. The "bandit" label remained prevalent among US depictions of Villa. The *Fort-Worth Star Telegram* in November 1917 didn't buy into notions of Villa reformism, declaring, "In spite of this bandit's profession that his aims are both 'patriotic' and 'noble,' there is no evidence that he is now any more than he ever has been, simply a lawless disturber of the peace, whose normal occupation is murder and robbery. . . . The real truth about Pancho Villa is that he is as wild and untamed as a timber wolf and has as much place in civilized society as a rattlesnake." The latter sentence, in particular, shows that the animalistic, dehumanizing language so prevalent in popular discourse about Villa remained dominant nearly two years after the attack on Columbus. Even after Villa semiretired from public life, the *Oregonian* maintained that Villa had never really changed or atoned for his past deeds. "The reformed bandit is not a heroic figure, or even a pitiful one," the newspaper wrote. "The misdeeds of a long life are not to be atoned by a few months of benevolence inspired by a desire to balance life's grim account."[46]

Grim, indeed, is how Villa's life ended. Although he had eluded the Americans' Punitive Expedition, his militia—and thus his influence in Mexican political affairs—dwindled. In July 1920, Villa agreed to lay down his arms against the Mexican government in exchange for amnesty, a *hacienda* in Durango, and pay for nearly 800 fighters loyal to him. During the next three years, he remained relatively out of the limelight. But there was some talk he was considering running for governor of Durango, where he remained popular. That never happened. Presumably under orders from jealous Mexican political rivals—perhaps even including then-President Obregón—gunmen on July 20, 1923, opened fire on Villa as he was riding in an automobile in Parral. He was hit nine times and died instantly. He was forty-five years old.[47]

IN THE UNITED STATES, popular reflections on Villa's death followed many of the same rhetorical patterns as previous ruminations about his life. He was still commonly mentioned as a "bandit" or "outlaw." Some outlets went further by describing him in subhuman terms. The *Washington Post* referred to him as a "human tiger who so often slaked his thirst by taking the blood of others." A *Los Angeles Times* writer portrayed Villa as a "primitive man" who had the "fury of some jungle beast." The piece continued that viewed from modern standards, Villa was a bad man, but "from animal standards, he was a splendid creature."[48]

Some publications took a different tack. The *Hartford Courant* noted Villa's strong leadership and called him "no ordinary man and students of United States history will realize it in years to come." A *New York Times* editorial about him made no mention of the raid on Columbus and asserted that "Francisco Villa was never so black as he was painted, nor did he receive credit for abilities of a high order." Indeed, the editorial seemed to lament wasted talent

Hunting the Outlaw 53

undermined by circumstance rather than his own choices. "After the worst has been said of Francisco Villa, after his crimes have been proved and his vices passed in review, the reflection is provoked that in a progressive and enlightened Mexico he might have been a useful servant of the State."[49]

Over the years, American animosity toward Villa softened as remembrances of his actions in Columbus faded from popular memory. Yet the "bandit" discourse persisted. For example, Avon Comics in 1950 released an edition titled "Pancho Villa: Mexico's No. 1 Bandit" that featured three short stories (very) loosely based on Villa's life. Although Villa is described as "the greatest 'bad man' of the twentieth century," each story offers a sympathetic depiction of him as virtuous and brave. Notably, his appearance is whitened and he looks more like actor Clark Gable than the historical Villa. The tales do not deny Villa's temper but show that he was justified in using violence against elites who provoked him or to defend his family and the local poor.[50]

A decade later, Villa posthumously received another honor. In 1961, the state of New Mexico dedicated Pancho Villa State Park on the site that had once housed Camp Furlong outside of Columbus. The name may have seemed like an odd choice, and locals were generally opposed to it. But according to the *New York Times*, state officials chose the name "not to honor the bandit, but to commemorate the battle and the peaceful relations between the United States and Mexico." Even in a gesture recognizing Villa, the "bandit" discourse remained firmly embedded within his legacy—albeit with less vitriol than had been the case nearly a half century earlier.[51]

THE US HUNT FOR VILLA was rife with frustration. Despite spending millions of dollars and committing thousands of troops to the pursuit, Americans failed to bring their target to justice. Moreover, Villa's ability to elude the Americans made him a hero among many Mexicans. This dynamic reflected a growing sense of anti-Americanism in places the United States tried to exert more influence and authority during the early twentieth century. US goals to maintain a sphere of influence in Latin America put it in conflict with more resisters, such as one in Nicaragua. Like Villa, Augusto Sandino refused to be cowed by American power and defiantly thumbed his nose at the Colossus of the North. This resistance, which goaded the United States into another frustrating pursuit, would also make him an inspiration to others.

CHAPTER THREE

A Plain Bandit
Augusto Sandino in Nicaragua

G. D. Hatfield had come a long way to not end up on the short end of an exchange.

In June 1927, the US Marine captain found himself in Ocotal, a small town in a remote corner of Nicaragua near the Honduran border. Perched nearly 2,000 feet above sea level, the town sat in a valley with a mountain ridge to the north and small streams running through it. Roads were scarce, and mountain passes were almost impossible to travel during the rainy season. It was home to roughly 1,400 people. But when Hatfield arrived, much of the town was already deserted, which was precisely why he was there.

Leading a detachment of approximately a dozen marines, Hatfield's orders were to protect the town from a potential attack by Augusto Sandino and his militia. A month earlier, Sandino had begun an armed resistance in the province of Nueva Segovia—where Ocotal was located—against the US presence in his country. Not only was he targeting marines but also fellow Nicaraguans he viewed as collaborators. Although he had no formal military training, the thirty-two-year-old Sandino more than made up for his lack of know-how with passion and chutzpah. Standing just five feet, five inches tall and probably no heavier than a boxing featherweight, Sandino could pack a rhetorical punch. He seemed to relish challenging, goading, and insulting his enemies.

Hatfield was one of the first Americans to encounter Sandino's vitriol when the two engaged in a lengthy telegraph correspondence that summer. Hatfield was trying to compel Sandino to surrender without bloodshed. But the contempt for which he held the Nicaraguan permeated—and surely undermined—his overtures. He snidely closed one of his notes with, "Trusting that you will soon come and salute me personally." In another, Hatfield wrote he was "hoping that you are a patriot and not a robber." Not to be cowed, Sandino challenged the marines to come and find him, warning Hatfield and his men to "make your wills beforehand." To which a fed-up Hatfield replied, "Bravo, General! If words were bullets and phrases were soldiers, you would be a field marshal instead of a mule thief."[1]

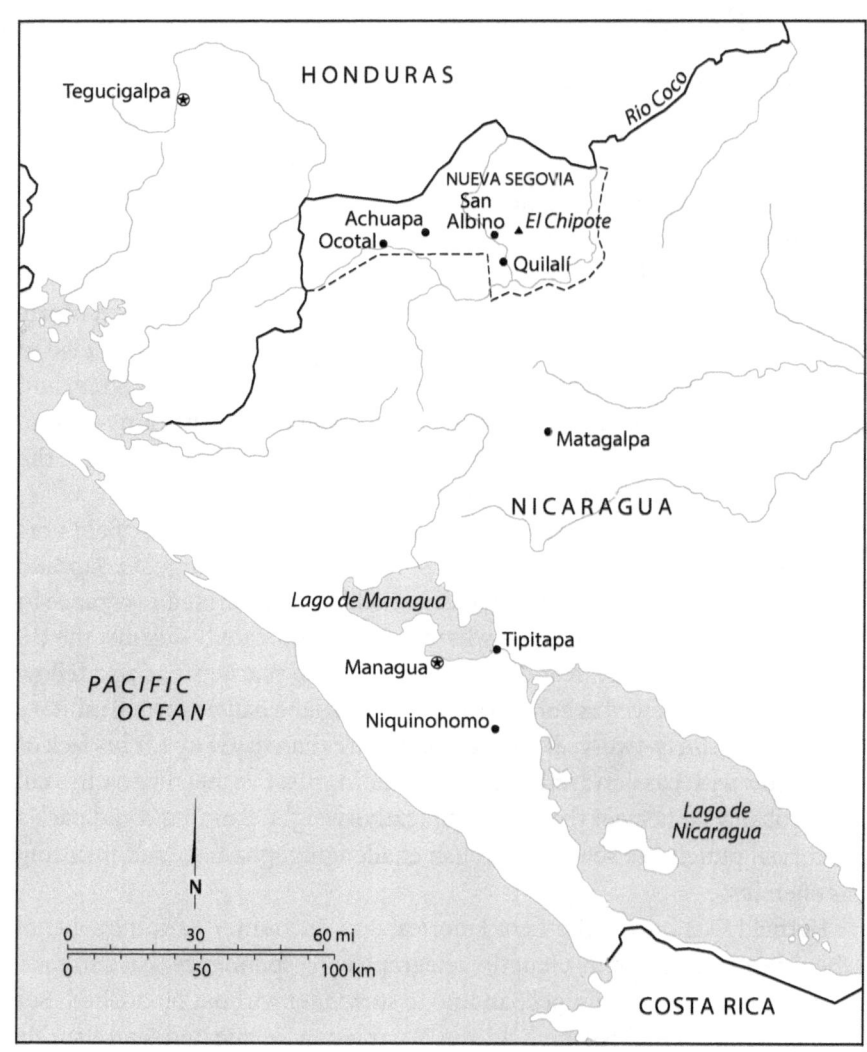

Western Nicaragua

Clearly frustrated by Sandino's stubborn resistance, Hatfield warned that if Sandino miraculously managed to escape, "you will be an exile and an outlaw, like a pig, hunted down and repudiated everywhere, awaiting your shameful death." Unbowed, Sandino responded that should the marines pursue him, the Sandinista militia "will leave several tons of dead bodies on the battlefield . . . and thus we will have the honor of irrigating the soil of our Native Land with traitors' and invaders' blood." In a public manifesto, Sandino referred to Hatfield as "[President Calvin] Coolidge's hired assassin and servant of Wall Street," adding that his pursuer was a "degenerate pirate [who does] not even know [his] father or [his] real language." Undaunted and reinforced by more than two dozen additional marines as well as forty-eight members of the Nicaraguan National Guard, Hatfield set a July 14 deadline for Sandino to surrender.[2]

Instead, in the dark morning hours of July 16, Sandinista forces—perhaps as many as 500—armed with machine guns infiltrated the town. After a marine spotted some of them at 1:15 a.m., a firefight ensued. The exchange went on for seven hours before a brief ceasefire. Now it was Sandino's turn to demand a surrender, promising Hatfield and the marines no harm if they agreed to give up their arms. Hatfield confidently declined the offer.

His assuredness was rewarded later that afternoon when the cavalry arrived—by air. Five US Marine biplanes dive-bombed Sandinista positions, first in aviation history, according to one historian. The operation proved a success. By late afternoon, the remaining Sandinista forces had fled back to their mountain hideouts. Hatfield estimated at least 300 Sandinistas had died, although that number was never confirmed. In contrast, one marine was killed and another wounded, as well as three wounded Nicaraguan National Guardsmen and four more captured. After getting the news from the battlefield, US Minister to Nicaragua Charles C. Eberhardt reported to Washington, "It is not supposed that Sandino will offer much further serious resistance."[3]

He was wrong.

Over the next six years, Sandino would remain a thorn in the Americans' side. When he wasn't insulting his American pursuers and their local allies, Sandino and his cadre of rural fighters were staging hit-and-run attacks while vying for the respect and admiration of the Nicaraguan peasantry. Although he never came close to seizing control of the country, Sandino's ability to elude US forces threatened the perception that the United States could maintain order and stability in a place of geostrategic interest. Moreover, it infuriated leaders in Washington, including President Herbert Hoover, who frustratingly referred to Sandino as "a plain bandit." The American chase for Sandino, particularly the justification of illegitimate means to accomplish the mission, bore many of the same characteristics as other pursuits, including the twenty-first-century global war on terror.

THE US MARINE PRESENCE in Nicaragua came during a spate of military interventions throughout the Caribbean region during the early twentieth century—including Cuba, Mexico, Panama, Haiti, and the Dominican Republic. It was an era in which US policymakers felt more confident asserting American influence in regional affairs. These interventions had a variety of justifications: protect American property and commercial interests; guard the access to—and the security of—an interoceanic canal; ward off European influence in the United States' "backyard"; and help so-called racially inferior peoples. Such rationales supported the US presence in Nicaragua as well.

At the turn of the twentieth century, US businesspeople and policymakers placed renewed emphasis on finding markets and resources abroad to support the nation's commercial interests. Business owners found Nicaragua advantageous because its weak government welcomed foreign capital and relied on trade with the United States to sustain itself. Easy access to the country's mines and lumber compelled American entrepreneurs to buy property and establish businesses there. The need to transport goods and produce to US markets more quickly was one factor that drove the United States to build an interoceanic canal in neighboring Panama. Before the United States acquired the Canal Zone in 1903, though, policymakers had considered Nicaragua. The idea held so much interest that the United States retained the option through the 1916 Bryan-Chamorro Treaty to build a second canal that would have further shortened the water route between New York and San Francisco. More important, the treaty prevented any rival European power from building a competing canal.

The desire to head off European influence also factored into American interest in Nicaragua. Various US policymakers had long considered the Caribbean region to be an American lake—more so after the defeat of Spain in 1898—and jealously guarded outside encroachment. Leaders in the United States feared European powers that owned significant commercial debt over a Caribbean or Central American nation could use it to justify political or economic concessions—or worse, the acquisition of a military base. Such debt often came about because of disorder and political instability. These situations not only posed significant risks to American businesses but also raised the potential of radicalism that could undermine broader US interests. One of the big national concerns in the 1920s was the onset of Bolshevism, which was gaining adherents internationally following the creation of the Soviet Union. Venerable US officials such as Henry Stimson, a secretary of state and two-time secretary of war, rationalized American efforts in defense of the region. "For a century," he wrote, "we have been the scrupulous protector of their independence, not only against Europe but sometimes even against themselves."[4]

The latter sentiment revealed a deep-seated paternalism that most US officials held toward the region's peoples. This sensibility was grounded in common racist attitudes of the early twentieth century that, not coincidentally, came during the height of Jim Crow segregation at home. White Americans at the time widely believed in a hierarchy of races that placed Anglo-Saxons at the top and nonwhites below. This popular ideology maintained that dark-skinned peoples of tropical regions were underdeveloped, lacked self-control, and did not have the wherewithal to marshal their own resources effectively or to govern themselves responsibly. Hence, it was the United States' duty to help such people, even if they resisted.

Formal US involvement in Nicaragua began in earnest in 1912 when, in the midst of a budding civil war between Liberals and Conservatives, the Nicaraguan government warned Washington about threats to American lives and property and asked for support. More than 2,000 US Marines helped quell the conflict, and a small contingent remained there until 1925. A year later, US forces returned as civil war erupted once again. In April 1927, President Calvin Coolidge sent Stimson to Nicaragua to broker an agreement between the warring sides. The resulting deal—known as the Tipitapa Agreement after the town where it was signed—kept the Conservative Adolfo Díaz as president, called for US-supervised elections in 1928 and 1932, and allowed for the establishment of a National Guard (Guardia Nacional, or GN). The marines would remain in the country for the duration to ensure the peace until the GN was ready. The country's Liberal leaders involved in the civil war all signed the pact—except one.[5]

AUGUSTO SANDINO remained the lone holdout. His refusal to go along did not register at first with many Americans or Nicaraguans as a matter of great importance. US Minister to Nicaragua Charles C. Eberhardt informed Washington that despite Sandino's truculence, "I believe this marks definitely the

A Plain Bandit 59

end of the insurrection." At the time, Sandino headed only a small militia of like-minded Liberals and was not well-known, even in his own country. He seemed to pose no threat to American interests.[6]

Indeed, very little in Sandino's personal background suggested he would one day become a Nicaraguan national hero. His enemies who called him a bastard were not entirely wrong. He was born out of wedlock in May 1895 in Niquinohomo, Nicaragua. His father, Gregorio, was a merchant and planter; his mother, Margarita Calderón, had worked in the homes and fields of the Sandino family. Despite his father's wealth and status, young Augusto grew up largely in poverty, raised by his mother. For a time, Margarita's failure to pay debts landed them in jail. By one account, Augusto was ashamed of his social condition and angry at his mother's promiscuity that produced an unknown number of maternal siblings. At age nine, he went to live with his maternal grandmother before eventually finding his way to his father, who took him in. Although his material conditions improved, his father and stepmother treated him differently from his three paternal siblings. Treated more like a servant, he had to do chores, eat with the help, and wear his younger brother's hand-me-downs.[7]

Sandino's life took a turn in June 1921 just when things were starting to settle for him. Working for his father and engaged to be married to a cousin, Sandino got into a dispute with a local rival, Dagoberto Rivas. Although the precise nature of the argument remains unclear, its results were not. Sandino shot Rivas, wounding him. Fearing arrest, Sandino went on the run and fled the country. He took up a variety of odd jobs to get by. The first was on a plantation in Honduras, followed by a brief stint on a United Fruit Company farm in Guatemala, and eventually as a mechanic and stockkeeper on an American-owned oil field in Mexico. On this last stop Sandino got word of the burgeoning civil war in his homeland. In May 1926, he quit his job to join the fight back in Nicaragua on behalf of the Liberals, to whom his father had allegiance.[8]

When Sandino returned to Nicaragua, however, the party's leadership gave the unknown and untested Sandino a chilly reception. Over the next year, the relationship did not improve. He developed a particular grudge against José María Moncada, one of the leading Liberal supporters of the Tipitapa Agreement. "He tried to soft-talk me into accepting the cease-fire," Sandino later recalled. "He assured me that it would be crazy to fight against the United States of the North because it is a very powerful nation with 120 million inhabitants. I could do nothing with 300 men under my command.

What would happen would be like what happens to a little lamb in the grasp of a tiger. From that moment, I felt a profound contempt for Moncada. I told him that I consider it a responsibility to die for Liberty."[9]

From that point, Sandino began his own rebellion in the sparsely populated Segovias of northwest Nicaragua. The group's formal name reflected their aim: Ejército Defensor de la Soberanía Nacional de Nicaragua (Army in Defense of Nicaraguan National Sovereignty). Given Sandino's position of leadership, though, they came to be known more informally as Sandinistas. According to one scholar, Sandino's militia "was made up primarily of hungry, barefoot, and ill-equipped *campesinos*, dressed in rags and with no military training." Many of the men were illiterate, had not been outside the region, and had never seen some of the new, modern conveniences of the age, such as electricity or automobiles. Sandino surrounded himself with a personal guard of about thirty men, some of whom were as young as thirteen years of age. Given the group's ragtag nature, material support from the local population was paramount to their survival. Sandino thus chose to curry favor by way of his personal conduct. A bit of a teetotaler, Sandino did not drink, smoke, or gamble. He expected his men to treat the locals with respect. Those who flouted the rules, stole, or abused peasants in any way could be subject to execution.[10]

Physically, Sandino was anything but intimidating. Short and slender, he amplified his presence by wearing a large brown Stetson hat and carrying a red-and-black kerchief with a .45-caliber pistol. His strength, rather, came from his convictions and the way in which he expressed them. In letters both public and private, he was often boastful about his abilities and savagely disparaged enemies at home and abroad. He referred to Nicaraguan collaborators with the United States as "eunuchs" and "sellouts." He called Conservative and Liberal leaders "a pack of dogs, cowards, and traitors." But he reserved his harshest vitriol for Americans, typically referring to US Marines as pirates, criminals, beasts, and morphine addicts. He also called the US eagle a "chicken."[11]

In his correspondence, Sandino never betrayed any doubt about his mission, nor was he overly circumspect about the way in which he went about it. As he stated in a July 1927 manifesto, "The Capitol Building in Washington will shake with the destruction of your greatness, and our blood will redden the white dome of your famous White House, the cavern where you concoct your crimes." This determination and gumption to challenge the United States led many observers to compare him to Pancho Villa. Some contempo-

Although short in stature, Augusto Sandino, shown here in early 1928, packed a rhetorical punch. He reveled in verbally disparaging his American and Nicaraguan enemies while carrying on a lengthy rural insurgency. Courtesy of the Library of Congress.

rary profiles of Sandino in the US press claimed that he had learned his rebellious ways from Villa while Sandino had been living in Mexico. However, there is no evidence to suggest that they ever met.[12]

Sandino wanted, above all, to remove US influence from Nicaraguan affairs. In his public manifesto addressed to "Nicaraguans, Central Americans, and the Indo-Hispanic race," he wrote, "I am not a mercenary, but rather a patriot who does not allow outrageous assaults upon our sovereignty." He advocated for the immediate removal of the roughly 5,500 US Marines in the country serving as peacekeepers—or invaders, as Sandino saw them. Moreover, the fact that Americans would oversee the 1928 presidential election, as agreed to at Tipitapa, galled him. If Nicaraguans needed help organizing and monitoring their own election, he much preferred such supervision come from other Latin American countries that he found to be more culturally aligned.[13]

HIS DEMANDS IGNORED, Sandino and his militia took up arms. His first move in June 1927 was to seize the San Albino gold mine owned by Charles Butters, an American mining engineer and metallurgist. A reported fifty Sandinistas confiscated some 500 pounds of dynamite, took over the mine, and kicked out all foreign workers. In an open letter to the Nicaraguan people two weeks later, Sandino justified his group's action by arguing he was defending the country's workers. He claimed that Butters had engaged in the sort of abusive practices that other American-owned companies, like United Fruit, had used elsewhere in Nicaragua and Central America—practices with which he was surely familiar from his time working on their plantations. "[Butters] defrauds my fellow citizens whom he obliges to work 12 hours a day," Sandino wrote. "He pays them with vouchers worth from 5 pesos to 5 cents, which are accepted only in his commissary in exchange for double-priced merchandise. *He believes that he is authorized by his nationality to commit these abuses, and gets by with them.*" By couching his argument in labor justice, Sandino also suggested how deeply pernicious US influence ran in Nicaraguan affairs.[14]

Days later, US Marines and their GN allies confronted Sandino in Ocotal. The marine victory, though overwhelming, was by no means decisive. From then on, Sandino's resistance shifted to a guerrilla campaign, staging small hit-and-run attacks on targets rather than squaring off against marines or the GN on a battlefield. As Sandino famously noted in an October 1927 letter, "Freedom is not won with flowers! It is with bullets that we must drive the enemy from power!"[15]

To that end, Sandinistas engaged in unconventional tactics—ranging from the comical to the profane—to stymie the marine pursuit. For example, before retreating in January 1928 from their mountain hideout at El Chipote, Sandinistas allegedly set up straw dummies armed with wooden rifles that US forces attacked as the militia made their escape. More severely, though, Sandinistas were apt to mutilate the bodies of fallen marines and their Nicaraguan allies. According to historian Neill Macaulay, the rebels used a variety of cuts—or *cortes*—such as these:

- *Corte de chaleco* (vest cut): The victim was decapitated via machete, with arms severed at the shoulders and a design etched on the victim's chest.
- *Corte de cumbo* (gourd cut): A portion of the victim's skull was sliced off, exposing the brain and causing hours of suffering before death.

- *Corte de bloomers*: The victims' legs were cut off at the knees, causing them to bleed to death.
- *Corte de corbata* (tie cut): The victim's throat was cut and the tongue pulled through the slit.
- *Corte de puro* (cigar cut): The victim's penis was amputated and put in his mouth.

Although such desecrations surely were driven, in part, by vengeance or sadism, they were meant to strike fear in the hearts of pursuing marines and GN forces. Sandino publicly admitted to engaging in such tactics but claimed that his men had done so only after marines had done it first. Indeed, there were rumors that the men of Marine Company M led by Lewis "Chesty" Puller carried on their belts the ears of dead Sandinistas. Still, it's clear that Sandinistas had taken some measure of pride in these mutilations. The group's official seal above the slogan of *"patria y libertad"* featured a drawing of a Sandinista preparing to behead a marine.[16]

SUCH SHOCKING language and behavior—in addition to operating without the sanction of either major political party—fueled US officials' contention that Sandino was a "bandit" or an "outlaw." In both public and private correspondence, the US Department of State commonly and uncritically used such terminology. In July 1927, Secretary of State Frank Kellogg wrote a letter to American Federation of Labor president William Green that the *New York Times* reprinted. Kellogg commented that "[Sandino's] activities cannot be considered to have any political significance whatsoever. . . . [Sandinistas] are in effect nothing more than common outlaws." Even within the State Department, such language permeated policy deliberations. Latin American Division head Dana Munro told Kellogg in January 1928 that US forces in Nicaragua did not have the "legal authority to hold bandit prisoners" and urged the department to declare a state of war in Nueva Segovia. Kellogg, however, refused to support the idea. Such a declaration, he argued, "would probably have the effect of converting Sandino's status from that of a mere bandit to that of leader of an organized rebellion."[17]

The "bandit" rhetoric of US officials was crucial, not just as a means to antagonize Sandino (which it did), but also to justify the continued occupation of Nicaragua and to sway public opinion. Above all, such discourse suggested the illegitimacy of Sandino's platform. Publicly and privately, Sandino maintained that his rebellion was nationalist and anti-imperialist. He sought no political office nor spoils of war. Nevertheless, US officials consistently denied that Sandino's rebellion was principled, altruistic, or spoke for all Nicaraguans. The "bandit" terminology proved to be a common shorthand to reflect that position, one used to casually denigrate and dismiss Sandino's grievances. Moreover, it ascribed criminality to Sandino and his fighters, suggesting they were operating outside the bounds of civilized behavior. By inference, going back to the 1904 Roosevelt Corollary to the Monroe Doctrine, it was the United States' responsibility to rein in and punish the Sandinistas' illegal activities.

As Michael Bhatia explained in a 2005 article, such disparaging language has been a common tactic among empires facing resistance to their presence—from Ancient Rome to Napoleonic France to the modern United States. He wrote, "An occupation's or empire's designation of an internal resistance as 'bandits' serves to demonstrate their control over territory and deny their opponent legitimacy. . . . The description or 'reduction' of a revolutionary movement to that of an insurgency removes the political or anti-occupation core of its actions, relegating it to a position of lawlessness and proposing it as an agent of disorder." The terminology, once ingrained in an audience, often leads to uncritical associations with particular motives and characteristics. In the case of the bandit: criminality, illegality, and illegitimacy.[18]

Consistently calling Sandino and his supporters "bandits" served another purpose. Positioning the Sandinistas as outside the bounds of legitimate resistance suggested that the US response to that resistance did not have to abide by legitimate methods either. According to historian Richard Grossman, persistent labeling of the Sandinistas as bandits "helped define the military tactics that were used. Since the United States was not fighting a legitimate military foe, it was argued, the rules of war (such as they were) did not apply." Indeed, US Marines did not consider captured Sandinistas as "prisoners of war" because of their methods of insurgency. The status was important because, as a signatory of a 1907 international agreement at The Hague, the United States was bound to treat captives humanely. However, one marine commander, R. H. Dunlap, argued that Sandinistas did not qualify for such protections "because of the fact that enemy forces do not wear uniforms, often do not bear arms openly and do not conform to the customs and usages of war; and because of the additional fact that we are at peace with the government of Nicaragua." As a result, he concluded, "I am unable to find any grounds, either moral or legal, upon which captured members of Sandino's bands can claim the status of prisoners of war." In other words, to recognize captives as "prisoners of war" would acknowledge their legitimacy as a movement. A century later, the administration of President George W. Bush would use a similar rationale to justify the harsh treatment and indefinite detainment of what it called "unlawful enemy combatants" in the global war on terror.[19]

The depiction of Sandinistas as criminal lawbreakers rather than soldiers permitted US Marines and their GN allies to pursue them with impunity. But their tactics and despoilment of local communities would lead to questions as to whether it was, in fact, the Americans who could be more aptly labeled the "bandits" in Nicaragua. Sandino had been suggesting as much early in his rebellion. He frequently noted the destruction of villages, rape of local women, and killing of civilians at the hands of marines and the GN. In January 1928, he wrote that the town of Quilalí had been "set on fire by the conquerors." He added that "hundreds of young girls and respectable matrons have been violated. Many of them died after their disgrace, murdered by those who are seeking to make the world believe in the unselfishness of their efforts to bring peace to our land."[20]

Sandino was particularly incensed by Americans' use of a relatively new weapon of war—the airplane. In the search for Sandino in Nicaragua's remote mountainous jungle, aircraft proved effective for reconnaissance. But US pilots also indiscriminately bombed suspected hideouts, a tactic that devastated the local population. In a January 1928 public statement justifying the confiscation of US-owned properties, Sandino called marines "piratical invaders ... [who] have sown terror, destroying in a cowardly fashion everything they have found in their way." Specifically, he noted that "to commit these acts of savagery they use fleets of airplanes and large-caliber cannon, contrary to all human law, certain of impunity because of their knowledge that our army lacks these elements of combat."[21]

These charges reached a broader audience in journalist Carleton Beals's nine-part series of articles published by the *Nation* in early 1928. Beals traveled to Nicaragua to meet with Sandino and gave a compelling account of the conditions faced by Sandinistas. Beals's reporting strongly suggested that Americans were doing the terrorizing much more than Sandino and his men. He relayed numerous Sandinista allegations of civilians killed, villages razed to the ground, and indiscriminate airplane bombing—with little evidence of the kind of rural infrastructure development that the US government had promised. At El Chipote, for example, Sandino told Beals that "we left because the marines were devastating the countryside and destroying the homes of our friends. They were destroying our food supply, not by attacking us but by terrorizing the *campesinos* who had previously brought us provisions." Such tales compelled a sympathetic Beals to comment, "I listened to stories of American atrocities that made our own tales of German misdeeds [in World War I] seem tame."[22]

ACCORDING TO ONE ESTIMATE, there were eighty-five engagements with Sandinista fighters during the first six months of 1928, though none on the scale of Ocotal. By that point, the US government estimated that Sandino had roughly eighty fighters left under his command. Eberhardt noted that "airplanes and ground patrols have been able to inflict serious damage" on the Sandinistas and that the "movement has lost practically all of its significance." He cautioned, however, that they still posed a threat because "it is very probable that such bands will continue to commit depredations and acts of terrorism from time to time."[23]

Indeed, most Sandinista activity during 1928 consisted of raids on mines and farms, principally foreign-owned ones, to reinforce Sandino's self-described nationalist agenda and to sustain the dwindling militia. On such occasions in which Sandino's forces seized Nicaraguan and non-US properties, they would provide receipts of materials taken. US-owned properties, however, did not receive the same courtesy. In April 1928, for example, Sandino left a note to the manager of an American-owned mine that his forces had attacked. It read, in part:

> Dear Sir: I have the honor to inform you that on this date your mine has been reduced to ashes, by disposition of this command, to make more tangible our protest against the warlike invasion your Government has made of our territory, with no other right than that of brute force. . . . The losses which you have sustained in the aforementioned mine you may collect from the Government of the United States—Calvin Coolidge, who is the only one truly responsible for the horrible and disastrous situation through which Nicaragua is now passing.

Sandino concluded the note by reiterating his demands from the previous year: the removal of US Marines and complete Nicaraguan autonomy to conduct its own election.[24]

Despite Sandino's threats and protests, the November 1928 elections were conducted safely and produced an 88 percent turnout of the electorate. José María Moncada, the Liberal candidate for president—and Sandino's bête noire—won convincingly. Given the success of the election that it was ostensibly there to protect, the United States then began a steady drawdown of its forces from a peak of 5,480 marines in 1928 to roughly 1,250 by June 1930. Yet the American military presence remained, much to Sandino's consternation. In March 1929, he reached out to the new US president. In a confident yet strident letter, he cautioned Herbert Hoover not to make the same mistakes of Coolidge. Sandino wrote:

> Coolidge and Kellogg are a pair of failed politicians. Their action in Nicaragua has sunk the land of Washington to the lowest depths of discredit. They have caused the shedding of blood and torrents of tears in my Homeland. They have also plunged many North American homes into mourning and caused weeping. You have only a tiny group of immoral friends in Nicaragua, who do not represent the sentiments of the Nicaraguan people. I represent, with my Army, the true sentiments of our citizens. The great majority of Nicaraguans are with me. I am aware of the material resources which your country has. You have everything, but "you are lacking God." If you continue the politics of Coolidge and Kellogg, you will continue to find Sandinos.[25]

By early 1929, though, Sandino's movement was floundering. He had failed to oust the marines or stop the US-sanctioned election. Nor was he able to recruit many more fighters into his ranks. Despite his outsized rhetoric, his rebellion was not attracting a great deal of support among Nicaraguans outside the rural Segovias. Certainly, there was a degree of popular antipathy toward the US presence, exacerbated by reports of marine and GN atrocities. In the capital city of Managua, one anti-US protest featured an estimated 6,000 marchers. But there were no signs or speeches referencing the Sandinistas. Although the Nicaraguan press often published articles about the war, many reports dismissed the group as "bandits." One estimate suggested that perhaps just 10 percent of Nicaraguans actively supported the Sandinistas. The more educated and propertied classes tended to blanch at Sandino's tactics. Moreover, he did not establish significant alliances with the politically likeminded. For as much as Sandino despised his fellow Liberal — and new president — Moncada, the feeling was mutual. "It is our duty to disown Sandino," Moncada wrote in a July 1927 open letter. "He respects neither life, liberty nor property. He is truthfully accused of assassinating defenseless persons.... Sandino has become the scourge of his own party."[26]

Given all the turmoil in his militia, it was time to regroup.

BY US ESTIMATES, Sandino's movement was on the ropes. Sandinista morale "had reached a low point," Eberhardt reported in March 1929. What remained of the group was low on food, clothing, and ammunition. More importantly, Sandino's charges "were evidently beginning to understand that Sandino had no real mission.... The so-called patriotic motives of Sandino were no longer evident to the most ignorant members of the outlaw bands."[27]

Shortly thereafter, Sandino traveled to Mexico in search of more outside support for his cause. Although Nicaraguans beyond the Segovias did not seem to take much interest in his rebellion, Sandino was much more popular elsewhere in Latin America. Newspaper editorials and officials across the region were sharply critical of the US intervention, citing it as another case of the "Colossus of the North" interfering in Latin American affairs. Sandino's anti-imperialist platform played well, particularly in Mexico. Since the 1830s, Mexicans had been resisting various forms of American expansionism and influence, including during their early twentieth-century revolution. Certainly mindful of this history, Sandino had hoped the Mexican government could provide desperately needed aid. He would be sorely disappointed.

Almost immediately, Sandino's plans went awry. Upon crossing the border, Mexican officials said he would not be allowed to travel to the capital, Mexico City. Instead, they instructed him to go to Mérida on the isolated Yucatán Peninsula, where he would remain for most of the next nine months. While Sandino would use the safe haven there to grant interviews and publicize his cause, he received little tangible aid from the Mexican government—just a few thousand pesos and a smattering of weapons. Unbeknownst to Sandino before he arrived in the country, US and Mexican officials—eager to repair long-strained relations—had agreed to neutralize him. In a May 1929 meeting, US Undersecretary of State J. Reuben Clark and Mexican Ambassador Manuel C. Téllez came to a consensus. The United States recognized Mexico's right to grant Sandino asylum so long as he did not use it as a base of operation against the Nicaraguan government, and the US pledged it would "prevent any injury to Sandino from the regular Nicaraguan forces and from the Guardia" while he was there.[28]

Not only did Sandino fail to secure much aid from the Mexican government, but other allies and sympathizers also separated from him. Mexico's Communist Party, for example, had been broadly supportive of Sandino's anti-imperialism, an alliance that had made US officials nervous. But while in Mexico, an unfounded story that Sandino had accepted money from Washington to sit out his own rebellion led to a break in relations with the communists. An angry Sandino rejected the party, ultimately producing a split with his own personal secretary, Farabundo Martí, an avowed Marxist. Martí would go on to gain notoriety for leading a rebellion in his native El Salvador, where government forces would capture and kill him in January 1932.[29]

AFTER A FRUSTRATED Sandino returned to Nicaragua in mid-1930, the tenor of his rebellion changed. Still expressly and avowedly anti-imperialist, he and his forces ratcheted up the violence. Pedro Altamirano, one of Sandino's key lieutenants, embodied this intensified approach. As described by historian Alan McPherson, the man known as "Pedrón" had a "barrel chest, tousled hair, thick eyebrows, a large mustache, and a hoarse voice." Altamirano perpetually had a cigar in his mouth and a .44 Winchester at the ready. Moreover, he was said to have been responsible for sixty beheadings and was the inventor of the aforementioned vest cut. Minister Eberhardt called Altamirano "a professional bandit" who was so focused on committing acts of violence that he did not seem too concerned "with the so-called patriotic ideals of Sandino." There is little evidence to suggest, however, that Altamirano operated beyond the bounds of Sandino's orders. The surge in violence compelled Stimson, now the secretary of state, to pressure the Moncada government to have the GN do more of the fighting and allow US Marines to take a back seat. Indeed, the GN spearheaded an offensive in late 1930 designed to cut off Sandinista supply routes to neighboring Honduras and flush out fighters.[30]

Even in a supporting role, however, marines remained in harm's way. That fact was most apparent on New Year's Eve 1930 when Sandinistas ambushed a group of ten marines charged with repairing a telephone line near Achuapa outside Ocotal. Eight marines were killed, and the two who escaped were wounded.

The news brought renewed scrutiny of the US mission in Nicaragua. From the start of the intervention, congressional support had been lukewarm. Opponents cited the expense, both in terms of money and international prestige, and questioned the benefits. The Senate, in particular, saw sporadic legislative attempts to end the mission through cutting funding or demanding outright withdrawal, though none succeeded. As Senator Burton Wheeler asked, "What right have we to send our boys into a foreign country to stamp out banditry? If we are to ask them to stamp out banditry, let's send them to Chicago to stamp it out there. As far as I'm concerned, I wouldn't sacrifice the lifeblood of one American boy for all the damn Nicaraguans." The Achuapa attack sharpened such congressional opposition yet again. The beleaguered Hoover administration realized something had to be done. But a surge in troops and money for an increasingly unpopular intervention did not seem palatable while the nation reeled from the worsening Great Depression. As a result, Stimson announced in February 1931 that all marines would be withdrawn from the country following the 1932 Nicaraguan elections.[31]

Yet Sandino and his militia continued fighting, determined not to lay down their arms until the last marine left. This persistence surely exasperated Hoover, whose frustrations boiled over at a press conference in Washington in April 1931. Initially he said, "I have no statement for quotation today," but then proceeded into a lengthy exposition about the Nicaraguan mission. Hoover denied that Sandino's rebellion was nationalist or idealistic. Instead, he saw him as an opportunistic criminal. "He heads no political cause," Hoover asserted. "He is just a plain bandit. He has all the qualities and character of a city gangster in the United States. He is no patriot." Over the course of his press conference, Hoover referred to Sandino and his followers as "bandits" five times, as "assassins" four times, and as "gangsters" twice. He made another unflattering comparison to connote Sandino's barbarism, saying that Sandinistas "have directed their activities towards isolated Nicaraguan and American plantations and have acted in a fashion that would do discredit to an Iroquois Indian."[32]

Although Hoover made a point to demean the rationale of Sandino's rebellion, he also took pains to downplay its threat. "It is not a national disturbance of the first order," he told the press. Indeed, Sandino's resistance remained mostly in the sparsely populated Segovias with perhaps fewer than 200 fighters under his direct command at that point. This dichotomy of the rebellion—as both a threat and a nuisance—illustrated the utility of the "bandit" discourse: connoting criminality that undermined order and stability on the one hand, while simultaneously suggesting the illegitimacy and frivolity of Sandino's cause on the other.[33]

A day after Hoover's press conference, Stimson issued a similar statement to the press. He noted that "we have a situation where small groups of confessed outlaws—treated as outlaws by the Nicaraguan Government—are making their way through the jungle to the east coast with the avowed intention of murdering and pillaging the civilian inhabitants of the country." Much like the president, the secretary of state reinforced to the public the portrayal of Sandino as a criminal whose political agenda had no validity.[34]

Not one to let an insult slide, Sandino responded with some invective of his own. In May 1931, Sandino released a statement pillorying the US president. "Like an impotent furious beast, the yankee president, Herbert Clark Hoover, throws himself into insults against the commander of the Army that

A Plain Bandit 71

is liberating Nicaragua," he said. "He and Stimson are modern assassins." The choice of the latter word was surely no accident. By redirecting one of Hoover's insults back to the president, Sandino not only showed that he remained unbowed but also that he saw the American leader as a criminal.[35]

Despite Washington's reflexive depiction of Sandino as a bandit, some American publications challenged the portrayal. Newspapers such as the *Washington Post* consistently referred to Sandino in such terms, yet others across the country—like the *Chicago Tribune* and the *Boston Globe*—more often called him a "general" or a "rebel," suggesting a more elevated reputation. Similarly, the venerable journal *Foreign Affairs* in 1931 wrote, "A purely objective view of the facts hardly warrants calling the Sandinistas 'bandits.'" Instead, the author insisted that any looting that Sandinistas may have been done was not for self-aggrandizement but merely to sustain the rebellion, a common practice in guerrilla warfare. Skepticism about the accuracy of the bandit label seeped into the American grassroots as well. Before Sandino's public split with communists, the Workers Party of America had actively supported his cause, holding antiwar rallies and raising money for the Sandinistas, and in April 1928 members even picketed the White House. One sign read, "Wall Street and Not Sandino is the Real Bandit."[36]

Some US personnel stationed in Nicaragua and tasked to quell the rebellion also questioned whether Sandino was truly a bandit. They concluded that the Sandinistas were driven more by the principle of Nicaraguan sovereignty and local authority than by any instinctual desire to loot and kill for the fun of it. The US consul in Matagalpa, for example, declared that Sandino's forces were "revolutionaries, bandit is a misleading term." Samuel Griffith, a marine who was part of the hunt for Sandino, said, "He was a patriot who was a nationalist." At a June 1929 party given in honor of Moncada, Lt. Richard Fagan allegedly declared, "I say that General Sandino is a patriot." Even those who insisted on Sandino's banditry sometimes struggled to uphold the argument. In a conversation between Beals and Gen. Logan Feland, the commanding officer in Nicaragua, the journalist challenged use of the term.

> BEALS: "[Sandino] is not a bandit, call him a fool, a fanatic, an idealist, a patriot—according to your point of view; but certainly he is not a bandit."
> FELAND: "Of course, in the army we use the word 'bandit' in a technical sense, meaning the member of a band."
> BEALS: "Then [John Philip] Sousa is also a bandit?"
> FELAND: "Guess you've got us on the hip there."

US Marines in 1932 display a captured Sandinista flag. Their success came as the long, frustrating mission in Nicaragua was nearing an end. Courtesy of the US National Archives and Records Administration.

Such comments from marines and officials charged with finding and capturing Sandino illustrate that despite the danger and frustration they faced, there was a grudging respect for his rebellion—that there was indeed some legitimacy to his cause, one that the "bandit" label obscured.[37]

Sandino, of course, never saw himself as a bandit. On more than one occasion, he declared that he was no more of a "bandit" than George Washington. Some six months into his rebellion, he privately doubted whether US officials themselves really believed what they were saying about him. He wrote, "Even my enemies themselves are convinced that our purpose is limited to the defense of our country's sovereignty, despite the insulting epithet they give us of 'bandits.'" Nevertheless, Sandino showed some concern about outside perception of him. At the close of his 1928 interview with Beals, Sandino asked: "Do you still think us bandits?" Beals replied, "You are as much a bandit as Mr. Coolidge is a Bolshevik." To which Sandino responded, "Tell your people there may be bandits in Nicaragua, but they are not necessarily Nicaraguans."[38]

As the battle over semantics continued, so, too, did the actual fighting on the ground. In 1932, more than 150 skirmishes took place between US/GN forces and Sandinistas, indicating an emboldened and strengthened rebellion. By that point, US Marines were playing more of a supporting advisory role in the hopes that the GN would be prepared to handle peacekeeping duties on its own in anticipation of a postelection US withdrawal. The results, however, were not encouraging. According to Macaulay, "The Sandinistas became increasingly aggressive; they made numerous attacks on Guard patrols and garrisons and, sometimes, stood their ground when attacked." Regardless of the battlefield results — so long as they remained in the hinterlands — the Hoover administration was dead set on removing US forces following the November 1932 Nicaraguan election.[39]

ON JANUARY 1, 1933, Juan Bautista Sacasa was inaugurated as Nicaragua's new president. The next day, US Marines left the country. US records counted 136 Americans and seventy-five GN soldiers killed — as well as 1,115 "bandits" killed in action. Over the six-year intervention, there were 510 lethal engagements, and the United States spent some $20 million to prosecute the war against Sandino and train GN forces.[40]

True to his word, Sandino formally agreed to end his rebellion one month after the Americans left. However, he was hardly on the brink of defeat. He had eluded US forces for nearly six years, never really coming close to capture. His popularity was growing, if not necessarily among Nicaraguan elites who paid little attention to the countryside, then certainly among Latin Americans who were galvanized by his anti-imperialism. In exchange for ending his rebellion, the agreement with the Sacasa government essentially gave Sandino and his men immunity and some land that they formed into a cooperative, and it allowed them to retain some weapons.

Sandino had pledged no interest in any formal role in government, but he nonetheless retained a degree of political influence in Nicaraguan affairs. In particular, he was publicly critical of the GN's growing power in the Nicaraguan government, criticism that rankled the GN's *Jefe Director*, Anastasio Somoza. During the years of Sandino's rebellion, the GN's power and resources expanded to meet the threat. Initially designed to consist of about 600 men, the organization grew to 300 officers and 2,300 soldiers. Its budget grew to some 25 percent of government expenditures and became the country's strongest institution. As its head, Somoza jealously guarded the GN's lofty position and found Sandino an unacceptable risk.[41]

On the evening of February 21, 1934, following a meeting with Sacasa, a detachment of GN soldiers arrested Sandino and five other men, including his father, Gregorio, and brother, Sócrates. Gregorio and another man were taken away, but Sandino and the other three were driven to an airfield. Lining the men in front of the headlights of a truck, GN soldiers proceeded to mow down the prisoners with a machine gun.[42]

The wide presumption was that the US government had something to do with Sandino's murder. Somoza told his other generals that he had the blessing of US Minister to Nicaragua Arthur Bliss Lane to eliminate Sandino because US government officials "consider him a disturber of the peace of the country." Lane, however, disputed that depiction, aware that such a perception would damage President Franklin D. Roosevelt's attempts to rebrand the United States as a "good neighbor" in Latin America. He reported to Washington that Somoza had indeed asked him about Sandino before the events of February 21 but that Lane had given no green light. "I had seen Somoza many times prior to [February 21] with a view to persuading him not to do anything rash," Lane wrote. "He gave me his word of honor on four separate occasions . . . that he would take no action against Sandino without my consent. He has since apologized to me for what he claims he could not prevent, the feeling among the Guardia officers being too strong against Sandino. Somoza has admitted to me, however, that the officers who participated acted under orders."[43]

Regardless of who gave the ultimate consent, the death of Sandino crushed what was left of the Sandinista movement. The following day, Somoza sent the GN to go after the remaining Sandinistas at their cooperative, and the group was essentially finished. With no one to challenge him, Somoza's power and authority in the GN grew. He forced Sacasa to resign the presidency in 1936 and took the office himself the following year. The Somoza family would go on to dominate the country for more than forty years.

Their dynasty would come to an end, however, in 1979. A new group, inspired by a rebellion from Nicaragua's past, challenged the Somozas' authority as well as the United States' steadfast support of it. That group called itself the Frente Sandinista de Liberación Nacional, more widely known as the Sandinistas.

ALTHOUGH SANDINO could not escape the wrath of Somoza, his ability to elude the United States endeared him to people across Latin America who had tired of Yankee meddling in regional affairs. In the mid-twentieth century, though, Washington's attention shifted more to great-power conflict elsewhere in the world—first with Nazi Germany and imperial Japan during World War II, then with the Soviet Union in the ensuing Cold War. Fear of spreading communist influence in the latter struggle brought the Americans back around to worrying about the Western Hemisphere, especially after the 1959 revolution in Cuba. One of that movement's leaders, Ernesto "Che" Guevara, was an outspoken critic of US influence in the region. Much like Sandino, his fearless opposition to US imperialism endeared him to a new generation of revolutionaries in Latin America willing to challenge the American-led order.

CHAPTER FOUR

The Elusive Guerrilla
Che Guevara in Bolivia

Where was Ernesto "Che" Guevara?

It was a question that reporters, politicians, and even the US Central Intelligence Agency often asked in the mid-1960s with few credible leads.

Guevara was one of the most famous men in the world. A native Argentine, he was a driving force behind the Cuban Revolution, the socialist experiment just ninety miles off the Florida coast whose endurance would frustrate US leaders for decades. Widely seen as eloquent, handsome, and charismatic, Guevara was a vociferous critic of American foreign policy, decrying what he saw as capitalist imperialism that brought misery to billions of people worldwide. As a de facto foreign minister of the Cuban government, Guevara often had audiences with international leaders and dignitaries during which he unabashedly expressed his outlook. His most notable example was at the United Nations General Assembly in December 1964, in which he took the United States to task for its history of intervention in Latin America, citing missions in Cuba, Mexico, Nicaragua, Haiti, the Dominican Republic, and Panama.[1]

More than mere rhetoric or moral suasion, Guevara argued that the oppressed should be willing to use violence to assert their autonomy. He even wrote a "how-to" book of sorts, *Guerrilla Warfare*, drawn from his experiences in the late 1950s during the Cuban Revolution. He arrived at three conclusions that were meant to inspire the downtrodden: "1. Popular forces can win a war against an army; 2. One does not necessarily have to wait for a revolutionary situation to arise; it can be created; 3. In the underdeveloped countries of the Americas, rural areas are the best battlefields for revolution."[2]

Such calls for rebellion and asymmetric warfare worried Cold War–era American powerbrokers who valued order, stability, and anticommunism consensus. To dismiss his platform, US critics often derided Guevara as a "professional revolutionary" who had his sights set on global domination. One columnist in 1961 claimed that Guevara "has been picked by Moscow to become the Communist military dictator of Argentina and extend a red empire across South America." An aide to Senator Hubert H. Humphrey met with Guevara and subsequently concluded that he was not to be trusted because "there is no hint of a doubt in my mind that Cuba is out to knife us. ... What is so frightening about a visit to Cuba is that irrevocably and undeniably that revolution is for export."³

Guevara's calls for guerrilla revolution abroad became more pronounced in the early 1960s. His ideas did not sit well with the Soviet Union, Cuba's primary patron, whose leaders rejected rural, agrarian rebellion as a way to institute socialism. Their opposition put Cuban leader Fidel Castro in a quandary. Although he sympathized with Guevara, he did not want to risk undermining Cuba's relationship with the Soviets. Moreover, Guevara's reputation as a bureaucrat, a role for which he seemed to have little enthusiasm, was taking a beating. He was both the minister of industries and head of the Cuban National Bank—and neither was performing well. Industrial production was well below prerevolution levels. Output of sugar, Cuba's main export, was its lowest in years. Consumers faced shortages of various commodities. It was becoming clear that Guevara was ill-suited for bureaucratic grunt work.

Following his address at the United Nations, Guevara embarked on a three-month, eight-nation tour that included stops across Africa. His aim, in part, was to shore up Cuban relations with the so-called third world that, in turn, would reduce dependency on the Soviet Union. When he returned to Cuba in March 1965, he was greeted by the country's top leaders and then went to a lengthy closed-door meeting with Castro. Following a speech at the Ministry of Industries, he took meetings with friends and colleagues telling people that he was going to cut sugar cane for a while.⁴

Then, he vanished.

Over the next two-and-a-half years, rumors circulated about Guevara's whereabouts. There were reported sightings in Argentina, Colombia, the Dominican Republic, Mexico, Peru, Venezuela, and Vietnam. Some suggested that Castro had Guevara jailed or executed. Others speculated that the United States had kidnapped and detained him, or that maybe he had defected and sold Cuban secrets for $10 million.⁵

The truth was that aside from a small circle of individuals—which didn't even include members of his own family—no one knew Guevara's whereabouts. The mystery added to his legend. In light of his fervent anticapitalist rhetoric and ideology, though, it was a legend that the US government was determined to snuff out.

WELL BEFORE he became a global icon of revolution, Ernesto Guevara de la Serna was an asthmatic child known by family and friends as "Ernestito."

He was born June 14, 1928, in Rosario, Argentina, the first of the five children of Ernesto Guevara Lynch and Celia de la Serna. The couple came from well-established landowning families of Spanish and Irish descent. Yet they sometimes struggled financially because they often lived beyond their means. Because of his precarious health, young Ernesto did not go to school until age nine. In the meantime, he remained at home where he developed a strong bond with his mother, who taught him how to read and write. Celia was known locally for flouting social conventions. She drove her own car, wore trousers, and smoked cigarettes. She also was a professed atheist in a staunchly Catholic nation. Well into adulthood, Ernesto would consult his mother often.[6]

As Guevara matured, traveling made a deep impression. Following his third year in medical school in 1950, he rode a bicycle fitted with a small engine around Argentina, eventually traversing some 2,500 miles over six weeks. Two years later, he traveled with a friend to five countries in South America over eight months in a journey that was later immortalized in print and in film as *The Motorcycle Diaries*. During his travels, Guevara was struck by the widespread poverty and inequality he witnessed in both his native Argentina and the rest of the continent.

After finishing medical school in 1953, Guevara set off again around South America before settling in Guatemala. His eight months there served as a political awakening. President Jacobo Arbenz was ushering in land reform at the expense of corporations like the United Fruit Company, which had dominated Guatemala's economy for years. Amid fears of socialism in its own hemisphere, the CIA in June 1954 orchestrated an overthrow of the democratically elected Arbenz. The coup d'état brought about a right-wing military government and eventually decades of civil war that would lead to 200,000 deaths. One Guevara biographer wrote, "The great lesson [in Guatemala] for the young Argentine revolutionary concerned Washington's a priori and ruthless opposition to any attempt at social and economic reform in Latin America. One must be prepared to fight US interference, rather than try to avoid or neutralize it." His next destination took him one step closer to that battle.[7]

GUEVARA'S PATH toward revolution reached a crucial juncture in Mexico. There, he reconnected with several like-minded people he had met in Guatemala. This group included Hilda Gadea, an exiled member of a leftist Peruvian political party who had worked with the Arbenz government. They married in August 1955 and had a daughter, Hildita. But the Cuban exile Nico López proved to be the more significant connection. Not only was López credited with bestowing Guevara with the nickname "Che"—a typical Argentine term Guevara often used that essentially means "hey"—but he facilitated Guevara's introduction in the summer of 1955 to Fidel and Raúl Castro.[8]

The brothers were in Mexico with a small cadre of Cubans after they had been released from prison. Two years earlier, they had orchestrated a failed uprising against the US-backed dictator Fulgencio Batista. They were making plans to try again. On the strength of Fidel's personality and conviction, Guevara was sold on the idea. He accepted an invitation to join the movement as the guerrillas' doctor and quickly developed a close bond with the brothers.[9]

His allegiance was tested in short order. In November 1956, Guevara was among eighty-two men crammed onto the dilapidated yacht, *Granma*, on the way to Cuba to begin a new offensive against Batista. The trip was a Murphy's Law of disasters: seasickness, poor navigation, bad timing, missed rendezvous. Worst of all, the rebels were spotted by Batista's military and nearly wiped out on the first day. Little more than a dozen survived, including Guevara, barely; he had been wounded in the neck and thought he would die. For the next year and a half, the remnants of the 26th of July Movement regrouped and consolidated in the remote Sierra Maestra mountains of eastern Cuba.

During that time, Guevara developed a reputation as a capable leader. He was promoted to *comandante*, a title he carried with him among Cubans for years afterward. He also more openly embraced socialism, which came at a time when the Castro-led rebellion was less ideological and more focused on eliminating Batista. Nevertheless, rumors about Guevara's socialist sympathies drew the attention of the US consulate in nearby Santiago, which dismissively concluded that he was merely "an idealistic adventurer."[10]

A beleaguered Batista fled the country on December 31, 1958, ushering in a new era in Cuban history. Although it was just one of many groups fighting against Batista, Castro's 26th of July Movement quickly emerged at the forefront of the revolutionary government. By virtue of his rank as *comandante*, Guevara had heavy responsibilities. One of the first was overseeing the tribunals of captured Batista-era officials accused of war crimes. Hundreds were sentenced to death via firing squad. Accounts vary about the extent to which Guevara second-guessed these executions. Nevertheless, the killings poisoned relations between Washington and Havana leading US officials and journalists to take a more jaundiced view of the Argentine revolutionary. In

December 1960, by which time the Cuban government was trending toward socialism, *Time* magazine ran a profile of Guevara. The cover featured him in the foreground between photos of Soviet premier Nikita Khrushchev and Chinese leader Mao Zedong underneath the headline, "Communism's Western Beachhead." The accompanying article called Guevara the "brain" of the Cuban Revolution, with Fidel the heart and Raúl the fist. It also referred to him as "the most fascinating, and the most dangerous, member of the triumvirate. Wearing a smile of melancholy sweetness that many women find devastating, Che guides Cuba with icy calculation, vast competence, high intelligence and a perceptive sense of humor."[11]

Yet Guevara lacked expertise in the two main positions Castro placed him—minister of industries and head of the Cuban National Bank. He struggled to overcome a steep learning curve. Three nights a week he took tutorials in economics and mathematics. More important for him, though, was to conduct the job according to his own personal aesthetic. He lived simply. His home, a confiscated mansion, was mostly empty. Any gifts Guevara received during his travels abroad were remitted to the state. He instructed his wife, Aleida—whom he had married in 1959 after divorcing Hilda that same year—to take the bus to run errands and not use the government car he had been given. By practicing what he preached, Guevara hoped he could inspire others to follow his example and create a more equitable, less materialistic society.[12]

GUEVARA EVENTUALLY determined that the biggest impediment to that goal was the United States, not only because of its long-standing political and cultural influence on Cuba but also, more importantly, because of its tightening trade embargo that crippled the Cuban economy. Initially, he tried to assuage US concerns that the Cuban Revolution would set off a domino effect of rebellion across the Western Hemisphere. "We have stated very clearly that Cuba does not export revolutions," Guevara said in March 1960. "Revolutions cannot be exported." But as US-Cuban relations deteriorated, Guevara's public rhetoric became more antagonistic. This shift was more pronounced after the failed Bay of Pigs invasion in April 1961, in which a cadre of CIA-trained, anti-Castro Cuban exiles attempted an uprising. Although an embarrassment for President John F. Kennedy's administration, Guevara was incensed. Speaking in August before the Organization of American States (OAS), Guevara said, "Cuba never will accept the hand of friendship extended by the United States which has bombed us, which has invaded us, which has decreed an economic embargo against us. We will never shake the hand of assassins like President Kennedy." In contrast to his statements the previous year, Guevara began focusing more on how to duplicate the Cuban model elsewhere. In particular, he emphasized Latin American and African countries that long had been under the thumb of US and Western European powers.[13]

His biggest contribution to that effort—at least while a public figure in Cuba—was the 1961 publication of *Guerrilla Warfare*. The slim volume provided both a rationale for creating revolution as well as guidelines for strategies and tactics. At its core, he wrote, the guerrilla "is a social reformer. He takes up arms in response to widespread popular protest against an oppressor, impetuously hurling himself with all his might against anything that symbolizes the established order." One of his caveats was that such uprisings could not take place against a government that came to power through a popular vote. "A guerrilla uprising cannot be brought about until all possible avenues of legal procedure have been exhausted," he wrote.[14]

Guevara differentiated tactics of guerrilla warfare from terrorism. Although targeted sabotage was acceptable, blanket use of such tactics was beyond the pale. "Indiscriminate terrorism against groups of ordinary people is inefficient and can provoke massive retaliation," he wrote. "However, terrorism to repay the cruelty of a key individual in the oppressor hierarchy is justifiable. But it must never be used to eliminate unimportant individuals whose death would accomplish nothing but invite retaliation." Strikes on enemy locations, resources, or businesses were acceptable, he reasoned, but not if it created mass starvation or unemployment that would undermine a revolution's broader goals. In a later section endorsing targeted killings, he wrote, "Under special conditions, assassinations of individuals guilty of major repressive actions are permissible. No indiscriminate terrorism is to be employed."[15]

Such ideas led American officials to view Guevara as a threat. In the halls of Congress, references to Guevara were tinged with apprehension. "A man like Guevara—bold, dashing and ruthless—is not one who would be expected to fight for democratic liberties," California congressman H. Allen Smith said. "He is a promoter of dictatorship." In contrast to other reports suggesting Guevara was a Soviet tool, Indiana congressman William G. Bray alleged that Guevara was the one instructing the Soviets. He claimed that Soviet generals were participating in Guevara-led schools that were teaching sabotage and revolution. Actually, Soviet leadership largely rejected guerrilla warfare as a means to promote socialism. But the Cold War climate trained most Americans to see a Soviet hand behind every challenge.[16]

The popular American press also depicted Guevara as dangerous for cloaking his ideology under an amiable facade. "Face to face, Dr. Guevara can be a pleasant, even charming personality," Tad Szulc reported in the *New York Times* in June 1960. Physically, Guevara was portrayed as harmless, even unmasculine. Wearing simple olive-green fatigues with a black beret, his "long brown hair curls gently down his neck." His facial hair was a "scraggly beard and mustache," and he had "slightly slanted brown eyes [that] give him his oriental air, oddly reminiscent of a younger, slimmer, shorter Ho Chi Minh." Moreover, Guevara had "an easy smile and soft, persuasive voice." But the description abruptly shifts, stating that "his eyes are hard. . . . He is said to have an icy ruthlessness." The profile ominously notes that "whether or not he is a Communist, Dr. Guevara's greatest obsession is his hatred of the United States in general and of 'Yankee imperialism' in particular." Although Guevara's public remarks would later bear that out, such depictions conditioned readers to see him as the next big Cold War threat, one hiding dangerous ideas behind weak and seductive features.[17]

Guevara, though, was venerated as something of a sex symbol. His magnetism piqued the interest of President Kennedy, a notorious womanizer. Laura Bergquist Knebel, a writer for *Look Magazine*, had once interviewed Guevara. Kennedy asked her what he was like. Knebel replied that she found him similar to the president in terms of personality—cool, pragmatic, smart—if diametrically dissimilar politically. To which Kennedy replied, "Something gives me the feeling you've got the hots for Che." Knebel protested, saying she had argued with Guevara during their interview. Undeterred, Kennedy said, "Yeah, but that kind of hostility often leads to something else." Knebel took offense at the sexual innuendo. She said his comments showed that to Kennedy, "Che was this attractive character by whom I'd been beguiled and bedazzled. . . . I had let the Che's male charm somehow befuddle my judgment." In a subsequent interview with Guevara, Knebel relayed her conversation with Kennedy. "Che was not amused," she said. "He was a dedicated revolutionary not given to personal chitchat. He had a wife to whom he was devoted, and such frivolities as Kennedy's remark, I think, were beyond him."[18]

Although the two men would never meet, Guevara had a surreptitious meeting with one Kennedy administration official. In August 1961, twenty-nine-year-old Kennedy speechwriter and Deputy Assistant Secretary of State for Inter-American Affairs Richard Goodwin had a chance encounter with Guevara at a late-night diplomatic party in Punta del Este, Uruguay. Sitting on the floor and assisted by two translators, the two talked frankly

US press and politicians widely viewed Che Guevara, seen here in 1960 with his customary cigar, as uniquely dangerous because he cloaked his political ideology under an amiable, attractive facade. Courtesy of the Cuban Heritage Collection, University of Miami Libraries, Coral Gables, Florida.

about their governments' respective political differences. Goodwin said that Guevara asked for a peaceful coexistence between the two countries, laying out some points for potential future discussion such as restitution for expropriated property and holding elections. As the meeting closed, Guevara gave Goodwin a box of Cuban cigars that were later presented to Kennedy.[19]

Within days, word of the meeting filtered out. The political climate of the day, though, compelled both sides to downplay it. Guevara called it "a short, polite, indifferent exchange." The Senate Foreign Relations Subcommittee on Latin America determined that it was "a casual and unimportant meeting at a cocktail party." But based on Goodwin's contemporaneous memos, it appears the encounter was cordial and friendly, even if the two men could not agree on anything. Goodwin recognized Guevara's humanity and depicted him as a rational actor, an uncommon concession about professed socialists in those days. It could have been a harbinger of future talks between the United States and Cuba. Yet both the Kennedy administration and Guevara had vested interests in demonizing the other side. Any acknowledgment of their opponents' concerns risked undercutting their own platforms. In the Cold War in which international politics was seen as a zero-sum game, neither side could afford to give in.[20]

DESPITE BEING a star of international politics, Guevara's record as a government bureaucrat had far less luster. The Cuban economy's performance and industrial production fell short of expectations, leading to questions about Guevara's effectiveness. He also had grown tired of subservience to the Soviet Union stemming from the Cuban Missile Crisis (in which Soviet leadership basically cut Cuba out of negotiations) and its reluctance to support guerrilla warfare in the so-called third world.

On his March 1965 return from Africa, Guevara resigned. Although he had considered the idea for more than a year, he wrote a letter to Castro on April 1 affirming his break. "I formally resign my positions in the leadership of the party, my post as minister, my rank of commander, and my Cuban citizenship," he wrote. Castro kept the letter in his back pocket; he did not publicly reveal its contents until October. In the meantime, as Guevara's public absence became more pronounced and rumors swirled of his whereabouts, Castro remained coy. When asked by journalists where Guevara was, Castro said, "The only thing I can tell you about Commander Guevara is that he will always be where he is most useful to the revolution." At the time, unbeknownst to all but a few, that usefulness was in the Congo.[21]

Taking part in a guerrilla war in central Africa checked a lot of revolutionary boxes for Guevara. The Congo had been a colony of Belgium for decades before attaining independence in 1960. Over the next few years, the country suffered significant turmoil, including the overthrow and assassination of its prime minister Patrice Lumumba, whom US officials believed to be pro-communist. New rebellions broke out in 1964 against the government of Moïse Tshombe, who was supported by US military aid, the CIA, as well as white mercenaries from South Africa and Rhodesia known as 5 Commando. To Guevara, if revolutionary movements in Latin America were not ready to take flight, the Congo presented the next best opportunity to strike a blow against US interests. He had hoped that a guerrilla war in the Congo would attract like-minded revolutionaries from across the region, who would then take their experiences and start wars of liberation in their own countries.

Shortly after submitting his resignation to Castro, Guevara departed Cuba under the pseudonym Ramón Benítez. He shaved his beard, wore thick, tortoiseshell eyeglasses, and exchanged his trademark olive-green fatigues and black beret for a gray suit and fedora. Even the Cuban ambassador to Tanzania, where Guevara arrived to begin his mission, didn't recognize him. Although Guevara was no longer an official member of the Cuban government, the Congo operation had Castro's full support. Over the course of the mission, he sent 129 Cuban soldiers to fight with Guevara on behalf of Congolese rebels called the Simbas. For the most part, Guevara kept his identity hidden; he went by the nickname "Tatu," the Swahili word for the number three. The head of the rebels, Laurent Kabila, was aware, but many other Congolese were not.[22]

By all accounts, even Guevara's, the mission was a disaster. "This is the story of a failure," he wrote. The reasons were plentiful. To begin, the Cuban contingent could not effectively work with the Congolese. Guevara and the Cubans had done little advance preparation with their nominal allies, who did not even know when they were arriving. The language barrier was difficult to overcome. Guevara had to speak in his rudimentary French to have it translated to Swahili for the Congolese to understand. The operation had a difficult time recruiting and training fighters, many of whom deserted. They often couldn't agree on appropriate missions. In one case, the Congolese insisted on attacking a well-defended hydroelectric plant. As Guevara had predicted, the assault failed, resulting in the precious loss of lives, weapons, and a diary that proved to be an important source of intelligence for the mercenaries and the CIA-backed Cuban exiles who were fighting the guerrillas.[23]

Compounding these issues were the difficult environmental conditions, in terms of not only terrain and amenities but also, especially, disease. Many Cubans came down with malaria. By July, some of them were begging to go home. But Guevara insisted they persevere, despite his own illnesses. He had chronic diarrhea and at one point likely had dysentery. By the time the mission ended in November, when the Congolese government and rebels reached a settlement that mandated all mercenaries and foreign agents leave, he weighed only 110 pounds.[24]

The extent to which the US government knew that Guevara was in the Congo is difficult to pinpoint. A secret CIA report in October 1965 asserted that there was "no evidence to support rumors which have located Guevara in a number of Latin American countries or in the Congo. Indeed there is no concrete evidence to permit conjecture whether he is still alive." But one study maintains that the radio transmissions from Guevara's team that the National Security Agency had been listening to via offshore listening posts indicated he was there. Moreover, CIA operatives in the field claimed years later to have known about Guevara's presence and were determined to get him. For example, Gustavo Villoldo, a Cuban exile working for the agency in the Congo, said he had been listening to Guevara's radio messages for months and was closing in on him before Guevara aborted his mission.[25]

Another operative, James Hawes, said he got even closer. The CIA selected the twenty-six-year-old Navy SEAL to lead a covert operation to create a Congolese navy on Lake Tanganyika, across which Simba rebels received supplies and weapons from Tanzania. To minimize American exposure, Hawes led a team of sixteen Cuban exiles, who in turn trained members of 5 Commando to run the navy. "Soon after arrival," Hawes wrote in his memoir, "we began to receive rumors of Che Guevara and his gang's presence with the Simba terrorists. Needless to say, this was extra motivation for a group of men dedicated to the eradication of communism anywhere and everywhere." Hawes credited the navy and the mercenaries for ruining Guevara's mission by interdicting supplies and engaging rebels on the battlefield. Most notably, he claimed that his navy engaged in a firefight with Guevara's band as they were retreating across Lake Tanganyika in November 1965. Just how close Guevara came to capture or death, however, is hard to discern.[26]

Nevertheless, Guevara spent the next eight months in the Cuban embassy in Tanzania and in Cuban safe houses in what was then Czechoslovakia. He took no visitors save his wife, Aleida. Castro asked that he return to Cuba, but Guevara resisted. Part of his reluctance could have been pride, given his bitter defeat in the Congo. Moreover, Castro had already made public Guevara's resignation letter. To go back to Cuba after such a well-publicized farewell could have been seen as a sign of weakness and thus might stymie broader objectives to bring socialist guerrilla revolutions elsewhere in the world.[27]

Ultimately, Guevara decided that to fulfill such a goal, he first would have to return to Cuba. On July 21, 1966, he flew back but remained in a safe house in eastern Havana, his presence known only to a select few, not even his five children. There, he began secretly planning his next mission, mindful of what had gone wrong in the Congo. "I learned certain things in the Congo," he wrote. "These mistakes I will never make again, others I probably will make again; and I will commit new errors. I have come out of this with more faith than ever in the guerrilla struggle, and yet we failed. My responsibility is great; I will not forget this defeat or its most precious lessons."[28]

ADOLFO MENA GONZÁLEZ arrived in the Bolivian capital, La Paz, on November 3, 1966. He was a forty-six-year-old Uruguayan businessman on an economic fact-finding mission for the OAS. He was balding with gray hair around his temples, wearing thick, tortoiseshell eyeglasses, and sporting a slight paunch.

He also was Che Guevara.

Brandishing another fake passport and unrecognizable disguise, Guevara was in Bolivia looking to duplicate the Cuban Revolutionary experience in the heart of South America. Much like his efforts in the Congo, Guevara had hoped that a small cell of fighters, a *foco*, would draw support from the local population as well as other like-minded guerrillas from around the continent and grow into a movement. Success in Bolivia, he figured, might then inspire similar rebellions in neighboring countries, including his homeland of Argentina, which was Guevara's grandest dream. Moreover, a proliferation of guerrilla movements might create a "second or third Vietnam" for the United States to confront. As he wrote in a message released the following year, "We must definitely keep in mind that imperialism is a world system, the final stage of capitalism, and that it must be beaten in a great worldwide confrontation. The strategic objective of that struggle must be the destruction of imperialism."[29]

In conjunction with Castro, Guevara determined that Bolivia was the ideal place to start, mostly for its geography—largely rural, bordering five South American nations—and its military-led government. Yet there were complexities in Bolivia's situation that Guevara failed to appreciate. The country had already experienced a leftist rebellion in 1952, when the Revolutionary Nationalist Movement (MNR) took power. Over the next twelve

Bolivia

years, it instituted agrarian reforms and nationalized its crucial tin industry. Although a military coup overthrew the MNR government in 1964, Bolivia held elections two years later that the OAS called fair and honest. The Bolivian government led by President René Barrientos, a general in the Bolivian air force, was staunchly anticommunist but not nearly as repressive as other right-wing governments that would dominate the region during the Cold War era. In sum, Bolivia did not seem ripe for revolution.[30]

Preparations for the Bolivian mission remained highly secretive. The small cadre of Cuban fighters were only told they would be part of an "internationalist mission." When they arrived for training, Guevara was already unrecognizable. He even remained in disguise during his last meeting with his family. Calling himself "Ramón," the code name he would use on the mission, he told his children that he was an uncle who had seen Che recently and passed along their father's love and advice. At their final dinner before his departure, Guevara and Castro shared a short, emotional embrace.[31]

ALMOST FROM THE START, the mission was a comedy of errors. An advance team had gone to Bolivia months before and purchased a 30,000-acre farm to serve as a base in remote Ñancahuazú, a mountainous, semitropical area in the country's southeast. The man who owned the neighboring property, though, quickly became suspicious of illegal activity; he thought the occupants might be manufacturing cocaine. To avoid attention of local authorities, the guerrillas set up camp deeper in the jungle where they were plagued by mosquitoes and ticks. Their long odds of success dwindled further after a fallout with the Bolivian Communist Party (PCB). The guerrilla band was purposely small at the outset—it would only have roughly fifty fighters at its peak—but expected to draw support from the PCB. When Guevara met on New Year's Eve with Secretary-General Mario Monje, the two men could not agree on who would lead. Guevara refused to cede authority over military matters. Monje determined that Guevara's insurgency was impractical and did not want to risk losing support from Moscow. Most inauspicious for the mission, though, was a disastrous training hike that started February 1, 1967. What had been planned as a two-week excursion turned into a forty-eight-day slog when the group got lost. The guerrillas endured heavy rains, insects, and hunger. They resorted to eating hawks, parrots, monkeys, and even one of their horses. Worse still, two men drowned trying to cross swollen rivers.[32]

Shortly after Guevara returned from the brutal training hike, another contingent of guerrillas had their first encounter with the Bolivian military. On March 23, a band of soldiers stumbled through the guerrillas' defensive perimeter. The guerrillas staged an ambush contradicting Guevara's standing orders to avoid confrontation. During the firefight, they killed seven soldiers and captured roughly a dozen, seizing a variety of weapons and ammunition while enduring no casualties. It was a stunning success for the bedraggled fighters. Yet the battle underscored problems on both sides.³³

Guevara determined that his foco was discovered too soon. With the Bolivian military aware of the guerrillas' presence—if not yet Guevara's—they lost the element of surprise before they could attract more fighters. Although the group had hoped to draw help from Bolivian communists, they wanted and needed the support of the local peasantry, the very people for whom this uprising was ostensibly designed. Over the course of the mission, the guerrillas failed to recruit a single person. Scrupulously avoiding the threat of force, Guevara insisted on paying for goods or food taken from villages. The guerrillas occasionally ran health clinics; Guevara himself did some dentistry work for patients. Yet the appeals went nowhere. Locals saw the guerrillas as foreigners; indeed, little more than half the foco were Bolivians, with the others mostly Cubans and a few Peruvians. None of them could speak the local Indigenous languages. Throughout his diary, Guevara often lamented his group's inability to recruit.³⁴

The Bolivian military, meanwhile, faced its own issues. It was widely seen as one of the weakest units in South America. Its recruits were poorly trained and equipped; some were still sporting weapons from the 1930s. The initial encounter with Guevara's guerrillas exemplified their shortcomings, as the band was defeated by a force of fewer than ten rebels. Embarrassed survivors claimed that dozens of guerrillas had attacked them and asserted that there were some 500 in the area.³⁵

These concerns compelled the Bolivian government to ask the United States for help. It requested not only modern guns but also tanks and planes to go against an indeterminate group of guerrillas. US Ambassador to Bolivia Douglas Henderson was dubious. He considered Barrientos's request a "shakedown," trying to obtain more aid by playing on Americans' anticommunist fears. Henderson worried that if the United States gave Barrientos everything he wanted, the Bolivian military might either use it indiscriminately and cause civilian casualties or poorly trained soldiers might lose it to the guerrillas and strengthen their position. In either case, Henderson did not want the United States to be blamed for Bolivian failures or take a heavy-handed approach that could feed impressions of a US intervention. "This is a Bolivian problem," Henderson said. "The Bolivians have to handle it." To that end, he advocated sending small arms, machine guns, field radios,

The Elusive Guerrilla 91

helicopters, and C rations—the kinds of aid that the United States was giving to Latin American militaries anyway in the name of anticommunism. Henderson also recommended stepping up the timetable for a long-planned program in which US Green Berets were to train a regiment of Bolivian Rangers.[36]

Under the command of Korean War veteran Maj. Ralph "Pappy" Shelton, sixteen American trainers arrived in Bolivia in May 1967 to teach a group of approximately 650 men. They set up camp at an abandoned sugar refinery near the town of La Esperanza. Conditions were less than ideal—dealing with bugs, disease, and heat—but they were meant to toughen an underwhelming group of recruits who were mostly illiterate and underfed. During their four-month crash course, the men were taught some of the basics, like marching and shooting. They also learned how to move at night, detect booby traps, engage in hand-to-hand combat, and operate as a unit.[37]

As the training got organized, intelligence and press reports about Guevara's presence intensified. Initially, these stories suggested that Guevara, who hadn't been seen publicly in two years, had been to Bolivia to organize guerrillas but had left the country. Further clues quickly emerged. In early April, the Bolivian army found the guerrillas' base camp, which contained documents, a diary, photographs, and drawings, including some that looked like Guevara. Later that month, the military captured two associates, Argentine artist Ciro Bustos and French writer Régis Debray, who were with the guerrillas but were trying to get back to Cuba. Under the threat of execution, they revealed that Guevara was, in fact, in Bolivia. US National Security Advisor Walt Rostow reported to President Lyndon B. Johnson that this was "the *first credible report that 'Che' Guevara is alive* and operating in South America. . . . We need more evidence before concluding that Guevara is operational—and not dead, as the intelligence community, with the passage of time, has been more and more inclined to believe."[38]

Indeed, the CIA remained skeptical but enlisted two operatives to investigate. Gustavo Villoldo, who had pursued Guevara in the Congo, and Félix Rodríguez were Cuban émigrés who had left their homeland after the revolution. Each of them had taken part in the Bay of Pigs invasion as members of the CIA-sponsored Brigade 2506 and served the agency in other covert operations against the Cuban government. Each was given cover as Bolivian military officers and assigned with the Bolivian Rangers in training. More importantly, when the Rangers were ready to be deployed, Villoldo and Rodríguez were to be the United States' only direct eyes and ears in the field in accordance with Henderson's recommendation that no US citizens be involved in combat activities.[39]

AS US AND BOLIVIAN EFFORTS ramped up, the guerrillas' morale was cratering. Not only were they unable to recruit any new fighters, but they had also lost radio communications with La Paz and Havana when their transmitters failed. This development made the prospect of outside reinforcements all but impossible. Moreover, as supplies dwindled, many in the group weakened and became ill. Some guerrillas started drinking their own urine to survive. Guevara struggled with his chronic asthma. At one point, he became so sick that he lost consciousness from vomiting and diarrhea. "My stench extends for a league," he wrote. When he finally was able to get cleaned up on September 10, 1967, he noted it was his first bath in six months.[40]

Despite their travails, the guerrillas generally enjoyed success whenever they engaged Bolivian forces. Between March and August, there were more than a dozen encounters. In that time, the military lost at least thirty-five men, with another twenty-five wounded and forty captured (and released). Among Guevara's forces, which were calling themselves the Bolivian Liberation Army, eight were killed. While the body count was certainly in their favor, given their small numbers, they were losses the guerrillas could ill afford to endure. Out of desperation, the rebels captured Samaipata, a village of nearly 1,700 residents, and held it briefly in early July. More than a show of force, they just needed food and medicine, for which they paid the townspeople. The news nevertheless shocked the US and Bolivian governments into stronger action.[41]

A decisive turning point came on August 31 with the eradication of Guevara's ten-person rear guard by a Bolivian military ambush. The group had been divided from the main force since April. Guevara had intended to keep this band of the sick and what he called "*resacas*" (dregs) apart only for a few days, but they could never find each other again. Using intelligence from a peasant whom the guerrillas had trusted, the military opened fire as the guerrillas were crossing what they had thought was a safe passage across a river. They were sitting ducks. Among the nine killed were Tania, the only woman in the group who would later be identified as an East German secret agent, and Moisés Guevara (no relation to Che), who was one of the few Bolivian communist leaders to join the guerrillas.[42]

The most important development in finding Che was the interrogation of José Castillo Chávez, a thirty-one-year-old Bolivian who had joined the group in February. Although the Bolivian military was eager to execute him, as it had two other ambush survivors, the CIA's Rodríguez considered him a valuable source of intelligence. Over the next two weeks, he carried out daily interrogations of Castillo, claiming he did so without torture or physical abuse that he considered "counterproductive." Their conversations yielded insights about the rebels' conditions and broader strategies. It compelled Rodríguez to recommend the Rangers cut their training short to get them into the field as soon as possible.[43]

THE NOOSE around Guevara tightened over the next month. The US-trained Rangers were in the field, assisted by two CIA operatives. A 50,000-peso reward (roughly $4,200 at the time) was offered to the public for his capture. In a bid to win international support, the Bolivian government shared evidence that Guevara was indeed in their country trying to foment rebellion. His band was down to seventeen men.[44]

On the run, Guevara went north where the terrain was more mountainous — reaching some 6,000 feet above sea level — but there was much less foliage and thus harder to hide. On October 7, 1967, Guevara wrote that the day began "bucolically." That afternoon, near the village of La Higuera, the guerrillas came across an old woman herding goats. "The woman gave no truthful news about the soldiers, saying that she didn't know anything," he noted. They nevertheless gave the woman fifty pesos to keep quiet. Listening on commercial radio, Guevara heard a report that soldiers were in a different area searching for the guerrillas. "The news seems to be diversionary," he wrote. It would be his last diary entry.[45]

The following afternoon, the Rangers closed in. Tipped off by a local peasant, they surrounded the guerrillas in a gully that was roughly 1,000 feet long and 200 feet wide. The only way out was to fight. Soldiers opened fire with machine guns and mortars. Early in what would be a four-hour battle, Guevara's weapon was hit by a bullet. He then was shot in the calf. Helped by a Bolivian, Simón Cuba (code name: Willy), Guevara tried to limp out of the gully. But the duo was quickly apprehended. Guevara's initial words to his captors are the subject of dispute. Some reports allege he said, "Don't shoot, I am Che Guevara, and I am worth more to you alive than dead." Others claim that he said, "I am Che Guevara and I have failed." There was no question, though, that Guevara was at the mercy of the Bolivians.[46]

Ranger leader Cap. Gary Prado Salmón recognized Guevara instantly, confirmed by a telltale scar on his left hand. But what he saw before him was a far cry from his captive's lofty reputation. According to Prado, Guevara was wearing "a completely filthy private's uniform, and a jacket with a hood. His chest was nearly bare because his shirt had no buttons." Guevara's footwear was simply pieces of leather tied with cord. A physical wreck, Guevara seemed resigned to his fate. Yet he did not totally submit despite being bound by his hands and feet. He offered to help treat a wounded soldier, but Prado declined. He wanted a drink from his canteen, but Prado feared Guevara would try to poison himself, so he offered up his own.[47]

As evening approached, the soldiers hiked a hobbled Guevara—along with Willy and the bodies of two dead guerrillas—to a nearby schoolhouse. He was confined to an eight-by-ten-foot room with mud walls and a dirt floor. A tiny window served as the sole source of light. Some Bolivian officers tried to question Guevara, but he mostly gave vague, generic answers. There are conflicting accounts about whether he was abused in any way or otherwise left alone overnight.[48]

Around daybreak on October 9, Col. Joaquín Zenteno Anaya and Rodríguez arrived in La Higuera by helicopter. Rodríguez's initial thought when he saw the bound and wounded Guevara: "He looked like a piece of trash." Almost immediately, Rodríguez photographed the contents of Guevara's backpack, which included a diary, codebooks, maps, a pistol, and some undeveloped rolls of film.[49]

Rodríguez then received Zenteno's permission to question the prisoner. Initially, Guevara was defiant. "Nobody interrogates me," he said. But Rodríguez claims he took a softer approach, complimenting Guevara for fighting for his ideals, untying him, bringing him a bench to sit on, and giving him a cigarette. The two discussed the state of the Cuban economy, why Guevara chose Bolivia, and why his mission failed. He refused to discuss tactical matters or what he did in Africa or to criticize Castro. At one point, Guevara surmised that Rodríguez was either a Cuban or Puerto Rican working for US intelligence; Rodríguez admitted that he was part of the CIA's Brigade 2506, to which Guevara responded "Ha!" During their conversation, Rodríguez brought Guevara outside to take a picture. The disheveled Guevara stands in the center with Rodríguez to his right and three Bolivian soldiers to his left. It would be Guevara's last photograph—alive.[50]

THE WRITING was on the wall that the Bolivian government had no intention of putting Guevara on trial. Its leadership feared security issues both in holding him during proceedings and in long-term incarceration. Killing Guevara would send a strong message against potential future guerrillas as well as undermine Cuba's attempts to foment socialist revolution elsewhere.

The call came shortly before noon from Bolivian high command: execute Che Guevara.[51]

The Bolivians' decision ran counter to what the CIA had wanted—to bring Guevara in for questioning at a US military base in Panama. When Rodríguez heard the orders, he begged Zenteno to ignore them. After thinking through potential ways to sneak out Guevara, Rodríguez determined it was a matter for the Bolivians to decide. "It was their war; Che was their prisoner," he recalled. "I was not in Bolivia to command, but to advise." Rodríguez said he informed Guevara of the Bolivians' decision. According to Rodríguez, Guevara initially turned pale but steadied himself and said, "It is better like this, Félix. I should never have been captured alive." Guevara then asked Rodríguez to pass along two messages: "Tell Fidel that he will soon see a triumphant revolution in America. And tell my wife to get remarried and try to be happy." At that point, Rodríguez claims, the two men embraced. "I no longer hated him," he wrote. "His moment of truth had come, and he was conducting himself like a man. He was facing death with courage and grace."[52]

Guevara seemed to be under the impression that Rodríguez would execute him. But the CIA operative had no desire. Instead, Sgt. Mario Terán volunteered to carry out the order. Rodríguez's only request was that he shoot Guevara from the neck down. There are differing accounts about Guevara's last words. Most seem to agree that he said to a hesitant Terán something along the lines of "Shoot, coward, you are only going to kill a man." Following two bursts from a semiautomatic rifle, Ernesto "Che" Guevara was dead.[53]

GUEVARA'S SAGA was not yet over, however. The Bolivian government was intent on showing off its prize to the world. Guevara's body was strapped to the landing skid of a helicopter and flown to the nearby town of Vallegrande. He was then put on display at a hospital where soldiers, reporters, photographers, and local onlookers could gaze upon the dead revolutionary. Lying on a stretcher over a washbasin, he was bare-chested with his head propped up and his eyes open. The official story was that Guevara, who an autopsy would show was shot nine times, succumbed to combat injuries while in captivity. Many contemporary observers, though, quickly surmised that those injuries would have resulted in immediate death. Wary of a burial place turning into a shrine, the Bolivian military said it cremated the body. In reality, it dumped his remains in an unmarked grave near the airfield in Vallegrande, where they would be discovered in 1997 and sent to Cuba for reburial.[54]

The dubious circumstances of Guevara's death and burial led to skepticism about what happened or if it was even truly Guevara. Ultimately, his

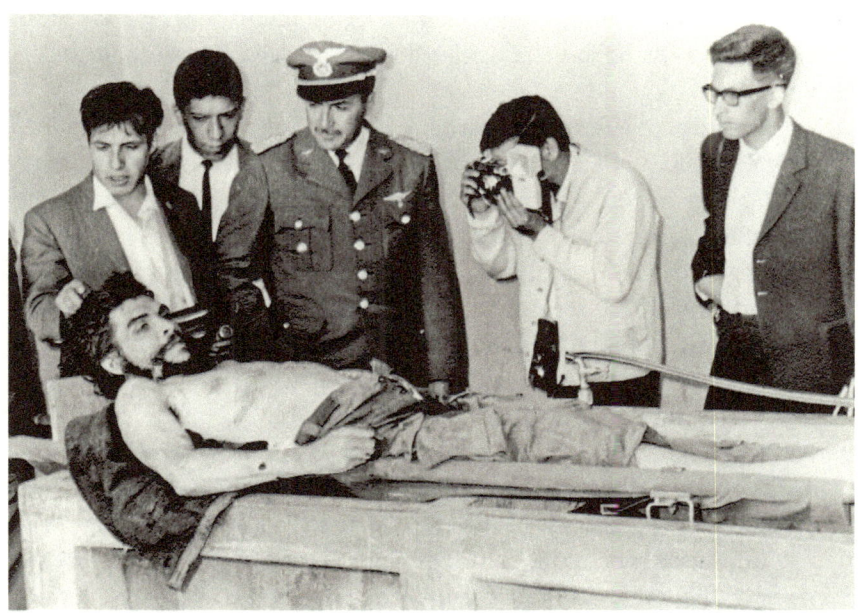

Intent on showing off its prize to the world, the Bolivian government put Che Guevara's body on display shortly after he was executed, in 1967. The nature of his wounds, though, belied the official story. Courtesy of the Associated Press.

hands were amputated for fingerprint analysis, which confirmed his identity. (The following year, a Bolivian official smuggled the hands, as well as Guevara's diary and a death mask, out of the country and gave them to Castro.) US National Security Advisor Rostow reported on October 11 to President Johnson that "we are about 99% sure that 'Che' Guevara is dead. . . . CIA tells us that the latest information is that Guevara was taken alive. After a short interrogation to establish his identity, General Ovando . . . ordered him shot. I regard this as stupid, but it is understandable from a Bolivian standpoint."[55]

For the most part, American opinion writers reveled in Guevara's demise. Obituaries and reflections often dismissively referred to him as a "professional revolutionary" as they did when he first came into national consciousness. One columnist in the *Boston Globe* opined that Guevara was "full of doctrinaire intolerances and suspicions, an arrogant, high-spirited adventurer confident that he knew the answers to all humanity's dilemmas, always prepared to live dangerously, contemptuous of those who challenged oppression and terror when it flew the flag of communism." A writer in the *Hartford Courant* called Guevara "a master of revolutions, destroyer of democracies

The Elusive Guerrilla 97

or any other form of government other than Communism. . . . His talent for destruction was diabolic." The *Washington Post* decried Guevara's "tactics of terror."[56]

Yet, reflective of Guevara's polarizing nature, some US observers lauded him. One *Washington Post* columnist hailed him as "the true revolutionary of the Western world." A *Philadelphia Tribune* writer called Guevara's death "a tremendous blow to the cause of freedom in Latin America. The rich and the privileged, concerned only with their tremendous profits garnered out of the exploitation of that area, are unrestrained in their glee." During a peace rally at the Lincoln Memorial later that month, a crowd of some 50,000 people held a moment of silence for Guevara.[57]

One writer aptly captured both sides of the Guevara divide. C. L. Sulzberger, a foreign correspondent for the *New York Times*, which his family owned, wrote a reflection coincidentally published the day Guevara was captured. While Sulzberger referred to Guevara as a "professional revolutionist" and "wholly ruthless," he added that "there is something gallant and even poetic about this man who against the greatest odds wishes to maintain an endless struggle. He is our enemy but, whether he lies in an anonymous grave or is again the one who got away, he merits respect and honor."[58]

WITH GUEVARA DEAD, so, too, was the Bolivian Liberation Army. Of the seventeen men trapped in the gully on October 8, 1967, only six made it out alive. One later died of fatigue. Two Bolivians were killed in separate shootouts with police in 1969. The remaining three were Cubans who escaped to Chile before returning to their homeland. One of them, Dariel Alarcón Ramírez, later had a falling out with Castro and defected in 1996 to the United States, where he would become friends with the CIA operative who was trying to hunt him down, Félix Rodríguez. As for Rodríguez, he remained with the CIA and was sent to Vietnam, where he allegedly was part of the infamous counterinsurgency Phoenix Program. He later was connected to the Iran-Contra Scandal in the 1980s.[59]

Among Bolivian leadership involved in Guevara's capture and execution, a "curse of Che" seemed to follow. President Barrientos died in a mysterious helicopter crash in 1969. Zenteno, while serving as Bolivia's ambassador to France in 1976, was gunned down on the streets of Paris by a group calling itself the "Che Guevara International Brigade." Prado was shot and paralyzed from the waist down during a revolt in 1981. Terán was said to be living for years in hiding, fearful of assassination by the Cuban government, before he died in 2022.[60]

If he cursed Bolivians, then the ghost of Che Guevara has continued to haunt American political discourse. During the 1984 presidential debate, candidate Walter Mondale was asked to repudiate outreach to Cuba made by his fellow Democrat, Rev. Jesse Jackson. In trying to establish some political distance, Mondale said, "I don't admire Fidel Castro at all. And I've said that Che Guevara was a contemptible figure in civilization's history." But that response was not enough to stop President Ronald Reagan from using it as an attack point in his campaign stump speeches. On at least ten occasions during the month of October, Reagan said, "My opponent failed to repudiate the Reverend Jesse Jackson when he went to Havana, stood with Fidel Castro, and cried, 'Long live Cuba! Long live Castro! Long live Che Guevara!'" In almost every instance Reagan mentioned it, his audience booed.[61]

Even into the twenty-first century, the specter of Guevara made for a powerful rhetorical device in Congress. Cuban-born Florida congresswoman Ileana Ros-Lehtinen, who served in the House of Representatives for thirty years, was a fierce critic of President Barack Obama's trip to Cuba in 2016. She was further incensed that he took a picture in Havana with a poster of Guevara in the background. "Che was a sadistic murderer and killer who executed Cubans during his reign of terror," she said. "Che, along with Fidel and Raúl Castro, is responsible for the suffering, misery, and oppression of the people of Cuba." The following year, she made a short address in the House to draw attention to a "No Che Noche" event she was attending that would "set the record straight on one of history's most sadistic murderers, Che Guevara."[62]

Such modern critiques, though, are generally at odds with the predominant view of Guevara as a venerable icon of "revolution," writ generically. His image has proliferated on t-shirts, posters, and films. Some companies have catered to tourists by creating a "ruta del Che" that retraces his last days in Bolivia. Even some of the locals, who didn't want anything to do with him when he was alive, have jumped on the bandwagon by creating shrines and selling Che-related trinkets. One study of Guevara wryly notes that "if Che had a dollar in 1967 for every 'sale' [of items with his image] he has made in the years since his death, he might have purchased the presidency of Bolivia and saved himself a lot of trouble." Although Guevara surely would have rejected the commodification of his image, one of the reasons it has become more popular is because the socialist ideals for which he fought seem less threatening in a post–Cold War world. The emphasis of his iconographic status is more rooted in recognition of his devotion and sacrifice for a cause that many casual observers may not fully understand.[63]

IT WOULD BE A STRETCH to argue that the United States deserves the lion's share of the credit in finding Guevara. It was a Bolivian mission, directed by Bolivian officers, run by Bolivian soldiers, dozens of whom died fighting guerrillas in 1967. Yet American influence cannot be discounted. The training and weaponry that the United States provided certainly sped the process of hunting down Guevara, affording him much less time to consolidate his fledgling movement that was essential for its survival. Moreover, American restraint—by not sending ground troops or heavier weaponry—denied Guevara one of his broader aims: to instigate a wider intervention and bog down the United States in "another Vietnam." Had Guevara enjoyed even a modicum of success in Bolivia or the Congo, American officials feared it would have created a domino effect of socialist revolutions that they could not allow in a Cold War world. The elimination of one of the United States' most prominent and vocal ideological enemies—while not losing a single American life in the process—was an impressive victory in its day. And his image continues to be a useful specter in American politics, especially when it comes to keeping pressure on the Cuban government abroad or decrying progressive ideals at home.

In the end, Guevara certainly did himself no favors. He made critical errors in judgment throughout his final mission, not least of which was choosing Bolivia in the first place. He seemed to ignore his own advice about guerrilla warfare from the very book he wrote—unable to attract support from the local population, unfamiliar with the terrain, moving around in the open. General Alfredo Ovando neatly summed up Guevara's predicament: "Guevara chose the wrong country, the wrong terrain and the wrong friends. He was a brave man but God was not with him."[64]

While the effectiveness of his means and methods can be questioned, Guevara was undeniably devoted to his cause. He was willing to endure great personal sacrifice to achieve what he believed would be a more just and equitable society. Although he essentially gave up life as a father to achieve revolution, he hoped to impart some of his ideas to his children. In a letter written before he left for the Congo in 1965, he asked them to "always be capable of feeling deeply any injustice committed against anyone, anywhere in the world. This is the most beautiful quality in a revolutionary."[65]

AT FIRST BLUSH, the US aim to eliminate Guevara was a success. One of the United States' most vocal antagonists was dead at relatively little cost to American lives and coffers. But in death, Guevara's reputation flourished. His efforts may have failed spectacularly in the Congo and Bolivia, but his devotion set a template for other like-minded revolutionaries in Latin America. During the 1970s and 1980s, various leftist groups emerged that drew inspiration in part from Guevara, such as the Revolutionary Armed Forces of Colombia (FARC), the Farabundo Martí National Liberation Front (FMLN) in El Salvador, and the Sandinistas in Nicaragua. These movements compelled many governments to initiate brutal campaigns to destroy them, often with American help. But not all such threats during this era were true revolutionaries. Colombia's Pablo Escobar, for example, threatened or initiated violence for much more self-interested motives. Although he posed a new kind of danger to US interests and security, he would nonetheless be framed in familiar ways.

CHAPTER FIVE
Dawn of Narcoterror
Pablo Escobar in Colombia

Robert Torricelli was outraged. He wasn't the first congressman to feel that way on Capitol Hill. And he wouldn't be the last. But he *was* furious enough to call a hearing.

As chair of the House Subcommittee on Western Hemisphere Affairs, the New Jersey representative held a day-long inquiry on July 29, 1992, titled "The Future of the Andean War on Drugs." Torricelli was apoplectic about how the world's most notorious drug kingpin, Pablo Escobar, could have escaped one week earlier from a Colombian prison and how it might impact the US government's decades-long "war on drugs." The previous October, Torricelli traveled to Colombia with two congressional colleagues and was pleased with the antinarcotics efforts he had seen, calling it "one of the bright spots in the war on drugs." Escobar's recent flight from justice, though, had "shaken our confidence."[1]

More than the escape, Torricelli was galled at the conditions in which Escobar was confined. It was no standard prison. Indeed, thanks to an agreement with the Colombian government, Escobar was allowed to build his own jail on the outskirts of his hometown of Medellín. The compound that had housed Escobar and thirteen of his associates since June 1991 was so formidable, it was known as *La Catedral*—the Cathedral. Given Escobar's fear of rivals and possible US extradition, the facility's security was designed as much to keep people out as it was to hold Escobar in. La Catedral had a double fence nearly ten feet high with fifteen rows of electrified barbed wire, seven watchtowers, and two guardhouses. It also had an antiaircraft battery because Escobar worried that competing cartels or US forces might bomb the prison.

Inside, its rooms resembled hotel suites. There were waterbeds and whirlpool baths, a woodburning fireplace, a stereo system, and a sixty-inch television. The facility also had a gym and a lighted soccer field. Two chefs prepared food for the residents. Prison guards doubled as waiters or bartenders during the frequent parties, which often included young prostitutes. As Escobar's brother and fellow inmate, Roberto, recalled, "There was a lot of sex at the Cathedral."[2]

More importantly, it was apparent that Escobar had maintained control over the infamous multibillion-dollar Medellín drug cartel, including overseeing murders of associates who had fallen out of favor. To Torricelli and many other American politicians, Escobar's deal, escape, and maintenance of power were miscarriages of justice. He had been reasonably accused of a variety of crimes—from drug smuggling to money laundering to murder—but seemed to face no consequences. It led Torricelli to question the Colombian government's ability to maintain order. If it could not bring drug trafficking to heel, he reasoned, then the United States must act. "The flow of drugs from Colombia is no different from an assault on our shores," Torricelli said. "They are a real and genuine threat to our country. And we would be within our rights to take unilateral action to deal with this threat, as we would be to deal with any other threat to our security."[3]

Escobar's danger to the United States came from more than just drugs. While he was head of a cartel that was supplying tons of cocaine entering the United States, he also was responsible for unleashing a wave of violence to protect that lucrative business. These attacks were aimed not only at rivals or double-crossers but also at authorities who tried to reel him in. Escobar operated by a policy of *plato o plomo*—silver or lead. Those who did not accept his bribes were subject to death. Throughout the 1980s and into the early 1990s, Escobar was connected to a series of murders and bombings that targeted politicians, journalists, judges, and police officers with hundreds of civilians caught in the crossfire. The US embassy drew down personnel and closed its consulate in Medellín because conditions were so dangerous.

The violence associated with drug cartels came to be known as "narcoterrorism." As the Cold War waned, Washington viewed this phenomenon as Latin America's principal threat to the United States in the late twentieth century. Although Escobar was not the only source of drugs or drug-related violence during this era, he was by far the most conspicuous. As the *Washington Post* editorialized, "Pablo Escobar personifies the evils of narcoterrorism." The US government thus committed a variety of resources to help the Colombian government find him. This aid included operatives from the DEA and CIA, Special Forces trainers, electronic surveillance, and hundreds of millions of dollars. Although the attempt to bring Escobar to justice would deepen American involvement in Colombian affairs, it ultimately had little impact on the broader war on drugs that would continue well into the twenty-first century.[4]

BEGINNING in the mid-twentieth century, Colombia was widely recognized by the United States as a reliable Cold War ally, part of the US aim to maintain a hemispheric consensus against communism. Colombia broke diplomatic relations with the Soviet Union in the 1940s, was the only Latin American nation to contribute militarily to the Korean War, and diplomatically supported the United States during the Cuban Missile Crisis. Yet during that time, Colombia faced steep challenges at home. After enduring the civil strife of La Violencia in the late 1940s and 1950s, in which an estimated 200,000 people died, a power-sharing agreement between the country's Liberal and Conservative Parties brought some measure of order. But in the countryside, a variety of disaffected socialist guerrilla groups emerged to wage war against the state for decades. These factions included the Revolutionary Armed Forces of Colombia (FARC), the National Liberation Army (ELN), and the 19th of April Movement (M-19). The presence of these combatants compelled the United States to provide hundreds of millions of dollars in military aid to the Colombian state in the name of anticommunism.[5]

Washington's attention to Colombia intensified with the onset of the war on drugs. The origin of the modern initiative is mostly attributed to President Richard Nixon. In June 1971, he declared, "America's public enemy number one in the United States is drug abuse. In order to fight and defeat this enemy, it is necessary to wage a new, all-out offensive." Such rhetoric, however, was not new. Politicians from both major parties had referenced some kind of "war" against drugs before. The Nixon-led effort, though, was widely seen by critics as a politically calculated effort against liberals and people of color.[6]

During the 1980s, President Ronald Reagan honed even more of the federal government's attention on illegal drugs. An antidrug crusader while governor of California, he brought that same sensibility to the White House. First Lady Nancy Reagan spearheaded the "Just Say No" campaign that was the centerpiece of her public agenda. She made frequent appearances—sometimes with the president—on television shows, news programs, and rallies to warn children about the dangers of drugs. But beyond moral suasion, the Reagan administration considered illegal drugs, particularly smuggling from abroad, as a matter of national security. In April 1986, Reagan signed National Security Decision Directive Number 221 that made it official US policy to work with other nations to halt the production and flow of illicit narcotics into the country. At a press briefing in July, he said, "Those who smuggle and sell drugs are as dangerous to our national security as any terrorist or foreign dictatorship." The broader American public seemed to agree. An April 1988 poll showed that 48 percent of respondents considered drug trafficking to be *the* principal foreign policy challenge facing the United States.[7]

Cocaine was the drug of most concern to the Reagan administration. A powerful stimulant, it derives from the coca leaf grown in the Andean region of South America. Its effects in powdered form were first developed in 1860. For decades, it was used as a surgical anesthetic and in commercial products (like Coca-Cola). Although its usage declined in the mid-twentieth century, cocaine made a comeback in the 1970s as a recreational drug favored among the wealthy and white middle class. By 1985, an estimated 5.7 million Americans used the drug regularly. This demand fueled an illicit economy worth billions of dollars a year. Most of those who dominated the supply chain were in Colombia, where approximately 80 percent of the cocaine in the United States was refined before shipment. These kingpins lived opulent lifestyles, seemingly above the law. But none conjured the specter of fear, power, and terror like Pablo Escobar.[8]

THE BROADER American public was introduced to Escobar in August 1983. ABC News ran an hour-long televised special, "The Cocaine Cartel," that examined how the drug trade operated in Colombia and its violent effects in the United States, particularly in the key entry point of south Florida. These cartels operated as consortiums, like businesses working together on the production, refinement, and transportation of cocaine. In this way, they could spread risk while maximizing reward. The most successful of these groups was based in Medellín, Colombia's second-largest city. The most powerful member of the cartel was Escobar.[9]

For a man who would eventually be named by *Forbes* magazine as one of the ten wealthiest men in the world, Escobar came from rather modest beginnings. Born December 1, 1949, he was the second of six children to parents Abel and Hermilda, a cattle farmer and a schoolteacher, respectively. In later years, Escobar would claim he came from poverty. In reality, his family was considered upper middle class for the province of Antioquia, where he was raised. A deeper look at the Escobar family tree suggests some foreshadowing about his path to power and criminality. According to his brother, Roberto, one of their great-great-grandmothers was a slaveowner from Spain. Their maternal grandfather was a bootlegger.[10]

Although his name and reputation would terrify people in later years, Escobar was physically unimposing. Standing five feet, six inches tall, he weighed around 160 pounds (but put on more weight after he escaped from

Dawn of Narcoterror   105

Pablo Escobar, shown here in 1988, came from modest beginnings in an upper-middle-class family. He would go on to become one of the wealthiest and most feared men in the world. Photograph by Eric Vandeville / Abaca / Sipa USA, courtesy of the Associated Press.

prison). Befitting a man who flouted conventions and prided himself on answering to no one, he had a host of idiosyncrasies, according to his family. Escobar cut his own hair, spent at least thirty minutes brushing his teeth, and took showers of up to three hours. He also wore a new shirt every day, often unbuttoned down to the middle of his chest. And while he generally avoided using cocaine and rarely drank alcohol, he smoked marijuana frequently. Although Escobar was a dedicated family man, he also was known as a sexual carouser with a preference for young women. In fact, he married one. When he was twenty-six years old, he married fifteen-year-old Maria Victoria Henao after dating for two years. The couple needed a special dispensation from the bishop because of her age. A year after their March 1976 wedding, they had a son, Juan Pablo. Their only other child, Manuela, was born in 1984.[11]

Before having a family of his own, Escobar spent many of his formative years as a petty criminal. While still a teenager, he sold answers to tests as well as forged diplomas. He also peddled contraband cigarettes and fake lottery tickets. His operation escalated to stealing cars, which resulted in

Escobar's first known arrest in September 1974. Yet his activity was successful enough that he convinced some people to pay him and his associates *not* to steal their cars, offering protection for a price. During this time, Escobar developed a reputation for casual, lethal violence. He sometimes would kidnap people who owed him money and kill the hostage if the family could not pay. As journalist Mark Bowden described it, "Pablo lived in a world where accumulation of wealth required the capacity to defend it."[12]

Sometime in the mid-1970s, Escobar began smuggling cocaine. He and other Colombian traffickers made connections to coca growers in Peru whose contacts in Chile had been cut off in 1973 following the rise of the right-wing autocratic government of Augusto Pinochet. Conditions in Colombia, in contrast, were fertile for such illicit activity. The state remained weak in the years after La Violencia. Men like Escobar who had experience smuggling contraband knew how to maneuver around the authorities. Moreover, the economy in Medellín was struggling following the decline of its textile industry. Thus, kingpins could draw from a population that could use the work as growers, guards, or muscle.[13]

The outlaw legend of Pablo Escobar was nearly snuffed out early. He was arrested in 1976 by Colombian police for transporting thirty-nine kilos of cocaine in the spare tire of a pickup truck. He remained in prison for three months until the judge overseeing his case was bribed to let him go. An appellate judge ordered Escobar rearrested, but before he could be found and tried, the arresting officers were killed, and the case was dropped. The episode was one of the earliest examples of his *plato o plomo* method.[14]

By then, Escobar was already working in a partnership with other like-minded cocaine traffickers in Medellín. This group included Jorge Luis Ochoa and his brothers, Juan David and Fabio; José Gonzalo Rodríguez Gacha (nicknamed "The Mexican" for his fondness of Mexico's culture); and Carlos Lehder, a German Colombian and self-styled neo-Nazi. According to Roberto Escobar, who served as an accountant and money launderer for his brother, the cartel was "an association of choice instead of a unified business." But over time, Pablo emerged as a first among equals, particularly through his ruthless use of violence. Collectively, the cartel had hundreds, if not thousands, of employees, including coca growers, guards, assassins, pilots, and lawyers. By the mid-1980s, they controlled more than half of the cocaine coming into the United States, up to fifty tons a year, for which they were earning an estimated $2 billion annually. The cartel made so much money that Roberto claimed it spent $2,500 a month just on rubber bands to keep the cash together.[15]

Colombia

With such a windfall, Pablo lived extravagantly. He held lavish parties. He played soccer on lighted fields, paid professional players to compete on those fields with him, and hired announcers to call his matches. He bought cars, paintings, and a range of properties, including a multimillion-dollar apartment complex in Miami that he allegedly paid for with two briefcases full of cash. His most ostentatious purchase was the $63 million Hacienda Napoles roughly 100 miles east of Medellín. The 7,000-acre property had ten separate residences, an airstrip, two heliports, 100,000 fruit trees, a motocross track, a gas station, a body shop to repair cars and motorcycles, and a zoo stocked with exotic animals, like hippopotamuses. The zoo was open to the public and was Colombia's most popular, with 60,000 visitors in 1983.[16]

Escobar also had a charitable streak. In Medellín, he funded improvements for roads, electric lines, and soccer fields. His most notable project was a housing development that came to be known as Barrio Pablo Escobar. In 1981, Escobar was impressed by the innovation of the homeless people he saw scavenging materials at a garbage dump. He formed a civic action group that collected donations from some of his fellow narcos and bought a tract of land on which to build 410 low-cost homes that were given to those who worked at the dump. For such largesse, Escobar was venerated in Medellín, especially among the poor. The Associated Press reported in 1991 that "hundreds of thousands of slum dwellers have considered Escobar a true-life fairy tale character — hoping he would enter their lives with a cash handout or free house."[17]

Such popularity compelled Escobar to try his hand at politics. He won a seat in 1982 as an alternate member of Congress. The position entitled him to the same privileges as the primary delegate, including judicial immunity. His biggest issue of political concern was Colombia's 1979 extradition treaty with the United States: Colombian citizens indicted by US courts could be sent to the United States for trial. Although it had not been enforced often, the agreement was the one thing members of the Medellín cartel feared most, because unlike in Colombia, they could not buy or bully their way out of an American jail. Escobar conveniently portrayed the issue as one of national pride. As Juan Pablo remembered, "My father thought it was humiliating for a country to hand over its citizens to another country's judicial system." In later years, Escobar and other drug kingpins would form an organization called "The Extraditables," dedicated to fighting the country's extradition policy. Their slogan was, "Better a grave in Colombia than a cell in the United States."[18]

For all his opposition to the United States, though, Escobar enjoyed certain aspects of Americana. Thanks to his diplomatic passport while in Congress, he traveled to the United States, hitting popular tourist destinations like Disney World, Graceland, and the White House. He even took a tour of the FBI building in Washington, DC. On a trip to Las Vegas, he allegedly met famed singer Frank Sinatra. Escobar had his own American Express credit card and displayed an American stagecoach at Hacienda Napoles.[19]

The tide in 1983 began turning against Escobar's public image as an upstanding politician and businessman. In an interview published in a Colombian magazine, Escobar claimed that his multibillion-dollar fortune stemmed from construction and a bicycle rental business he began at age sixteen. Most politicians were too cowed to challenge such an absurd notion. But Rodrigo Lara Bonilla, Colombia's minister of justice, called his bluff. He denounced Escobar, the broader cartel, and the drug money corrupting Colombian politics. The newspaper *El Espectador* printed Escobar's mug shot from his 1976 arrest for drug trafficking, something he had tried to keep hidden. His political party expelled him, and Congress moved to strip him of judicial immunity. An infuriated Escobar left his seat in January 1984 publicly claiming frustration with politicians who neglected the plight of the poor. Privately, he was planning vengeance against those who challenged him, setting the stage for an onslaught of violence that would make him infamous.[20]

THE YEAR 1984 would be pivotal for Escobar. In March, Colombian authorities—assisted by the DEA—found one of the Medellín cartel's largest cocaine processing laboratories deep in the Colombian jungle. The raid at Tranquilandia resulted in the seizure of 13.8 tons of cocaine valued at $1.2 billion. Although the seizure did not cripple the cartel, its ripple effect raised the street price of cocaine for the first time in three years. Moreover, it gave the DEA a clearer idea of the scale of the cartel's operations.[21]

Authorities in the United States gained more intelligence on Escobar in June. An American, Barry Seal, secretly took pictures of Escobar helping him load duffel bags of cocaine into an airplane. Seal was a pilot who had been smuggling for the cartel for years. Facing a lengthy jail sentence for trafficking when caught by authorities, he cut a deal with the federal government to become an informant. Using this intelligence, as well as what the DEA found in Tranquilandia, the US government in November 1986 issued a thirty-nine-count indictment of Escobar and the other cartel leaders for the production, transportation, and distribution of cocaine. It was the first in what would be at least ten separate federal indictments against Escobar over the next six years.[22]

Escobar concerned Washington for another reason. It suspected he was cooperating with anti-American governments in Latin America that allowed him to use their countries as transshipment points for cocaine smuggling. Seal's pictures of Escobar had been taken in Nicaragua, then led by the socialist-leaning Sandinista government that the Reagan administration had been undermining for years. Cuba was also identified as a way station for the cartel's drugs, although whether Fidel Castro was aware of the arrangement remained murky. The cooperation of Panama's Manuel Noriega was less in doubt. The country's strongman allowed Escobar's traffickers to use Panama as a transshipment point for a fee of $100,000 per load. Escobar also paid Noriega $5 million to be allowed to operate in Panama. By the end of the 1980s, Noriega himself was the subject of a drug indictment that would lead to the US invasion of Panama and his eventual capture and imprisonment.[23]

Feeling the pressure from the United States and Colombian governments, Escobar and the cartel lashed out. They were suspected of arranging the April 1984 assassination of Lara, who was killed by motorcycle-riding gunmen. Escobar and the cartel also were thought to have funded the deadly February 1986 hit against Seal in which the assassins were offered $1 million to capture him alive or $500,000 to kill him.[24]

These killings were part of an existing, though intensifying, pattern of violence. Designed principally to intimidate authorities into relaxing counternarcotics efforts, such brutality was dubbed "narcoterror." A CIA report in July 1984 was one of the first examinations of the concept. Initially, it linked the violence of drug traffickers with such insurgent groups as FARC. Indeed, there were some areas of cooperation. Narcos were known to pay guerrillas to guard drug laboratories in rural areas of guerrilla control. A collection of drug lords, including Escobar, funded M-19's November 1985 seizure of the Palace of Justice that destroyed a variety of incriminating court records but also killed ninety-five people, including eleven of the country's Supreme Court justices. Such alliances, though, were generally ad hoc. And Escobar did not look upon the guerrillas fondly. He allegedly said, "They accuse me of being a narcotrafficker. But to portray me as a member of the guerrillas is unacceptable because it hurts my personal dignity. I am a man of investments, and for this reason could not be allied with guerrillas who fight against private property."[25]

Nevertheless, the CIA identified the heart of the problem of narcoterrorism: "Although there are fundamental differences between the aims of traffickers and [insurgents], the systematic use of violence by drug traffickers can delegitimize and erode the authority of the state in the same manner as traditional terrorist activity." Combined with the corrupting effect of drug money in all levels of the Colombian government, some US officials started to worry that the Colombian state could turn into a narcocracy. Charles Gillespie Jr., who served as US Ambassador to Colombia from 1985 to 1988, had just such a fear. "Colombia had democratic institutions and was apparently not under imminent threat of being taken over by the narcotics traffickers," he recalled. "However, you could see the beginnings of such a takeover, if you let yourself think about it, as I did then."[26]

According to his brother Roberto, Pablo wanted to be president of Colombia someday. But such political ambitions were not the driving force behind the violence he unleashed. His motivations were much simpler: getting Colombian and US authorities off his case so he could continue to conduct his illicit business. In this way, he was different from a traditional terrorist, whose violence or threat thereof is motivated by a political or social impulse. General William G. "Jerry" Boykin, who led a Delta Force team in Colombia after Escobar's escape from La Catedral, recognized this distinction. He wrote that Escobar "wasn't a terrorist in the political sense, one who terrorized in the pursuit of some religious or political belief. Escobar had simpler tastes: Money and power." Likewise, Bowden saw through Escobar's platitudes to the poor or his claim that US extradition was an affront to Colombian sovereignty. For Escobar, "his only cause, ultimately, was himself. At his most grandiose, he identified his own ambitions with those of his countrymen, but there was no rationale or ideology behind this parallel."[27]

REGARDLESS OF MOTIVATION, the scale of violence in Colombia worsened. Much of it was directed at judges, police, politicians, and journalists. One December 1988 estimate counted the narcoterror death toll at fifty-seven judges, at least 250 reporters, and more than 1,000 mayors, city council members, and drug enforcement officers. These brazen attacks included the murder—or attempted murder—of presidential candidates. The most notable was Luis Galán, who had denounced Escobar, favored the US extradition treaty, and was the odds-on favorite to win the presidency in 1990 before he was shot to death in August 1989. Three months later, five kilos of dynamite took down Avianca Flight 203 shortly after takeoff, killing 110 people, including two Americans. The main target was César Gaviria, Galán's deputy, who would go on to become Colombia's next president. Gaviria was supposed to be on the flight but backed out at the last minute. Escobar would later be indicted in the United States for the bombing. His codefendant in the case, Dandeny Muñoz-Mosquera, eventually was captured and convicted in US federal court under a 1986 terrorism statute. He received ten consecutive life sentences in prison.[28]

Officials in Washington had long worried about the narcoterror threat against Americans in Colombia. The danger in Medellín seemed particularly acute. The US consulate there closed in 1983 because of security concerns. DEA agents in Colombia could stay in the city only a few days at a time. Gillespie recalled taking two trips there during his time as US ambassador but never stayed the night. The capital, Bogotá, seemed little safer. In the mid-1980s, the State Department ordered the drawdown of US personnel at the embassy because of threats. Those who continued to work there received danger pay and a hardship bonus.[29]

These threats led to a growing undercurrent of outrage in the United States, especially at the Colombian government's inability to bring Escobar to heel. Following Galán's murder, the *Hartford Courant* wrote that "Pablo Escobar . . . and other kingpins in the Medellín drug cartel pose a greater threat to the United States than the Marxists on Grenada or Moammar Gadhafi [in Libya] did." The not-so-subtle inference was that if those threats warranted US military intervention, then why not against Escobar in Colombia? Indeed, President George H. W. Bush in 1989 offered to send US troops there to fight the narcoterror threat. But Colombian president Virgilio Barco Vargas politely rejected the proposal. Surely mindful how such an overt display of American force might look in relation to Colombian sovereignty and his own authority, Barco preferred a more tactful approach. Instead, the United States sent trainers, weapons, equipment, and aid money.[30]

This covert assistance included advisers from Delta Force and the DEA. One DEA agent, Steve Murphy, was excited to get the assignment. "I was determined to get Pablo Escobar," he wrote. "Months of research had convinced me that he was an evil monster. I knew I would have absolutely no problem putting a bullet in his head." US aid also included a shadowy military intelligence unit called Centra Spike that specialized in eavesdropping on radio and telephone conversations, pinpointing source locations. Much of the work done by the unit was from nondescript Beechcraft airplanes flying over areas of suspected cartel activity. Only a handful of US embassy personnel were aware of this secretive mission.[31]

Americans tasked with hunting Escobar worked most closely with the Colombian police task force Bloque de Busqueda—Search Bloc. At its peak, the unit had 600 people working around-the-clock to search for Escobar. Over the years, Search Bloc conducted more than 10,000 raids and killed nearly 150 suspected members of the Medellín cartel, including Escobar's cousin Gustavo Gaviria, a key partner of Escobar's well before they got into narcotrafficking, who was killed in a shootout with police. At least that was the official story. In many instances, suspected cartel members who wound up dead were said to have been killed in a police shootout, which widely became interpreted as a euphemism for execution. According to one reporter, "The Bloque de Busqueda were brutal killers, who once threw two suspects out of a helicopter because they were worried they just *might* have identified the Activity operators working alongside them as Americans." Such extralegal activities dogged the unit for the remainder of its existence and gave some US officials pause about continuing to work with it.[32]

But the persistent narco-violence led officials to swallow their concerns. In addition to murders and kidnappings, car bombings became more frequent, killing as many as 500 people between 1989 and 1993. Police, especially in Medellín, were the most targeted. Escobar paid a bounty of roughly $4,000 for each officer killed. Many of those who took him up on the offer were poor, teenage *sicarios*, or hitmen. The Associated Press estimated that Escobar was responsible for the death of 10 percent of Medellín's police force. Escobar, though, did not claim credit for all the violence. According to Juan Pablo, they would review the newspaper in the morning and his father would admit to the murders attributed to him. "He'd say, 'I didn't do that one,' and then, 'I did that one.'"[33]

The brazen violence led to contrasting conclusions in the United States and Colombia. Descriptions of Escobar in the US press tended to dehumanize him. The *Los Angeles Times*, for example, referred to him as "wily and nervous as a hunted fox, and maybe a little crazed." Similarly, a *Wall Street Journal* op-ed called him and other narcos an enemy "barely human in its brutality." These types of depictions suggested not only that Escobar was dangerous and unpredictable but also that extreme measures might be necessary to end the threat he posed.[34]

Colombians, though, recognized that Escobar would not have had nearly as much money, power, and influence at his disposal if not for Americans buying his product. Gillespie recalled that during his time as US ambassador, "Colombians would say, 'If the United States didn't provide this market, we wouldn't have this problem. We'd have a much more manageable problem.'" Similarly, the *Washington Post* reported that Barco told US Attorney General Edwin Meese in a December 1988 meeting that "the American people put up most of the cash that the Medellin cartel uses to corrupt governments, hire assassins and undermine law enforcement throughout the Western Hemisphere." Privately, Bush acknowledged that American demand exacerbated the power of narcotraffickers like Escobar. His administration dedicated more resources to curbing demand, which yielded an estimated decline in regular cocaine users from 5.7 million in 1985 to 1.8 million by 1991. But this trend had little immediate effect on the violence.³⁵

DESPERATE TO END the plague of murder and kidnapping afflicting his country, Colombian President César Gaviria in October 1990 offered all suspected narcos, including Escobar, a plea bargain. If they surrendered and confessed to the least significant charge against them, they could escape prosecution of the other charges. Some Medellín cartel leaders, including the Ochoa brothers, took the offer. Escobar, though, held out for a written guarantee that he would not be extradited, that he could control conditions of his imprisonment, and that the state would guarantee the safety of his wife and children. In June 1991, hours after the Colombian congress voted to end extradition, Escobar surrendered to begin his imprisonment at La Catedral.³⁶

The deal came at an opportune time for Escobar. He was exhausted from years on the run. He could no longer stay at his luxurious homes and was sometimes forced to sleep in the woods to avoid the authorities. Afraid his phones were tapped, he communicated only through couriers. The surrender of members of his cartel and the deaths of his cousin and a brother-in-law also gave him pause. The deal guaranteed he could avoid his worst fear—extradition—and gave him a safe port in which to regroup. Escobar acknowledged just one crime: acting as a middleman in a French drug deal arranged by his cousin, Gustavo. When he went to court as part of his plea deal, Escobar described himself as a "livestock farmer" who got involved in the business of "buying and selling cars, livestock, and land investment." He denied knowing anything about cocaine or being involved in narcotrafficking.³⁷

US officials and newspapers were nearly unanimous in their condemnation of the deal. Boykin called it "almost literally, a deal with the devil." The *Los Angeles Times* described it similarly as "a proverbial deal with the devil." Law enforcement working on the case saw the arrangement as an injustice. DEA agent Javier Peña, who had been in Colombia since 1988, said the agreement was "a crushing blow to our efforts to bring him to justice." Former DEA chief Peter Bensinger wrote a blistering op-ed in the *New York Times* in which he argued that "the so-called surrender of Pablo Escobar . . . is not only the surrender of the world's biggest drug dealer but also the surrender of justice by the US and Colombia." He referred to Escobar as "chief of a deadly terrorist organization . . . [who] should be on death row, not in a posh mountain retreat."³⁸

Hearing the American criticism, Gaviria published a rebuttal in the *Washington Post*. He wrote, "Those who question our commitment to waging war on drugs overlook recent history. They forget the high price that our nation has already paid." He continued that such plea deals were necessary because the Colombian judicial system "had been rendered impotent by terrorism." He also acknowledged that the fight against narcotics trafficking was not Colombia's responsibility alone. "We have an obligation to see that justice is done, just as other countries have an obligation to stop the demand for drugs that drives this criminal violence." The *Hartford Courant* was one of the few US outlets that empathized with Gaviria. "Mr. Escobar is a detestable human being and undoubtedly deserves much worse than he is getting," it wrote. "But for Mr. Gaviria the first priority is to stop the violence. If treating Mr. Escobar leniently can save many lives, it is worth a try. If not, the president should renege on his deal with this murderer."[39]

Privately, President Bush was skeptical about the deal but sympathetic with Gaviria's position. Referring to Escobar as "a really bad egg," Bush told the English-speaking Gaviria that the United States "would have preferred extradition. But I know you are under a lot of pressure." Gaviria appreciated the sentiment and tried to alleviate Bush's concerns about the conditions in which Escobar was incarcerated. "The press has reported that it is a luxurious jail," Gaviria said. "That is not true. It's not luxurious. You can verify that, it's no better than any other."[40]

Whether he sincerely believed that or was in denial, Gaviria was dead wrong about Escobar's living conditions. Escobar enjoyed too many amenities and liberties to think otherwise. More importantly, his means of incarceration made it easier to exercise control over the cartel. And he wasn't afraid to use such power. According to one report, while in jail Escobar was suspected of authorizing the kidnapping and killing of up to two dozen associates who fell out of favor for one reason or another. An informant approached the DEA and the Colombian attorney general about two of them — Gerardo Moncada and Fernando Galeano. Escobar thought they had stolen $20 million and demanded they pay him restitution of $200,000 for every shipment of cocaine they sent abroad. The duo, Escobar's childhood friends and associates for years, balked. An enraged Escobar was said to have beaten the men with a stick, then had his *sicarios* finish them off. The men's bodies were burned and chopped up, their charred penises sent to their wives.[41]

REPORTS OF THESE KILLINGS — in addition to the parties, contraband, and continued oversight of the cartel — reached the highest levels of the Colombian government. Joe Toft, the head DEA agent in Colombia, recalled that Gaviria initially refused to believe the news. But eager to avoid embarrassment, the Colombian president approved a raid on La Catedral to bring Escobar to a higher security prison in Bogotá. The move was a disaster. The military was reluctant to go in, giving Escobar time to prepare. His men seized the vice minister of justice, who had been sent to inform Escobar about the prison transfer. Hours later, when the military assault finally commenced, Escobar escaped by kicking out a weakened brick wall. Under the cover of night, he and a handful of men then cut through a wire fence and traveled down steep cliffs from the mountain compound to elude their pursuers. Escobar's son and brother refuted army reports that he was dressed as a woman and bribed the soldiers to let him walk out.[42]

American audiences were aghast that Escobar was free again. Congressman Robert Torricelli called a hearing on Capitol Hill looking for answers. Speaking for the Bush administration, Press Secretary Marlin Fitzwater framed the problem in stark terms, saying that "Escobar and his ilk represent a threat to law-abiding, civilized societies throughout the hemisphere, and they must be brought to justice." The *Hartford Courant* opined that the United States should get involved in finding Escobar. Calling to mind the "wanted" posters of the mythic Old West, it noted, "If he does not surrender soon, no effort should be spared to bring in the multiple murderer—dead or alive."[43]

Gaviria indeed sought US assistance, which came quickly. The day after Escobar's escape, DEA agents Murphy and Peña were at La Catedral looking for leads on where he might have gone. The following day, Centra Spike started picking up Escobar's cell phone conversations. In less than a week, an eight-man Delta Force team led by two-time Purple Heart winner Boykin arrived with orders to train and support the Colombian police and military but refrain from going into the field. Despite the limitations, Boykin was eager for the assignment. "I thought it was a prime opportunity to rid the world of a gory and unrestrained killer," he wrote. "I hoped we would capture Escobar quickly, but I knew the best scenario for everyone was to simply kill him. By then I had come to believe that some men in the world were simply evil. They could not be bargained with. They could not be rehabilitated. . . . I came to believe such men just needed killing. Pablo Escobar was one of those men."[44]

While Escobar focused most of his war against Colombian authorities, he still seemed to most fear the Americans. He justified his escape by claiming that the Colombian government's attempt to move him would have jeopardized his safety and that a prison transfer was merely a prelude to US extradition. He suspected that the Americans were involved in the raid at La Catedral. Escobar's concerns likely were exacerbated by news of a June 1992 US Supreme Court ruling that the US government could abduct suspects from foreign countries to stand trial in the United States. One of Escobar's lawyers decried the apparent impunity with which the US government could pursue his client and claimed that President Bush was trying to score political points as he was running for reelection. "We know the DEA has carte blanche to kidnap anyone in the world," José Salomón Lozano said. "It would be a big coup for George Bush, who is losing in the polls, to be able to say to the American people, 'Here is Public Enemy No. 1.'" Such animosity led some US officials to worry that a desperate Escobar might stage a vengeful bombing campaign in the United States. The US embassy even received a fax the day Escobar escaped. Signed by the Extraditables, it stated that should anything happen to Escobar, "We will target the United States Embassy in the country, where we will plant the largest quantity of dynamite ever."[45]

With so much at stake, the renewed hunt for Escobar led to tension between US and Colombian officials. Some Americans, like Murphy and Peña, lauded the courage of their Colombian counterparts in the field. But others thought that Colombians were too timid in their pursuit. Bowden recounted a joke at the US embassy: "How many Colombian prison guards and soldiers does it take to let Pablo Escobar escape? Answer: Four hundred. One to open the gate and three hundred and ninety-nine to watch." Boykin was particularly critical of Search Bloc's leadership for moving too slowly on the time-sensitive signals intelligence it received from Centra Spike. One Colombian military leader was nicknamed "Pajamas" because he once answered the door wearing them when Delta Force went to his house to press him into action. "In the end, we gave him the benefit of the doubt and decided he was more likely a coward," Boykin wrote. Among Colombians, some politicians complained that the US presence was too overbearing. At one point, the United States, with the permission of the Gaviria administration, had seventeen aircraft flying over Colombia searching for Escobar. Local leaders complained to Gaviria that the flights were causing "panic among the citizenry." Three Colombian congressmen decried "the raping of our air space."[46]

But for all the frustrations of Escobar hunters, their quarry shared one thing with them: he didn't want to be on the run either. Moving from place to place around Medellín was exhausting and costing him $1 million a day, according to one estimate. It was difficult to communicate with his family, with whom he spoke frequently. Centra Spike intercepted a conversation Escobar had with his lawyers saying he preferred to return to La Catedral despite his fear of an American kidnapping or assassination attempt.[47]

The most important aspect that La Catedral provided was safety. This facet would become more important as a mysterious group began staging attacks on Escobar-related targets. The organization called itself Los Pepes, derived from the phrase *Perseguidos por Pablo Escobar*—Persecuted by Pablo Escobar. Members issued a press release in January 1993 explaining their mission. "We want to make Pablo Escobar feel the effects in his own flesh of his brand of terrorism," they wrote. "Every time that Pablo Escobar carries out an act of terrorism against defenseless people, we will respond with a similar act." Over the next few months, Los Pepes was suspected of staging deadly assaults against a variety of people linked to Escobar, including relatives, lawyers, accountants, and even tutors and maids who worked for the Escobar family. The US Defense Intelligence Agency estimated that Los Pepes killed nearly fifty people associated with Escobar during the first four months of 1993. Los Pepes members were also blamed for car bombs at the apartments where Escobar's mother, sister, wife, and children lived. The *New York Times* noted the irony that Escobar was "a veteran practitioner of terrorism [who] is suddenly squirming as a target of terrorism."[48]

The widely held belief at the time was that Los Pepes was led by disaffected members of the Medellín cartel, particularly brothers Fidel and Carlos Castaño, with financial help from the rival Cali cartel. Many US officials also suspected that members of Search Bloc either were part of the group or were sharing intelligence with it. Initially, some members of the DEA were OK with such an arrangement. But that support faded once it became clear that the Cali cartel was involved and that Los Pepes was targeting tangential connections, such as the eighteen-year-old son of one of Escobar's lawyers. Murphy wrote, "If we ever harbored any sympathy for Los Pepes or secretly cheered them on for going after Escobar and his associates, those sentiments quickly faded after the grisly murders of [Guido] Parra and his innocent son." According to a US embassy report, Ambassador Morris Busby met with one of Gaviria's advisers to express his concerns about any potential police-Pepes alliance. The same report alleged that Gaviria ordered intelligence cooperation to end and told a police commander to instruct Los Pepes to stop its activities, a move that suggested Gaviria was aware of a connection. Escobar, for one, was certain. Juan Pablo recalled that his father asked him, "What should I do to fight a corrupt police force and government that are allied with Los Pepes? Haven't you noticed that I'm the only narco they're going after? At least I chose to be a bandit, and that's what I am." Notably, it seemed to be one of the few times that Escobar acknowledged his criminality.[49]

IF PABLO ESCOBAR had a weak spot in his aura of invincibility, it was his wife and children. Despite remaining in hiding, he often tried to secure safety for his family. In February 1993, he encouraged them to go to the United States. Maria Victoria, Juan Pablo, and Manuela all had proper travel visas, but Ambassador Busby canceled them on the grounds that children under the age of eighteen had to travel with both parents. Angry but desperate, Escobar later tried to curry favor with Busby by sending him a handwritten letter stating that he had nothing to do with the February 1993 attack on the World Trade Center that had killed six people and injured more than 1,000. (At the time, it was not yet clear who was responsible, and drug cartels were not ruled out.) The outreach failed to move US officials. In November, the Escobar family once again tried to leave the country, this time taking a flight to Germany. But under pressure from the United States, the German government refused them entry.[50]

Throughout his time in hiding, Escobar frequently spoke to his family, sometimes four times a day. Using a radiophone, he needed a direct line of sight to their location, an apartment complex in Medellín. Knowing this limitation, search teams were confident that Escobar was somewhere in the city. To throw off his pursuers, Escobar started calling his family in a moving car. This tactic made it difficult for eavesdroppers to get a fix on his location. Escobar often spoke to his sixteen-year-old son through whom he was negotiating with Colombia's attorney general on terms of a surrender. Escobar wanted to go back to the *status quo ante*—that is, back to a Catedral-like facility without extradition—and get his family out of the country. But once US officials got wind of such discussions, they adamantly opposed any deal and blocked potential destinations, like Germany.[51]

Desperate and frustrated, Escobar spent more time on the phone and for longer durations. This enabled Centra Spike and Search Bloc to get a better fix on his location. On the afternoon of December 2, 1993—one day after his forty-fourth birthday—Escobar had a long conversation with Juan Pablo, who was relaying a journalist's questions for an interview. His eavesdroppers narrowed his position to the Los Olivos neighborhood of Medellín, a residential district of two- and three-story row houses. A small unit of officers led by Hugo Martínez Jr., son of the Search Bloc chief, drove around the area looking for the source of the signal. Incredibly, Martínez spotted through a second-floor window an overweight, bearded man with long, curly black hair. It was Escobar.[52]

Within ten minutes, an assault team entered the house. After breaking through a heavy metal front door, police found the first floor empty but heard commotion upstairs. Escobar's lone bodyguard, Alvaro de Jesús (nicknamed Limón), tried to make a break for it by leaping out a back window onto an orange tile roof that was surrounded by walls on three sides. Search Bloc snipers on the ground gunned him down, his body tumbling to the yard below. Escobar followed outside. He took off his flip-flops and jumped out the window to the roof. He initially stayed near the roof wall to give himself some cover, then tried to make a run for it across the roof toward a back street. A barrage of gunfire ensued, killing Escobar.[53]

The official autopsy report states that Escobar was hit three times—in the right leg, his back, and in the head. The source of that last wound—the killshot that went from his right ear, through his brain, and out by his left ear—is in some dispute. Colombian authorities insisted that Escobar was killed amid a hail of gunfire as he was shooting at police. Outside observers, though, were dubious given the tendency of suspects to die in shootouts in Colombia. Boykin, for example, did not buy the official account. "I'd say it's more likely the Colombians downed him with a shot in the ass, then walked up and put a coup de grace bullet in each side of his head," he wrote. "There you go, Pablo, payback for two decades of murder." Bowden suspected likewise. In his account of Escobar's death, Bowden asserts that Escobar fell and then was shot in the head at close range. He also intimates that Delta Force may have had a hand in it, but there is no evidence to support that idea. In contrast, Escobar's son and brother claimed that Escobar died by his own hand, killing himself as the police closed in. Such a version is a way to provide Escobar one last measure of agency—to die on his own terms—and deny Colombian (and American) authorities the satisfaction of taking him out. Few other accounts, though, support the theory of death by suicide.[54]

Regardless of who delivered the final shot or how, there was much celebrating among Colombian and American authorities. DEA agent Murphy arrived on the scene shortly after getting word of the shootout. Escobar's body was still sprawled on the roof. He was barefoot, wearing jeans cuffed around the ankles. His t-shirt was raised halfway up his torso exposing a protruding belly. Dried blood caked his face and right arm. Murphy joined with the Search Bloc team in taking pictures of themselves around the body, like it was a big-game trophy. The inference that Escobar was some exotic animal or that US personnel were part of the shootout did not cross Murphy's mind at the time. "Like everyone else around me, I was caught up in the euphoria of the moment," he wrote. "I was overjoyed."[55]

As were many other Americans who empathized with the terrible toll that chasing Escobar had taken on Colombia. "I want to offer my congratulations to you and the Colombian security forces for your courageous and effective work in this case," President Bill Clinton wrote to Gaviria. "Hundreds

On the rooftop of his hideout in Medellín, Pablo Escobar was killed by Colombian police in December 1993. Search teams took celebratory photos afterward. Photograph by Medellin Police / AFP Collection via Getty Images.

of Colombians—brave police officers and innocent people—lost their lives as a result of Escobar's terrorism. Your work honors the memory of all of these victims." The *Chicago Tribune* concurred, noting that "Escobar terrorized the country. . . . With his elimination, Colombians have regained their country, and the government has taken out a new lease on the future. A heinous enemy of the state, a symbol of extreme violence and lawlessness, is gone." Murphy's DEA partner, Peña, had been stationed in Colombia for five years pursuing Escobar. Aware that some people in Medellín openly mourned Escobar's death, he rejected notions that Escobar had any good intentions or benefits to Colombians. "He was no hero," Peña wrote. "He may have spent a small fraction of some of his billions he made selling cocaine to fix up Medellín shantytowns and build a soccer stadium, but his brutality had brought Colombia to its knees for years."[56]

Not everyone agreed. Escobar's funeral in Medellín brought out thousands of mourners, many of whom shouted "Viva Pablo!" as he was taken to his final resting place. Aside from those supporters, there was little outrage or criticism about the circumstances of his death. Such silence suggested a wide consensus that Escobar deserved what he got, that he was too dangerous to be tried and put in prison for his crimes. Colombia's former minister of government, Humberto de la Calle, wrote in the *Washington Post* that

Escobar's death was a major achievement for Colombia that "lifted a palpable cloud of terror from us." Peña was more succinct in his assessment: "Escobar was pure evil."[57]

AS THE LIVED MEMORIES of the terror and violence he wrought have faded, Escobar's image has enjoyed a revival in twenty-first-century popular culture. This shift has coincided with a broader rise in so-called narcoculture that romanticizes the life and luxury of powerful drug traffickers like Escobar. As explained by Latin American studies expert Aldona Bialowas Pobutsky, this phenomenon upholds Escobar as an antiestablishment icon. "Like Che Guevara, albeit in a different context," she wrote, "Escobar, the criminal and the terrorist, has been redefined in popular culture as the daredevil, with associations of freedom, rebellion, guts, and individuality."[58]

He has appeared as a character in a variety of television shows and films, including portrayals by A-list Hollywood actors such as Javier Bardem and Benicio del Toro (who also played Guevara in another film). Most of these depictions have framed Escobar less as a villainous narcoterrorist and more as a complicated antihero. The prime example is the Netflix series *Narcos*. Escobar is one of the main characters in the first two seasons, which dramatizes the rise of the Medellín cartel and the DEA's pursuit of him. Murphy and Peña, who served as consultants to the series, are also central characters. The series does not frame Escobar as a thug or terrorist but as ambitious and complex. Series cocreator Doug Miro explained that he saw the Colombian-born Escobar in very American terms. "He pulled himself up from his bootstraps, a poor kid on the farm, by sheer force of will and intelligence, to being the biggest drug dealer in the world," he said. "And that is an American story if there ever was one." While such a view oversimplifies Escobar's upbringing and ignores his criminality, it sheds light into how he has come to be viewed more favorably—or at least with less anxiety—in modern American popular culture.[59]

Much like Guevara, Escobar's image has also become commodified into a brand. But unlike Guevara, such branding is in keeping with Escobar's business-oriented mindset. He's been featured on t-shirts, sweaters, and key chains. He's also been referenced in music by artists, including Kanye West and Lil Wayne. Restaurants around the world have borne his name. For example, the rapper 2 Chainz opened an eatery in Atlanta called Escobar Restaurant and Tapas (later changed to Esco).[60]

The starkest example of Escobar's tempered legacy is the rise of narcotourism. A subset of so-called dark tourism, in which travelers go to dangerous or macabre places, a cottage industry has developed catering to those who want to see where Escobar lived or staged his violence. Tours range from a few hours to a couple of days. In 2013, a *New York Times* reporter indulged in one such junket, visiting Escobar's family home, the site where he was gunned down, and his grave. After enduring the tour and sampling the nightlife, the reporter's traveling companion remarked, "I'm getting more and more Pablo by the minute."[61]

Some of Escobar's closest associates have also cashed in on the trend. His brother, Roberto, who served fourteen years in prison, holds his own tours and sells DVDs and photos. One of Escobar's top *sicarios*, Jhon Jairo Velásquez (a.k.a. "Popeye") did likewise after he was released from prison in 2016. His added touch was to go to the graves of people he killed and describe to tourists how he killed them. An episode of the Netflix series *Dark Tourist* enlists Popeye, who died in 2020 of esophageal cancer, to reenact one of his murders.[62]

For the most part, such tours cater to foreigners. Usually, governments welcome tourists from abroad for their infusion of capital. But the Colombian government has tried to turn the page from the Escobar era. In 2019, officials approved the destruction of the Monaco building in Medellín that had become a popular tourist destination because Escobar had lived there. La Catedral was allowed to fall into disrepair until it was taken over in 2007 by Benedictine monks. Hacienda Napoles was repossessed by the state and reopened as a theme park and zoo. It still has hippopotamuses, whose population in the mid-2010s had grown to an estimated sixty from the original four that Escobar imported. As embodiments of danger and awe, these animals seem an apt symbol of how many Americans have come to view Escobar.[63]

OSTENSIBLY, the death of Pablo Escobar was supposed to be a prominent victory in the war on drugs. But even at the time of Escobar's demise, there was great skepticism that his passing would have any effect. "Unfortunately, the victory over Escobar does not amount to a big win in the war on drugs," the *Chicago Tribune* editorialized. "It is not expected to have much of an impact, if any, on the flow of cocaine from Colombia to the US." As the *New York Times* similarly recognized, so long as "demand from users remains insatiable" there would be willing suppliers. Indeed, much of that demand for cocaine would come to be supplied by the Cali cartel. Considered to be less brutal, though by no means nonviolent, they were able to fill the vacuum left by Escobar and the Medellín cartel. Well into the twenty-first century, Colombia remained the world's largest producer of cocaine.[64]

And still the United States assisted Colombia in its antinarcotics efforts. Even without a notable villain like Escobar to personify the drug war, US aid rose from $26 million in 1994 to $800 million in 2000, making Colombia the third-largest recipient of American money behind Israel and Egypt. It was but a drop in the bucket compared to the estimated $1 trillion the US government has spent during the war on drugs over the last half-century. Such largesse compelled one historian to characterize US antidrug policy as a "military industrial narcotics complex."[65]

Much of the same rationale used to justify supporting Colombia in the 1980s and 1990s continued well into the twenty-first century. In fact, a President Bush offered the same sunny rhetoric in both eras. In 1990, George H. W. Bush traveled to a celebrated drug summit with other Andean leaders in Cartagena, Colombia. Signaling a healthy optimism that success against narcotrafficking was right around the corner, he hailed the meeting as "the dawn of a new era in the war against drugs." Fourteen years later, his son George W. Bush visited the same city to talk about antidrug efforts. "Defeating [drug traffickers] is vital to the safety of our peoples and to the stability of this hemisphere," he said. "This war against narcoterrorism can and will be won, and Colombia is well on its way to that victory." It was a sad commentary that more than a decade after the death of the world's most notorious narcoterrorist, notions of "victory" in the war on drugs were still seen as distant.[66]

FOR A TIME, Escobar was the face of the broader US fight against illegal drugs. It was a battle whose beginnings predated him and continued to simmer well after he died. The war on drugs, though, would not be the last time the United States declared war on a concept. In fact, the next one was just getting started even before Escobar's death. The war on terror, officially articulated after the September 11, 2001, attacks but essentially in place years before that, placed the Saudi-born Osama bin Laden in America's crosshairs. Like Escobar, bin Laden was widely reviled as the preeminent example of this new conflict, one that would endure despite a successful pursuit.

Afghanistan and Pakistan

CHAPTER SIX

The Terrorist Apotheosis
Osama bin Laden in Afghanistan

The world's most wanted man was cornered, trapped 14,000 feet above sea level in some of the most rugged terrain on Earth.

Since the mid-1990s, the US government had been chasing Osama bin Laden, the Saudi-born millionaire suspected of financing and organizing terrorist attacks against American targets around the world. The hunt initially featured surveillance and cruise missile strikes. But following the devastating attacks of September 11, 2001, the administration of President George W. Bush intensified the search as part of a global war on terror (GWOT). These efforts included sending American forces to Afghanistan, where bin Laden had been enjoying safe haven. In early December 2001, it seemed like the mission was about to pay off.

American intelligence determined that bin Laden and hundreds of hardened fighters in his al-Qaeda network were holed up in Tora Bora, a mountainous area near the Afghanistan–Pakistan border. It was US forces' best estimate of bin Laden's location in three years. Approximately forty members of the First Special Forces Operational Detachment—commonly known as Delta Force—were assigned to the mission. Roughly a dozen Green Berets, six CIA operatives, Air Force special tactics commandos, signals interceptors, and a dozen British commandos assisted Delta Force. The conditions, though, made an attack difficult. Field commander Thomas Greer, who went by the pen name "Dalton Fury," described Tora Bora as "a vertical no-man's land, a hellish place of massive, rocky, jagged, unforgiving, snow-covered ridgelines and high peaks separated by deep ravines and valleys straddled with mines." Al-Qaeda fortified the area with camouflage bunkers, heavy machine guns, mortars, and rocket-propelled grenades.[1]

There were more complications. Eager to avoid the perception of the American military as a foreign invader, US officials instructed Delta Force to work with local Afghans to capture or kill bin Laden. The CIA secured this assistance in exchange for several million dollars given to two warlords. A US Senate report later described one of them as a bully with a fourth-grade education and the other as a drug smuggler. Combined, they commanded a force of nearly 2,000 men whom Greer dismissed as "a fractious bunch of AK-47-toting lawless bandits and tribal thugs." Perhaps not surprisingly, given the circumstances of their employment, they proved unreliable. Although they engaged in firefights during the day, the Afghans surrendered hard-won ground at night. When Delta Force wanted to press the advantage, the warlords preferred to hold back. At one point, the Afghan allies negotiated a ceasefire with al-Qaeda that proved to be merely a stall tactic.[2]

Nevertheless, thanks to unchallenged air power, Americans rained fire upon al-Qaeda. Over nearly two weeks, US forces dropped at least 1,100 precision-guided bombs, 550 so-called dumb bombs, and the 15,000-pound BLU-82 "Daisy Cutter." The CIA's Gary Berntsen, who was on the ground during the battle, described the fusillade's devastation: "trees shredded to knee-high stumps, small caves and tunnels destroyed, huge craters bored into the rocky ground and mud buildings blown to bits." Bin Laden seemed despondent. US forces intercepted one of his radio transmissions in which he told his men, "Our prayers have not been answered. Times are dire. . . . I'm sorry for getting you involved in this battle, if you can no longer resist, you may surrender with my blessing." The hunt for bin Laden appeared to be nearing an end.[3]

But with fewer than seventy-five Americans on-site, there was skepticism about whether they had enough of a presence to finish the job. Berntsen sent a request to US Central Command (CENTCOM) for 800 Army Rangers but received no response. Afterward, General Tommy Franks, head of CENTCOM, said he did not send more troops because he wanted to maintain a light US footprint in Afghanistan, an approach that had been successful up to that point. Moreover, he was not sure that additional forces could arrive in time to help. He was unconvinced that bin Laden was even in Tora Bora. It turned out to be a severe miscalculation.[4]

Despite killing at least 220 al-Qaeda fighters and capturing more than 50, US forces could not produce the biggest prize. After bin Laden's radio went silent, some thought he might have been killed in an airstrike, buried in a collapsed mountain cave. Turns out, shortly after his last transmission, bin Laden, two of his sons, and one of his chief deputies, Ayman al-Zawahiri, slipped out of Tora Bora. Initially, he and his entourage went to Kunar Province in eastern Afghanistan, where he enjoyed the protection of local warlords. Sometime between 2003 and 2005, he relocated to Pakistan, where he was marginalized yet maintained leadership of his diminished network.[5]

Although the Bush administration insisted that the GWOT was bigger than just one man, many Americans still fixated on bin Laden. As was the case with Aguinaldo, Villa, Sandino, Guevara, and Escobar, bin Laden was similarly reviled in the popular American discourse but with a greater intensity given the scale of the 9/11 attacks. "If I could get my hands on bin Laden, I'd skin him alive and pour salt on him," one man told the *New York Times*. Americans, including President Bush, widely referred to bin Laden not just as a terrorist but also as evil incarnate.[6]

The failure in December 2001 to capture or kill the 9/11 mastermind kept in place the key pillar justifying the GWOT. This conflict not only held US forces in Afghanistan for nearly twenty years but saw the American military presence spread further around the world. Over two decades, the United States conducted counterterrorism operations in more than eighty countries, including sustained campaigns in Iraq, Pakistan, Syria, Yemen, and Somalia. Counterterrorism concerns impacted the home front as well. These effects were chiefly evident in such revamped security measures as intrusive surveillance, harsher policing, and more stringent border protection. Fear of additional foreign terrorist attacks bred suspicions of Muslim Americans and immigrants, especially those of Middle Eastern descent. Although al-Qaeda was not able to conduct another attack on the United States anywhere near the scale of 9/11, the cost for such prevention was steep. By one estimate, from 2001 to 2022 the United States spent or committed some $8 trillion in the GWOT while getting involved to varying degrees in conflicts that killed more than 900,000 people.[7]

DURING THE MID- TO LATE twentieth century, the Middle East was a region of prime importance to the United States. This interest stemmed from two principal concerns: having access to oil and warding off communist influence (that might threaten access to oil). As a result, the United States became the most prominent foreign power in the region.

The Soviet Union's December 1979 invasion of Afghanistan challenged this presumption. Although Afghanistan was not a US strategic interest, President Jimmy Carter's administration feared that an unchecked invasion would embolden the Soviets to continue into neighboring Iran and thus provide it a stronger foothold in the oil-rich Persian Gulf region. Such a prospect was unacceptable. In January 1980, the president announced the so-called Carter Doctrine. While he acknowledged that reliance on foreign oil was a national security concern, Carter nevertheless asserted that the United States would use force, if necessary, to defend its interests in the Persian Gulf. To that end, he called for a 5 percent increase in the defense budget, expanded the US military presence in the region, and covertly began arming the loose coalition of Afghan rebels known as the mujahideen to try and turn

Afghanistan into the Soviet Union's version of the Vietnam War. Over the next decade, the United States provided an estimated $2 billion in aid and weapons to Afghan fighters.[8]

The Soviet invasion had angered not only Afghans and Americans but many Muslims around the world as well. Among those outraged was a wealthy young Saudi man looking for a purpose.

Osama bin Laden's revolutionary zeal was not something into which he was born. The man who would one day become America's public enemy number one was the seventeenth child (out of fifty-five) sired by Mohammad bin Laden. Osama's father founded what would become a multibillion-dollar construction company. Over the years, Mohammad took on many wives, including a teenaged Alia Ghanem when he was fifty years old. Although the couple remained married for only two years, the union produced one child, Osama, in March 1957. By most accounts, Osama did not know his father well, perhaps meeting just a handful of times. Consequently, he was much closer to his mother.[9]

Mohammad's death in a September 1967 plane crash, though, deeply affected Osama. According to biographer Peter Bergen, "Osama, always a grave child, became even more subdued, and he increasingly embraced fundamentalist Islam." In addition to praying five times a day, bin Laden fasted twice a week to emulate the Prophet Mohammad, the seventh-century founder of Islam. He did not smoke, drink, or gamble. Most teachers and friends from that time remember him as pious and soft-spoken. Thanks to the family fortune, bin Laden and his many half-siblings had access to some of the best schooling in Saudi Arabia. As a student, though, he was rather unremarkable. Bin Laden eventually enrolled in King Abdulaziz University to study economics and business administration. He then worked for the family business. By this point in his life, bin Laden was wealthy and religious yet somewhat aimless.[10]

The Soviet invasion of Afghanistan provided him with that missing sense of direction. Indignant that a communist and atheistic government invaded a Muslim-majority nation, bin Laden determined to do something about it. At first, those efforts involved collecting donations on behalf of the Afghan mujahideen. But as he met other like-minded supporters from elsewhere in the Arab world, he become more deeply involved. He joined a "services office" to assist Arab volunteers looking to help the Afghans. Through this bureau bin Laden made frequent trips to Pakistan to drop off donations and money to Muslim recruits.

Bin Laden crossed a threshold in 1984 when he entered Afghanistan for the first time and saw the fighting up close. The experience strengthened his determination. Although not a trained fighter, he was useful to the cause because he had money and connections. His group's contributions were not a decisive factor in the broader scope of the war, at least compared to Afghan resolve and US aid, but they did draw the Soviets' attention. In May 1987, bin Laden and a cadre of about sixty men fortuitously survived a three-week assault by Soviet forces at Jaji, near Tora Bora. He escaped with only a wound to his foot. Yet the injury and his willingness to expose himself to great personal risk established his bona fides among other fighters, particularly religiously motivated Arabs like himself. As the war wound down the following year, the survivors at Jaji drew inspiration from the battle and deliberated about what to do next.[11]

IN AUGUST 1988, bin Laden was among nine men who formed an organization dedicated to fighting the enemies of Islam. Inspired by their experience at Jaji, a place they had called "the base," the group adopted the same name in Arabic: "al-Qaeda." They sought to replicate their success against the Soviets by providing financial and logistical support to jihadis—that is, militant Islamists—waging similar battles elsewhere. Their primary opponents, often referred to as the "near enemy," were secular autocrats who ruled countries in the Middle East through repression and corruption. Such leaders often aligned with a second foe, the "far enemy." This adversary was Western influence that supported those autocrats, ensured the survival of Israel, and exposed the Middle East to materialistic and sinful customs that undermined what it meant to be a good Muslim. Defeating these enemies would enable bin Laden and his followers to one day restore an Islamic caliphate, a single Muslim state that would spread from the Middle East to North Africa. A strict following of the Qur'an, Islam's holiest text, and the hadith, the purported statements and actions of the Prophet Mohammad, guided their vision of an ideal society. Their ideology reflected the tenets of Salafism, an ultraorthodox movement within Sunni Islam that aims to restore the purity of the faith by focusing on its origins.[12]

Very quickly, bin Laden emerged as al-Qaeda's emir, or leader. More commonly, he was referred to as the sheikh as a sign of honor. The title reflected the deep respect he commanded among his supporters for living the example he wanted others to follow. Bin Laden rejected modern comforts, often sleeping on the floor, eating little, and dressing modestly. He subjected his growing family to such spartan conditions too. By the time of al-Qaeda's creation, he had taken four wives, which he believed to be the most permissible under Islam, and had nine children. (He later granted a divorce to one wife who had grown tired of the hardships, married another, and eventually had twenty-four offspring in total.)[13]

Bin Laden's attention began turning to the United States in 1990. In August, Saddam Hussein's Iraq invaded its tiny, oil-rich neighbor Kuwait and threatened its larger, even more oil-rich neighbor Saudi Arabia. Hussein was one of the Middle Eastern autocrats that al-Qaeda considered the "near enemy." Bin Laden did not want to see such a man take over his homeland. Calling to mind the jihad, or struggle, that his group had been a part of against the Soviet Union in Afghanistan, bin Laden proposed to the Saudi government that he lead a similar mission against Hussein, claiming to be in command of tens of thousands of fighters. Saudi officials did not buy bin Laden's exaggerated claims. Besides, they had already reached an agreement with another would-be defender: the United States. More than a half-million US troops eventually arrived in the kingdom in the lead-up to the Desert Storm campaign that expelled Iraqi forces from Kuwait in 1991. After the war, the United States maintained a military presence in Saudi Arabia to enforce no-fly zones in Iraq designed to keep Hussein contained.[14]

The arrangement infuriated bin Laden. He was offended at the idea of infidels, nonbelievers in Islam, setting up camp in Islam's holiest land. In an appeal to Saudi monarch King Fahd, bin Laden wrote, "It is unconscionable to let the country become an American colony with American soldiers—their filthy feet roaming everywhere—for no reason other than protecting your throne and protecting oil sources for their own use. These filthy, infidel Crusaders must not be allowed to remain in the Holy Land." Bin Laden's remarks underscored a deep-seated repugnance for the United States. He viewed Americans as physically and morally dirty. Moreover, this letter was one of many instances in which he compared Americans to the Crusaders of a millennium ago who waged bloody and largely failed campaigns to take Muslim-controlled territory. The comparison suggested that bin Laden read US interest in the region as part of a broader historical continuity of Christians attacking Muslims.[15]

In the early 1990s, though, al-Qaeda remained more of a support system than an operational force capable of carrying out its own attacks. Its emphasis was on financing or training other jihadists to fight the "near enemy," like the governments of Egypt or Yemen. During this time, bin Laden grew his network from the relative safety of Sudan, which had become a haven for a variety of disaffected extremists. While some of the militants that al-Qaeda supported targeted Americans, including in the February 1993 World Trade Center bombing and the "Black Hawk Down" incident that October in Somalia, neither attack appears to have been planned by the group.[16]

Nevertheless, US intelligence agencies started to notice bin Laden. An August 1993 CIA report referred to bin Laden as a donor to a new generation of jihadists who stood out for his "religious zeal and financial largesse." But the true depth of bin Laden's ambition, even the name of his fledgling organization, was still unknown. A big break came in June 1996 when Jamal al-Fadl, a Sudanese man and an early al-Qaeda recruit, went to the US embassy in Eritrea looking for protection. He had stolen more than $100,000 from al-Qaeda and feared bin Laden would kill him. Fadl then became a US government witness under FBI protection. Over months of questioning, he shed light on the inner workings of al-Qaeda. By then the CIA was already surveilling bin Laden with Sudanese agents and a dedicated twelve-person unit called Alec Station. Meanwhile, counterterrorism officials in President Bill Clinton's administration were considering options about how to get bin Laden.[17]

Aware of the Americans' intensifying interest in bin Laden, the Sudanese government compelled him to leave. He could not go back to Saudi Arabia, which had stripped him of his citizenship, frozen his assets, and pressured his family to cut ties because of his repeated criticisms of the Saudi government. The only place that was even remotely welcoming was the country where he had started his path toward global jihad—Afghanistan.

THE SOVIET INVASION of Afghanistan had made the country a Cold War cause célèbre for the United States. But following the Soviet withdrawal in 1989, US attention and aid waned. Meanwhile, the Soviet defeat provided Afghanistan little respite. With a weak central government in place, the country descended into civil war. Warlords, backed by private militias, dominated various sectors of the country where they ruled with impunity.

Into this morass stepped a collection of religiously inspired fighters called the Taliban. They considered themselves students of Islam who sought to bring order and justice to Afghanistan according to their fundamentalist interpretation of Islam. In 1994, led by the group's founder, the one-eyed cleric Mullah Mohammad Omar, the Taliban began taking out warlords one by one, first in the southern province of Kandahar before spreading throughout the country. Many Afghans seemed to welcome the demise of the warlords and the institution of some semblance of security. But the cost would prove severe. In the areas they controlled, the Taliban closed schools for girls and rarely permitted women to leave their homes unless covered from head to toe and accompanied by a male family member. They banned virtually all forms of entertainment, including television, music, and sports. To keep people in line, the Taliban staged public executions of those found guilty of capital crimes. By 1996, the group controlled roughly 90 percent of the country, including the capital of Kabul.[18]

As the Taliban were claiming effective control of Afghanistan, bin Laden returned. He did not meet an enthusiastic reception. Although al-Qaeda and the Taliban had similar ideologies, the Taliban were more parochial in their concerns. Some Taliban leaders feared that bin Laden, a foreigner pursued by the Americans and the Saudis, would bring more trouble than he was worth. Nevertheless, Omar allowed bin Laden to remain. Over the next five years, a symbiotic relationship developed. Bin Laden swore allegiance to Omar as "Commander of the Faithful" and provided training, weapons, and fighters to help the Taliban against the holdout Afghan warlords who had formed a loose coalition of resistance called the Northern Alliance. In exchange, the Taliban provided a sanctuary for al-Qaeda that allowed the group to recruit and train fighters, strategize, and import weapons with little to no interference.

Emboldened by this protection, bin Laden in August 1996 made a public pronouncement that signaled his determination to start targeting the "far enemy" at a time when other Middle East jihadi groups were being decimated in their respective fights against the "near enemy." He released the "Declaration of Jihad" in which he blamed the death of Muslims worldwide on "the blatant imperial arrogance of America." He bemoaned the continuing US military presence in his homeland and claimed that the United States and Israel were in a Judeo-Christian alliance against Saudi Arabia and Palestine. As a result, he called for Muslims around the world "to share with them in the jihad against the enemies of God." In an interview with an Australian publication later that year, bin Laden further justified his calls for jihad by pointing to the crippling effects of US-led sanctions on Iraq, its support of Israeli oppression of Palestinians, and its use of the atomic bomb during World War II.[19]

Bin Laden's increasingly strident rhetoric compelled the Clinton administration to consider ways to neutralize him. One idea described by CIA director George Tenet was to support a team of Afghans to kidnap bin Laden and "literally roll him up in a rug, take him to the desert, and hide him away" until US forces could come get him. Another suggestion proposed an assault

Osama bin Laden, shown here in 1998, gave many interviews to journalists in which he denounced the United States and presaged attacks to come. By then, the Clinton administration was considering ways to capture or kill him. Photograph by Rahimullah Yousafzai, courtesy of the Associated Press.

on bin Laden's 100-acre compound at Tarnak Farm near the Kandahar airport. It would have been a complex and dangerous mission, not least because the compound, in the words of Clinton's chief counterterrorism coordinator Richard Clarke, "looked more like Gunga Din's fort than Dorothy's farm in *The Wizard of Oz*." The complex had several dozen houses surrounded by a twelve-foot wall with a machine gun nest in each corner and two tanks parked outside. There also were questions about the capability of the Afghan team and what to do about the women and children at the location. Despite staging three rehearsals, the plan was scrapped before it went to President Clinton for his consideration.[20]

In February 1998, bin Laden upped the ante. He released a so-called fatwa, cosigned by four other men, claiming that it was "an individual duty incumbent upon every Muslim" to kill Americans and their allies, whether they were civilian or military, for crimes committed against Muslims worldwide. In interviews with Western journalists, however, bin Laden insisted he was no more of a terrorist than the US government. "The US today . . . has set a double standard, calling whoever goes against its injustice a terrorist," he told CNN. "It wants to occupy our countries, steal our resources, install collaborators to rule us with man-made laws, and wants us to agree on all these issues. If we refuse to do so, it will say we are terrorists." A year later, bin Laden made similar claims on ABC's *Nightline*. He told reporter John Miller, "We believe that the biggest thieves in the world are Americans and the biggest terrorists on earth are the Americans. The only way for us to fend off these assaults is by using similar means."[21]

Despite the hard edge to bin Laden's anti-American rhetoric, the journalists noted a softness to the man that may have undercut how seriously American audiences considered him a threat. They all cited his weak handshake. "It's not like a great handshake," Miller said. "It's kind of like yeah-I've-got-to-shake-your-hand handshake." CNN cameraman Peter Jouvenal likewise said, "I just remember this rather limp sort of handshake. Not a proper handshake. I remember his hands were cold, like sort of shaking hands with a fish." Such impressions of an effete greeting suggested a deficiency in manliness, at least by Western standards. Moreover, bin Laden was incredibly soft-spoken. Miller noted that "if you didn't lean in to bin Laden, you couldn't hear him. As he spoke in a very kind of almost high pitched, but very soft voice." Peter Bergen, who was part of the CNN team, maintained that bin Laden's oratory style was partly by design because he wanted to present himself as cleric "rather than as the fire-breathing leader of a global terrorist organization." But bin Laden's gentility toward his interviewers belied the severity of his convictions and his designs against the United States. American audiences would continue to underestimate bin Laden at their peril.[22]

ON THE MORNING of August 7, 1998, a truck bomb exploded outside the US embassy in Nairobi, Kenya. Nine minutes later, a second bomb went off at the US embassy in Dar es Salaam, Tanzania. The twin attacks killed 224 people, including twelve Americans, and injured more than 4,000. Investigators later traced the explosives to the same Egyptian man who was al-Qaeda's most expert bomb-maker. This finding showed that al-Qaeda—in the process of merging with Ayman al-Zawahiri's Egyptian Islamic Jihad group—had shifted focus from providing funds, training, and weapons for allied groups to organizing and executing its own attacks.

American politicians and the press framed the attacks as acts of war, presaging the more formal global war on terror that was to come. After visiting both bombing sites, Secretary of State Madeline Albright said, "It's a war— that's what it looks like." The *Washington Post* called the attacks "an act of war" and insisted that the United States had both a right and an obligation to fight back. One writer in the *Wall Street Journal* took it a step further, arguing that "in the war against terrorism—against those who are killing Americans—the US must be willing to kill terrorist chiefs." Such sentiments reflected demand for a high-profile response.²³

Clinton obliged on August 20. US intelligence determined that bin Laden was planning to meet with other al-Qaeda leaders at an Afghan base near Khost. American ships that night lobbed some seventy Tomahawk cruise missiles into Afghanistan as well as approximately a dozen more at a chemical plant in Sudan suspected of having ties to al-Qaeda. The strikes killed an estimated twenty-four al-Qaeda operatives in Afghanistan and one person in Sudan, a night watchman at the pharmaceutical factory later shown to have had no link to the terror group. Bin Laden escaped unscathed.²⁴

Reaction to the cruise missile strikes was mixed. Some lauded the "resolve" of the Clinton administration in fighting back and praised the righteousness of the strikes. One *Washington Post* writer, for example, credited the president for endeavoring to "destroy and deter bandits hiding out in two broken states that lack the will or ability to control them." Such framing bore distinct hallmarks to similar reprisals against Villa and Sandino decades earlier. Yet skepticism abounded about Clinton's motivations. In the summer of 1998, the president was embroiled in a scandal about an affair with a White House intern that would eventually lead to his impeachment Critics openly wondered whether Clinton had ordered the strikes to distract from his personal predicament. They called it a "wag the dog" strategy after the 1997 film by the same name in which a fictional president fabricates a conflict with a small nation to divert attention from an embarrassing domestic scandal. The parallels to reality seemed to sap public enthusiasm for further high-profile bombing raids.²⁵

Frustrated by the strikes' failures and the tepid public support, the Clinton administration considered other ways to get bin Laden. One was by trying to starve al-Qaeda of funds. Clinton signed an executive order placing economic sanctions on bin Laden, al-Qaeda, and, later the Taliban. In the hopes of enticing an informant, the FBI placed bin Laden on its Ten Most Wanted list, which included a bounty that eventually grew to $25 million. Another approach was to continue to find opportunities for a raid. But those options proved fleeting, not least because of the logistics. It was tremendously difficult to pinpoint and target bin Laden. Often, intelligence indicating his location came from a single source, who could not always be trusted. If the information was indeed valid, there would have to be enough advance notice for the information to get to the president for authorization and for the operation to take place, whether it be a raid or a missile strike. Clarke estimated that bin Laden would have had to remain at one location for at least six hours for any operation to have a chance at success. Moreover, planners had to weigh the potential of civilian casualties. Officials in February 1999, for example, decided against striking a hunting camp where bin Laden was believed to be staying because it was also attended by princes of the United Arab Emirates, an important US ally in the Middle East. It would prove to be one of the last, best leads on bin Laden's whereabouts before 9/11.[26]

The US failure to find bin Laden was put into stark relief in October 2000. Two al-Qaeda operatives steered a small boat laden with explosives up to the USS *Cole*, an American destroyer docked at a port in Aden, Yemen. The attackers detonated their cargo, killing themselves and seventeen American sailors, wounding thirty-nine more. The explosion left a forty-foot-wide hole in the ship. Only heroic efforts by the stunned crew saved it from sinking. An investigation took months to determine that it was indeed an al-Qaeda attack. As the White House was transitioning from Clinton to Bush, there would be no formal US retaliation. In the meantime, bin Laden was planning something deadlier.[27]

FOR THE INCOMING Bush administration, terrorism seemed to be less of a national security concern than challenges from states like Russia, China, and Iraq. Richard Clarke, who remained as head of the Counterterrorism Security Group in the White House, tried to reorient the new administration. Just five days after Bush's inauguration, Clarke wrote to National Security Advisor Condoleezza Rice asking *"urgently"* for a principals-level (that is, primarily cabinet-level) review of al-Qaeda, which he described as "not some narrow, little terrorist issue" but a group that posed a "transnational challenge to the US and our interests." Rice later claimed the principals had already been briefed and wanted a more comprehensive counterterrorism strategy before conducting such a meeting. That meeting did not take place until September 4, 2001.[28]

In the meantime, intelligence reports during the summer of 2001 indicated that al-Qaeda was planning . . . something. "The system was blinking red," Tenet later said. But what, precisely, could not be determined. On August 6, Bush received a President's Daily Brief (PDB) with the ominous title, "Bin Laden Determined to Strike in US." The report noted that the FBI was conducting seventy field investigations in the United States related to bin Laden and that they had discovered "patterns of suspicious activity in this country consistent with preparations for hijackings or other types of attacks, including recent surveillance of federal buildings in New York." The warning, though, did not register with Rice or Bush. "None of us even remembered the PDB until May 2002, when CBS Evening News referred to its contents," Rice wrote in her memoir. In a 2004 press conference, Bush said the PDB did not tell him anything he did not already know: "What I wanted to know was, is there anything specifically going to take place in America that we needed to react to? . . . But that PDB said nothing about an attack on America. It talked about intentions, about somebody who hated America—well, we knew that."[29]

The missed warning signs proved devastating. On the morning of September 11, 2001, nineteen al-Qaeda operatives hijacked four passenger aircraft and used those planes as guided missiles against the twin towers of the World Trade Center in New York and the Pentagon in Arlington, Virginia. The fourth flight, likely aiming for the Capitol Building or White House, crashed in Pennsylvania after a group of courageous passengers—aware of the other three attacks—tried to stop the hijackers. The carefully orchestrated mission killed 2,977 people and caused tens of billions of dollars in damage, to say nothing of the emotional trauma to the psyche of a nation that had not been struck by a foreign foe like that since World War II.

Almost immediately, US counterterrorism officials like Clarke suspected al-Qaeda. In statements and interviews he gave in the weeks after 9/11, though, bin Laden was coy about his group's responsibility. Yet he strenuously justified the attacks, which cost just $500,000 to execute. He praised the hijackers for retaliating "on behalf of their poor, oppressed sons, their brothers and sisters in Palestine and in many of the other lands of Islam." He asserted that the victims who died at the World Trade Center "were part of a financial power. It wasn't a children's school!" And he told the al Jazeera network that "if killing those that kill our sons is terrorism, then let history witness that we are terrorists."[30]

Despite meticulous planning, bin Laden made some severe miscalculations. First, even he was surprised by the lethality of the attacks, not expecting both World Trade Center towers to collapse. The scale of the devastation perhaps contributed to the second misjudgment—the reactions. He anticipated that the attacks would lead to an outcry among the American public about US policy toward the Middle East and put pressure on the US government to withdraw its military forces from the region. Any retaliation would likely be in the form of missile strikes, as in 1998, or targeted commando raids. In that event, bin Laden expected that other jihadists and the broader Muslim world would come to al-Qaeda's aid. Yet such support was virtually nonexistent. Many jihadis had, in fact, long opposed bin Laden's shift to a "far enemy" strategy for fear of provoking an overwhelming US military response that would put other Islamist movements at risk.[31]

That is precisely what happened.

INDEED, THE UNITED STATES prepared for war. The conception was rife within the popular discourse. *Washington Post* columnist Charles Krauthammer maintained that the scale of the 9/11 attacks went beyond terrorism. "This is not a crime. This is war," he wrote. "You bring criminals to justice; you rain destruction on combatants." *New York Times* columnist Thomas L. Friedman called it the beginning of a third world war.[32]

Bush did not shy from employing such rhetoric either. Just days after the attacks and bolstered by a congressional authorization for the use of military force (AUMF) to pursue the 9/11 planners, Bush announced a "war on terror" against al-Qaeda and "every terrorist group of global reach," including nations that harbored such groups. He frequently referred to himself afterward as a "wartime president." Years later, he explained his thinking about why America's counterterror approach became more military-centric than criminal justice–focused. "On 9/11, it was obvious the law enforcement approach to terrorism had failed," Bush wrote. "Suicidal men willing to fly passenger planes into buildings were not common criminals. They could not be deterred by the threat of prosecution. They had declared war on America. To protect the country, we had to wage war against the terrorists."[33]

In the lead-up to war, the Bush administration pursued two tracks. The first was to pressure the Taliban to deliver bin Laden to the United States. Publicly, Mullah Omar was obstinate, claiming it was against custom to surrender a guest, much less one with whom he was ideologically sympathetic. Privately, he was more conflicted. The 9/11 attacks had been planned without the Taliban's knowledge, bringing unwanted attention from the United States just as the Taliban were on the verge of defeating the Northern Alliance. Many Taliban leaders lobbied Omar to surrender bin Laden. Omar even authorized his top deputy to meet with the CIA station chief in Pakistan to discuss the matter. Omar offered to send bin Laden to a neutral third-party country, but the Bush administration refused to negotiate. "Osama is like a chicken bone stuck in my throat," Omar said. "I can neither spit him out nor swallow him."[34]

As discussions continued, the Bush administration initiated a second track. A seven-member CIA team code-named JAWBREAKER arrived in Afghanistan on September 26, led by fifty-nine-year-old Gary Schroen. Its mission was to establish a cooperation with the Northern Alliance against al-Qaeda and the Taliban. Armed with $3 million in cash, the team secured the desired partnership. It paved the way for the United States on October 7 to initiate Operation Enduring Freedom, a sustained military campaign that primarily featured air strikes and Special Operations missions against al-Qaeda and Taliban targets.

The JAWBREAKER mission did not end there, however. According to Schroen, Cofer Black, the CIA's head of counterterrorism, added one more aim: "I don't want bin Laden and his thugs captured. I want them dead. Alive and in prison here in the United States, they'll become a symbol, a rallying point for other terrorists. . . . They must be killed. I want to see photos of their heads on pikes. I want bin Laden's head shipped back in a box filled with dry ice. I want to be able to show bin Laden's head to the president." The directive seemed to shake the longtime operative. "It was the first time in my thirty-year CIA career," Schroen wrote, "that I had ever heard an order to kill someone rather than to effect their capture and rendition to justice."[35]

Black's sentiment reflected a broader conception among the American public that there could be no reasoning or negotiating with bin Laden because he was evil incarnate. On this score, Bush was the rhetorician in chief. In press conferences and speeches after 9/11, the president reflexively referred to bin Laden as "evil." He most elaborated on the idea during a September 26 exchange with reporters. When asked if he considered bin Laden a religious or political leader, Bush said, "I consider bin Laden an evil man. . . . This is a man who hates. This is a man who's declared war on innocent people. This is a man who doesn't mind destroying women and children. This is a man who hates freedom. This is an evil man. . . . He has got evil goals. And it's hard to think in conventional terms about a man so dominated by evil that he's willing to do what he thinks he's going to get away with. But he's not going to get away with it."[36]

Beyond the language of evil, Bush also was central in framing bin Laden as primitive or barbaric. To wit, he frequently claimed that bin Laden was living in a cave. "We'll smoke him out of his cave, and we'll get him eventually," Bush said during a nationally televised press conference. The rhetoric suggested that bin Laden was not only uncivilized and animalistic but also a coward. "This man wants to destroy any semblance of civilization for his own power and his own good," Bush told reporters. "He's so evil that he's willing to send young men to commit suicide while he hides in caves." *Washington Post* columnist David Ignatius aptly argued that these popular assertions distorted bin Laden into "a brutal but primitive fanatic—a sort of 21st century throwback to the hashish-crazed Muslim sect of 'assassins' in ancient times."

The threat was much more nuanced given the wealth and privilege in which he was raised.³⁷

Bush's off-the-cuff remarks about bin Laden reflected his emotional state. "My blood was boiling," he recalled when hearing about the 9/11 attacks. "We were going to find out who did this, and kick their ass." At one point, he told reporters that he wanted bin Laden "dead or alive," which compelled a variety of news outlets to print "Wanted" posters in the style of the mythic Old West. Bush later admitted his quip may have been too blunt; his wife, Laura, reportedly told him to "tone it down, darling." Another line that spurred backlash—though tempered in the post-9/11 haze of grief, fear, and anger—was Bush's reference to the GWOT as a "crusade." It played right into bin Laden's consistent framing of his own struggle against the West. Historian Bernard Lewis excused Bush's rhetorical faux pas but recognized that the term "still touches a raw nerve in the Middle East, where the Crusades are seen and presented as early medieval precursors of European imperialism—aggressive, expansionist and predatory." Press Secretary Ari Fleischer gently walked back the term saying that "the President would regret if anything like that was conveyed," but he was using it "in the traditional English sense of the word. It's a broad cause."³⁸

The heated rhetoric no doubt fed the popular desire for vengeance. "Bury Osama bin Laden with pigskin," one retired truck driver from Wyoming told the *New York Times*. Another man said, "Find them and kill them. No court. No trial. Electrocute them." Even a pastor in Indiana could not resist the temptation to strike back. "I don't like the word, revenge," he said. "The word, retaliate means much the same thing. But I believe there needs to be some retaliation."³⁹

Desires for vengeance also were expressed through mockery, with a dash of capitalism. Anti–bin Laden paraphernalia became a cottage industry. A variety of T-shirts, coffee mugs, posters, golf balls, and dartboards were sold with bin Laden's image and likeness—even toilet paper going for as much as twelve dollars a roll. "I wanted to be the first to put his face where it belongs," one entrepreneur said. Likewise, the popular animated television show *South Park* produced a biting satire of al-Qaeda's leader (and the US war in Afghanistan) in an episode titled "Osama bin Laden Has Farty Pants." The show portrays bin Laden as a vain, dimwitted leader who talks gibberish and is outsmarted by the main characters, four ten-year-old boys, in a slapstick fashion similar to the Looney Tunes cartoons of the 1940s. The episode was nominated for an Emmy Award in 2002.⁴⁰

LEERY OF APPEARING as invaders like the Soviet Union two decades earlier, the US military purposely entered Afghanistan with a light footprint. The US strategy of arming the Northern Alliance and supporting them with air strikes and Special Forces operations succeeded in toppling the Taliban from power before the end of 2001. It paved the way for the creation of a new, democratic Afghan government, though one that struggled with rampant corruption and was propped up by hundreds of billions of dollars in international aid and US military support over the next twenty years.

But bin Laden slipped away. After his escape from Tora Bora, the trail went cold. In March 2002, Bush tried to downplay the United States' inability to find the world's most wanted man. "We haven't heard from him in a long time," Bush told reporters. "And the idea of focusing on one person is—really indicates to me people don't understand the scope of the mission. Terror is bigger than one person. And he's just—he's a person who's now been marginalized.... I truly am not that concerned about him." Bush's apparent indifference to finding the 9/11 mastermind frustrated writers like Maureen Dowd of the *New York Times*. "When President Bush realized he couldn't catch Osama quickly, he was downgraded faster than a telecom stock," she wrote. "Osama went from Wanted Dead or Alive to Forgotten but Not Gone."[41]

By then, the Bush administration was fixating on another villain—Iraqi leader Saddam Hussein. Convinced that Hussein had weapons of mass destruction that he would either use against the United States or share with a terrorist like bin Laden, the Bush team was ramping up for a war that began in March 2003. The conflict shifted attention, resources, and manpower away from the continuing struggle in Afghanistan.

In the meantime, bin Laden remained in hiding. For a time, he stayed in northeastern Afghanistan's Kunar Province, a mountainous region with dense trees and evergreen shrubs that made air detection difficult. Locals generally were hostile to outsiders, and they had little contact with the new Afghan government. It was an ideal place to lay low. Sometime between 2003 and 2005, though, bin Laden slipped into Pakistan. Its government had long been an inconsistent ally in the GWOT, occasionally helping the United States capture al-Qaeda suspects but more often turning a blind eye to the presence of extremists because of sympathy among some Pakistani officials. Once there, bin Laden balanced self-preservation with a desire to remain relevant. Afraid of American electronic surveillance, he rarely met lieutenants in person and communicated only via courier. Such an arrangement challenged his ability to maintain command and control over what was left of al-Qaeda. Moreover, affiliates like al-Qaeda in Iraq (AQI) dominated the headlines with their campaign of violence and bloodshed there, overshadowing bin Laden's organization and leadership. Occasionally, bin Laden released an audio or video statement in which he echoed familiar refrains against the United States. But they did not attract nearly the same attention as they had in the weeks and months after 9/11.[42]

As the fifth anniversary of 9/11 approached and bin Laden remained at large, there was more public reflection about the GWOT. By then, the United States was bogged down in two wars with an expanded military presence throughout the Middle East (and later into Africa). The USA PATRIOT Act, passed overwhelmingly by Congress weeks after 9/11, allowed more intrusive government surveillance. Moreover, the Bush administration supported the use of "enhanced interrogation techniques" against detainees deemed "unlawful enemy combatants." Such techniques, though, were essentially forms of torture that included waterboarding, beatings, stress positions, nakedness, and sexual humiliation. Hundreds of prisoners were held indefinitely without charges at Guantánamo Bay Naval Base in Cuba. A public outcry against such measures emerged following the release of photos of prisoner abuse at Abu Ghraib prison in Iraq. Although the Bush administration would walk back many of these practices, the damage was done to the United States' posture as a champion of human rights. The *New York Times* pinned much of the GWOT's underside on Bush, who enjoyed expanded presidential powers as a wartime commander in chief: "The president's constant efforts to assert his power to act without consent or consultation has warped the war on terror. The unity and sense of national purpose that followed 9/11 is gone, replaced by suspicion and divisiveness that never needed to emerge." Fruitless searches, endless wars, and government overreach in the name of fighting terror were exhausting America.[43]

SHORTLY AFTER TAKING OFFICE in 2009, President Barack Obama met with some of his top national security advisers and told them to prioritize finding bin Laden. At the time, there were no hard leads, only presumptions that al-Qaeda's leader was living in an urban area because other top lieutenants had been captured in cities.[44]

A year later, a lead emerged. The CIA began tracking a man in Pakistan identified as Abu Ahmed al-Kuwaiti, who was thought to be a bin Laden courier. They traced him to an unusual compound in Abbottabad, a city of some 200,000 people. The property was in a middle-class neighborhood on a small dirt road about half a mile from the main highway. The compound had barbed wire, security lighting, and walls between twelve and eighteen feet high. Inside the walls were a main house of three stories, a smaller guesthouse, and a courtyard with goats and chickens. But the detail that most intrigued analysts was drone footage of "the pacer." He appeared to be a tall man who wandered around the property for hours during the day but never left the compound or helped anyone working in the courtyard.[45]

Intelligence analysts at the time didn't know it, but the person was Osama bin Laden.

Kuwaiti had purchased the land and oversaw the compound's construction in 2004. Bin Laden likely moved in around August 2005 and was joined by three of his four wives as well as twelve children and grandchildren. Including the families of Kuwaiti and his brother, a total of twenty-seven people lived on the grounds. The inside of the main house was spartan in keeping with bin Laden's frugality. The beds were made from boards hammered together. The house used minimal electricity and had no heating or air-conditioning. There was no phone line or internet service. Residents burned their trash and rarely left the premises.[46]

Although marginalized in his hideaway, bin Laden still schemed about ways to attack the United States and to keep al-Qaeda relevant. He considered plans to assassinate Obama and to stage simultaneous attacks on oil tankers around the world to spur a global economic crisis. With the help of two adult daughters, he was drafting a statement in response to the Arab Spring, a series of popular protests that began in 2011 against the same kinds of repressive governments that bin Laden had long opposed. To that end, he considered rebranding al-Qaeda to emphasize its "friendliness" through a commitment to no further attacks against Muslims. He planned on using the upcoming tenth anniversary of 9/11 as the opportune moment for such an announcement.[47]

He never got the chance.

ON THE EVENING of May 1, 2011, two Black Hawk helicopters filled with twenty-three Navy SEALs, an interpreter, and a dog left a base from Jalalabad, Afghanistan, on a surreptitious, tree-top-skimming, ninety-minute flight into Pakistan. Their mission was to capture or kill Osama bin Laden at his suspected compound in Abbottabad. But there was no clear consensus from intelligence analysts or a tight-knit circle of advisers in the Obama administration that bin Laden was even there. Obama recognized it as a fifty-fifty call. He rejected the idea of an air strike out of concern for civilian casualties, the potential for harming Pakistani relations, and the difficulty of

The Terrorist Apotheosis 145

The compound in Abbottabad, Pakistan, where SEAL Team 6 found and killed Osama bin Laden in May 2011. The Pakistani government demolished the site a year later. Photograph by Anjum Naveed, courtesy of the Associated Press.

proving bin Laden's presence. Instead, he opted for a riskier, but more surgical, Special Operations mission—dubbed Operation Neptune's Spear—that was planned by Admiral William McRaven, who had commanded or carried out more than 1,000 missions in his career. In preparation, SEAL Team Six staged weeks of rehearsals near Fort Bragg in North Carolina, where a full-scale mockup of the compound had been constructed.[48]

The operation hit a snag upon arrival. One of the helicopters lost lift over the compound and did a hard landing into the animal pen. By all accounts, only the extraordinary skill of the pilot averted disaster though the helicopter was no longer operable. Almost immediately, the team had to improvise. The other helicopter was supposed to drop off some SEALs on the roof of the main house and work their way down, but that approach was aborted. Instead, all team members were dropped off on the ground either in the courtyard or outside the north gate.

The SEALs methodically worked their way into the compound. As they tried to blast open the door of the guesthouse, Kuwaiti began shooting at them from behind the door. The SEALs returned fire. When they entered the room, they found Kuwaiti dead with his wife holding a baby and shielding three other children. On the first floor of the main house, the SEALs exchanged fire with Kuwaiti's brother, Abrar, killing him and his wife. As they moved up to the second floor, the SEALs spotted bin Laden's twenty-two-year-old son, Khalid. One of the SEALs calmly whispered to him by name. As soon as Khalid poked his head into the stairway, he was shot in the face and killed instantly.[49]

There was one floor to go.

At the top of the stairwell, the SEALs saw a tall man behind a curtain. The point man fired. As he got to the top of the stairs, the point man encountered two women screaming. Fearing they might be wearing suicide vests, he jumped on them to shield his comrades from any potential blast. What happened next is a matter of dispute between two competing accounts later written by SEALs at the scene.[50]

Robert O'Neill, who had more than 400 previous missions to his credit, described what he saw as he entered the bedroom behind the point man. "Osama bin Laden stood near the entrance at the foot of the bed, taller and thinner than I'd expected, his beard shorter and hair whiter. . . . He had a woman in front of him, his hands on her shoulders. In less than a second, I aimed above the woman's right shoulder and pulled the trigger twice. Bin Laden's head split open, and he dropped. I put another bullet in his head. Insurance."[51]

Another account, written by Matt Bissonnette under the pen name "Mark Owen," insisted that the point man's initial shots, not O'Neill's, were the first to hit bin Laden in the head. "Blood and brains spilled out of the side of his skull. In his death throes, he was still twitching and convulsing. Another assaulter and I trained our lasers on his chest and fired several rounds. The bullets tore into him, slamming his body into the floor until he was motionless."[52]

In the moment, the SEALs were not totally sure it was bin Laden. They asked one of his daughters to confirm his identity, then they proceeded to take photos, blood, and saliva samples. Because of the blunt trauma from the shooting, it was hard to decipher facial recognition. "Bin Laden's head was a mess, split wide above his eyebrow like a melon dropped from a tile floor," O'Neill wrote. He pressed the head back together to try to restore some recognizable features. At that point, the raid commander radioed McRaven, who relayed the message back to a nervous White House that had been following along via satellite. "Geronimo, EKIA," he said, which meant "bin Laden, enemy killed in action."[53]

Over the next half hour, the SEALs loaded up bin Laden's body and collected a treasure trove of intelligence in the form of hard drives, videos, and notebooks. In all, the mission lasted forty-eight minutes. The SEALs blew up the downed helicopter and escaped thanks to a backup helicopter that had been on standby. Ninety minutes later, the team was back in Afghanistan. After DNA analysis confirmed bin Laden's identity the next morning, the body was taken to the USS *Carl Vinson* and dumped into the Arabian Sea.

After spending nearly twenty years instigating a war with the United States, bin Laden did not put up much of a fight when the Americans came to his doorstep. His youngest wife, Amal, later told Pakistani authorities that the sounds of the helicopters had woken them up. "American helicopters have arrived," bin Laden said to his family. "All of you must leave this room at once." It would still take nearly fifteen minutes for the SEALs to arrive at his bedroom, time to prepare some kind of defense (futile though it may have been) with the AK-47 and pistol found nearby that he apparently never touched. "He was just kind of frozen, the classic deer in the headlights," O'Neill wrote. Perhaps he was resigned to his fate, determined to become a martyr. Bissonnette considered a simpler reason — cowardice. "He had no intention of fighting. He asked his followers for decades to wear suicide vests or fly planes into buildings but didn't even pick up his weapon. In all my deployments, we routinely saw this phenomenon. The higher up the food chain the targeted individual was, the bigger a pussy he was."[54]

As news filtered out about bin Laden's demise, Americans across the country took to the streets in celebration. Many of the revelers were college students who rejoiced as if their team had won a national championship. The *Hartford Courant* recognized that for young people whose earliest memories were shaped by 9/11, bin Laden's death was essentially the "V-E Day of their generation." *Washington Post* columnist Alexandra Petri, herself a recent college graduate, argued that people in her age range viewed bin Laden as a real-life version of a fictional villain. "Osama bin Laden is our Voldemort," she wrote. "He's our Emperor Palpatine." The spontaneous ebullient reactions produced some mild hand-wringing, however, because they seemed to emphasize vengeance over justice. While conceding the point, one psychology professor from the University of Virginia argued that the celebrations ultimately were "good and healthy" because they produced a "communal joy."[55]

For his part, Obama consistently framed the bin Laden killing as justice. On the night he announced the raid, Obama said, "Justice has been done." In a lengthy interview days later with the CBS News program *60 Minutes*, he reiterated that idea. "As nervous as I was about this whole process, the one thing I didn't lose sleep over was the possibility of taking bin Laden out," he said. "Justice was done. And I think that anyone who would question that the perpetrator of mass murder on American soil didn't deserve what he got needs to have their head examined." Other widely read columnists, though, had no qualms calling the raid revenge. Dowd of the *New York Times* argued that "the really insane assumption behind some of the second-guessing is that killing Osama somehow makes us like Osama, as if all killing is the same. Only fools or knaves would argue that we could fight Al Qaeda's violence non-violently.... Morally and operationally, this was counterterrorism at its finest. We have nothing to apologize for." Krauthammer of the *Washington Post* was more blunt. He maintained that capturing bin Laden for trial, as many other previous cases of terrorism had been handled, "would have been insane, gratuitously granting him a second life of immense publicity on a worldwide stage from which to propagandize. We came to kill. That is what you do in a war."[56]

MUCH LIKE THE 9/11 ATTACKS, Osama bin Laden's death brought about some semblance of national unity. But it proved fleeting. Within days, Republicans challenged the Obama administration's initial version of events, including the idea that bin Laden took aim at the SEALs and had been using women as human shields. Rather than chalk it up to the fog of war, political enemies seized on the inaccuracies to accuse the Obama administration of exaggerating the raid's inherent dangers. The questioning reflected the increasingly bitter partisanship taking hold in the country. "The high of the raid, the ability to just feel good about something, dissipated quickly," Deputy National Security Advisor Ben Rhodes reflected. "If the country's politics couldn't even allow us to enjoy *this*, then literally nothing would bring the country together." The questioning and skepticism showed that one of the utilities of the global war on terror—rallying together against a common enemy—was losing effectiveness.[57]

While the GWOT warded off another big attack on the US homeland and decimated al-Qaeda, the cost of the conflict was enormous. In the name of fighting terrorism, the United States committed to two protracted wars. The Afghan war—spurred by the US aim to bring bin Laden to justice—ended in August 2021 with the Taliban back in power. The United States spent or committed an estimated $2.3 trillion and lost the lives of more than 2,300 servicemen and -women as well as nearly 4,000 civilian contractors. The toll for Afghans was far worse—at least 168,000 people killed in the fighting, with millions more displaced. Meanwhile, the United States also engaged in a war in Iraq from 2003 to 2011. The forces unleashed from that conflict—namely, ISIS, which tried to carry out bin Laden's vision to such a sadistic level that even he disavowed them—compelled Obama in 2014 to send US troops back to Iraq where they remain through a fourth presidential administration. Over that time, the United States has spent or committed an estimated $2.9 trillion and lost the lives of 4,600 servicemen and -women as well as nearly 3,700 civilian contractors. The death toll among Iraqis was at least 300,000.[58]

Perhaps if bin Laden had been caught in Tora Bora, all that blood and treasure could have been saved. But his evasion of US forces justified the expansion of a global war on terror that was underwritten by steadily increasing defense budgets and a military commitment in at least eighty countries. These measures also conveniently helped to ensure American influence in a post–Cold War world. Even years after bin Laden's death, the GWOT continued, if reduced to a simmer on the back burner of US national security concerns. Vice President Dick Cheney predicted as much in October 2001 when he said about the GWOT, "It is different than the [1991] Gulf War was, in the sense that it may never end. At least, not in our lifetime."[59]

Conclusion

The death of Osama bin Laden and the degradation of al-Qaeda provided little respite in the global war on terror (GWOT). In 2014, another even more deadly enemy emerged that compelled US forces to chase the next threatening bandit.

One of the tragic ironies of the GWOT is that the longer the conflict continued, the more extremism multiplied. By one estimate, there were nearly four times as many jihadists in 2018 as there were on 9/11. They were not all necessarily cultivated by US intervention; many were instigated by other factors such as the Israeli-Palestinian conflict, Russian and Iranian regional influence, and the persistence of corrupt autocracies. But the continuing US military presence nevertheless provided added motivation for many such fighters.[1]

The Islamic State of Iraq and al-Sham (ISIS) was the most prominent example. Founded by Abu Musab al-Zarqawi in the late 1990s as Tawhid wal Jihad, it was a scuffling organization until the 2003 US invasion of Iraq provided it with a renewed sense of purpose. A year later, the group became al-Qaeda in Iraq (AQI), an affiliate of bin Laden's organization at a time when al-Qaeda was desperate to remain relevant. Under Zarqawi's leadership, AQI was the deadliest agent of chaos among all the insurgent groups in war-torn Iraq. It took aim not only at the United States and its allies but also at Shia Muslims in an attempt to foment an all-out Iraqi civil war. US warplanes killed Zarqawi in 2006. Soon thereafter, many Sunni Muslims, ostensibly the people on whose behalf AQI was fighting, tired of the violence and turned on AQI. By the time US forces left Iraq in 2011, AQI, which by then had rebranded itself the Islamic State of Iraq, was essentially finished.

The remnants of the group, though, gained new life thanks to the civil war developing in neighboring Syria. The Syrian government's brutal attempts to stomp out its opposition provided fertile ground for new recruits. At the same time, ISIS took advantage of the lingering sectarian tensions in Iraq as well as the broader ineffectiveness and unpopularity of the Iraqi government. With political turmoil in both countries, ISIS grew in numbers and began doing something few other terror groups had done before: capture and govern territory. Their haul included Mosul, Iraq's second-largest city of more than 1 million residents. Emboldened by its victories and territorial holdings, ISIS in June 2014 brashly proclaimed a caliphate. Caliphates had existed in various forms for centuries, but none had been internationally recognized since the Ottoman Empire dissolved after World War I. Reviving such an entity had been one of bin Laden's long-term aims, but one he did not expect to see in his lifetime. The leaders of ISIS had less patience.

ISIS ran its so-called caliphate as if it were a country. It established a court system, made its own weapons, and operated bureaucracies that produced driver's licenses and birth certificates. Most of these efforts were funded by the taxes they collected from residents, which also required its own bureaucracy. At the same time, ISIS committed appalling acts of violence—some of which they uploaded to social media—to keep people in line and to attract more followers from abroad. The group publicly executed criminals and prisoners via beheadings, stonings, and crucifixions. There were tales of ISIS throwing people off buildings, blowing them up in cars, running them over with a tank, drowning them, and, in the case of a captured Jordanian pilot, burning him alive in a cage. They also systematically raped many captured women and frequently used child soldiers to carry out executions. Such brutality compelled al-Qaeda leader Ayman al-Zawahiri, bin Laden's successor, to renounce any ties or connections to ISIS.[2]

The leader who sanctioned this ruthless violence and briefly became America's new public enemy number one was Ibrahim Awwad Ibrahim al-Badri—more widely known by his *nom de guerre*, Abu Bakr al-Baghdadi. Born July 1971 in Samarra, Iraq, Baghdadi came from a middle-class family. From a young age, he was considered stern and deeply devout; his school-age nickname was "The Believer." Poor eyesight kept him out of the Iraqi military, so he pursued graduate studies, presumably with an academic career in mind. He eventually earned a master's degree and a doctorate in Koranic Studies.[3]

Baghdadi's most formative experience in his path to jihadism came in 2004 when he was arrested by US forces while visiting a friend that American officials wanted for questioning. Baghdadi was held for nearly a year without charges. His detention seemed to further radicalize him. He was held at Camp Bucca in southern Iraq, a place that some would later call a "jihadi university" for enabling extremists, insurgents, and other like-minded individuals to network. Baghdadi similarly was able to forge key alliances and relationships that paved the way for him to join AQI after his release. In 2010, when ISIS was at its nadir, he was chosen as the group's emir.[4]

Four years later, though, ISIS was at its apex. Its followers were running roughshod through Syria and Iraq, holding territory roughly the size of Virginia in which nearly 12 million people lived. In July 2014, the camera-shy Baghdadi took a victory lap at the Grand Mosque in Mosul in his first public appearance. Purposely evoking the Prophet Mohammad in his manner of speech and black-clad robes, he declared himself Caliph Ibrahim and exhorted Muslims around the world to support the caliphate. Thousands of jihadists answered the call, augmenting a force that at its peak the CIA estimated to be more than 30,000 fighters. With the US-trained and equipped Iraqi army on its heels, Iraq's capital of Baghdad appeared vulnerable. Meanwhile, ISIS fighters were setting their sights on wiping out the Yazidis, a religious minority group in Iraq that had had thousands of its women captured and sold into sexual slavery.[5]

In August, less than three years after leaving the country, the US military returned to Iraq to support Iraqi forces and Kurdish militias in their resistance to ISIS. The key component of Operation Inherent Resolve, a mission that ultimately included a coalition of more than seventy-five nations, was airstrikes against ISIS targets. In light of the well-documented atrocities committed by ISIS, there was little backlash against the move. Supporters couched the fight against this new jihadist threat in terms similar to the one against al-Qaeda. "We don't understand real evil, organized evil, very well," former US Ambassador to Iraq Ryan Crocker said. "This is evil incarnate." Likewise, the *New York Times* editorialized that ISIS was unique among other jihadist groups. It wrote that "no Islamist group before . . . has so nakedly adopted a cult of sadism" and compared the violence of ISIS to that of the genocides of Rwanda, Cambodia, and the Holocaust. "Even to call what this group does 'crimes against humanity' is to put a legalistic spin on raw evil," it concluded.[6]

Despite the US bounty on him growing to $25 million—the same as bin Laden—Baghdadi did not carry quite the same cachet among the American public as the late al-Qaeda emir. There were fewer editorials, polemics, or satires about the ISIS leader. A few factors help explain this disparity. First, unlike al-Qaeda, ISIS was not able to stage a coordinated attack on US soil. The group took credit for mass shootings in San Bernardino, California, and Orlando, Florida, by gunmen who claimed to be inspired by ISIS. But those connections were specious at best. Second, whereas bin Laden gave a variety of interviews and statements to remain in the public eye, Baghdadi was rarely seen or heard. Aside from his 2014 appearance in Mosul, Baghdadi released only a few audio messages. Third, the United States had only recently

Conclusion 153

celebrated dispatching bin Laden, widely considered to be the most notorious terrorist of the modern era. Gearing up for the next one so soon may have been too emotionally exhausting.[7]

Yet Baghdadi was responsible for more death and devastation than bin Laden. Beyond the sadist violence the group committed, ISIS from 2013 to 2018 killed more than 28,000 people in terrorist attacks or in territory it controlled, far more than al-Qaeda. This estimate does not include the acts of groups in countries such as Afghanistan, Egypt, Nigeria, and Libya that pledged allegiance to ISIS and committed similar attacks in its name. Between its affiliates and "lone wolf" fanatics who claimed loyalty to the organization, ISIS inspired acts of terror in more than three dozen countries. Moreover, Baghdadi was reported to have held sex slaves of his own, including American humanitarian aid worker Kayla Mueller, who was captured in Syria in August 2013. Over eighteen months, she was allegedly beaten and raped repeatedly by Baghdadi himself before she either died in an airstrike or was executed by ISIS.[8]

With this record in mind, President Donald J. Trump in 2019 called finding Baghdadi "the top national security priority of my administration." But much like past chases for foreign bandits, US intelligence leads were frustratingly few despite battlefield successes. In the previous five years, the US-led coalition retook all ISIS-held territory, killed or captured tens of thousands of fighters, and compelled most of the rest to go underground.[9]

Literally, in Baghdadi's case.

Through the interrogation of one of Baghdadi's wives and a courier, US and Kurdish intelligence surmised in the summer of 2019 that Baghdadi was hiding at a compound in northwest Syria near the border with Turkey (now officially Türkiye). They traced him to a house in Idlib Province that had a series of tunnels supported by lights and a ventilation system. One tunnel was reportedly eight yards long by five yards wide and featured a library of religious books. Kurdish spies confirmed his presence through a stolen pair of underwear and a blood sample.[10]

In a scene reminiscent of the bin Laden raid, eight helicopters carrying a few dozen members of Delta Force took off from Erbil, Iraq, on the night of October 26, 2019, en route to Baghdadi's suspected location. They flew low, occasionally taking fire during a seventy-minute flight over hostile territory. Upon arrival, some of the compound's residents, including eleven children, surrendered and were removed. The team then blasted through a wall of the compound to avoid the main door they suspected was booby-trapped and killed five people who refused to surrender, including four women. With a US military dog in pursuit, Baghdadi went into one of the tunnels and detonated a suicide vest that killed himself and two children. After clearing the debris, Delta Force took DNA samples to confirm Baghdadi's identity and later buried what was left of him at sea. US forces, who suffered only minor injuries to two personnel and the dog, then leveled the compound with drones and warplanes to prevent it from becoming a shrine.[11]

Back in Washington, Trump's announcement of the raid tapped into many of the same tropes as past threats of Baghdadi's ilk. First, there was the dehumanizing, animalistic depiction. Trump boasted that Baghdadi "died like a dog." The line suggested that Baghdadi met an undignified death, one devoid of any honor or decency. Trump underscored that point later in the press conference when he added that Baghdadi "was an animal, and he was a gutless animal." That framing merged the dehumanization with a second trope: the gendered suggestion that Baghdadi was unmanly because he lacked bravery. Trump underscored the point saying that Baghdadi "died after running into a dead-end tunnel, whimpering and crying and screaming." Trump repeated the words "whimpering," "crying," and "screaming" at least four times each in his remarks, even though there was no sound to the live feed he watched of the raid, nor could any officials confirm Trump's assertion. Nevertheless, the idea was made clear that despite Baghdadi's record of grievous violence, Trump saw him as weak and cowardly.[12]

Baghdadi and the caliphate may have been dead, yet US forces remained in Iraq and Syria ostensibly to guard against an ISIS revival. Their continued deployment went against Trump's initial instincts. Just three weeks before the Baghdadi raid, Trump had announced that he was pulling all 2,000 US troops out of Syria, part of his pledge to end US involvement in what he called "stupid endless wars." But a host of US military and civilian officials pushed back on the idea and Trump relented, agreeing to maintain a residual force in Syria.[13]

Rather than uttering platitudes about a mission of principle, responsibility, or security, Trump's rationale was more nakedly transactional. During the same press conference in which he announced Baghdadi's death, Trump said that he would keep enough US soldiers in Syria "to secure the oil." He acknowledged that access to Syrian oil "can help us, because we should be able to take some also. And what I intend to do, perhaps, is make a deal with an ExxonMobil or one of our great companies to go in there and do it properly." Dispelling any doubt his comments about appropriating another country's resources were a mistake, Trump reiterated the idea during a speech the following day. "We don't want to be a policeman [in Syria] . . . but

Conclusion   155

we're keeping the oil, remember that," he said. "I've always said that: 'Keep the oil.' We want to keep the oil. Forty-five million dollars a month? Keep the oil." Rarely had such commercially imperial objectives been expressed so starkly by an American president in public. Critics who considered the GWOT to be merely a convenient justification to preserve American access to Middle Eastern oil could point to Trump's comments as confirmation of their suspicions.[14]

THE BAGHDADI EPISODE showed that the nexus of terrorism and imperialism remained firmly in place as the United States entered the 2020s. The threats that nonstate actors like Baghdadi presented to the United States were still being described in many of the same ways as foes like Emilio Aguinaldo, Pancho Villa, Augusto Sandino, Che Guevara, Pablo Escobar, and Osama bin Laden had been. Some of the precise terms may have changed over time—bandit, savage, guerrilla, terrorist—yet the general ideas remained the same. These actors were widely viewed as criminal, uncivil, and illegitimate for the violent ways in which they pursued their platforms and for daring to challenge US interests.

These challengers, though, were useful in justifying incursions abroad to protect places of strategic importance. Such areas expanded considerably over the course of the twentieth century as the United States developed into a global empire, a moniker that most US leaders have denied. President George W. Bush, for example, said in 2004, "We're not an imperial power.... We are a liberating power." Despite this rationalization, the United States unquestionably has held considerable authority over many areas of the world. This sway has not always been determinative; the United States cannot always compel other countries—including allies—to do what it wants. But its influence has been significant nonetheless.[15]

The men considered here violently confronted American empire to varying degrees. Some were more principled about it than others. Sandino, for example, was driven to preserve Nicaraguan independence as demonstrated when he voluntarily laid down his arms after US forces left. Guevara, while fighting in Bolivia, refused to threaten or intimidate the locals that he was trying to recruit to his flailing insurgency. In contrast, Escobar's main aim was intensely personal, to preserve his illicit drug cartel and to avoid extradition. Bin Laden had no compunction taking aim at thousands of civilians. Baghdadi and ISIS wantonly slaughtered anyone who did not cooperate with their mission.

Nevertheless, Americans generally saw them all within a similar framework. It helps to explain why certain rhetoric has persisted over the years and has been effective in generating popular support for US policies because it identifies distinctions between "them" and "us." If these threats in opposition to the United States are seen as subhuman, barbaric, or evil, then by extension it means that Americans must be humane, civilized, and good. This line of reasoning reinforces a sense of American exceptionalism, a concept whose roots can be traced to the puritans of the seventeenth century, that Americans are somehow special and unique compared with those of all other nations. Moreover, such terminology has been useful in justifying the bending or breaking of established rules of military engagement. If laws of war are for the benefit of legitimate, state-sanctioned combatants, then it stood to reason that illegitimate, nonstate actors—like bandits and terrorists—were not entitled to those protections. This rationale enabled the Bush administration to support torture and indefinite detention of prisoners during the GWOT. But such precedents had long been established in prior pursuits and conflicts.

Whether the US missions to find these bandits and terrorists have been effective is another question entirely. In cases where the United States failed in its pursuit, the broader objective of quelling the threat was nonetheless achieved. The hunts for Villa and Sandino are cases in point. Both chases failed in the sense that the United States did not kill or capture them. But the threats that both men presented—to the US-Mexico border and to US interests in Nicaragua, respectively—dissipated over time despite their ability to elude the United States, even if they were not able to escape national rivals after their American confrontations.

Where US forces got their man, though, conflicts continued. In the case of Aguinaldo, his capture stymied the Philippine insurgency but did not end it entirely. Indeed, the worst defeat US forces suffered in the Philippines—the uprising at Balangiga—occurred six months after Aguinaldo was detained, and the Moros of the southern Philippines continued clashing with Americans for years. After Guevara had been killed, he served as an inspiration to other anticapitalist groups that challenged governments across Latin America, the presumed backyard of the United States. The desire to stomp out leftists compelled several US presidential administrations in the late twentieth century to support autocratic governments in places such as Argentina, Chile, El Salvador, and Guatemala, all of which committed an array of atrocities against their own people in the name of anticommunism.

Other successes seemed to be but a blip in the wider battle. Escobar's death in 1993 did little to halt the flow of illegal narcotics into the United States, and the broader war on drugs endures. Although narco-violence was indeed curtailed somewhat in Colombia, it has become much more prominent in recent years in Mexico instead. Similarly, bin Laden's celebrated death did not end the global war on terror. It did not even end the US military engagement in Afghanistan. That mission did not conclude until 2021, nearly twenty years after it began. Nevertheless, US forces remain deployed elsewhere around the world in the name of keeping jihadist groups like al-Qaeda, ISIS, and their metastasizing affiliates in check.

The paradoxical results of these missions—objectives achieved in failed chases, whereas objectives failed in successful pursuits—show the broader importance of recognizing limitations of military power. Relying so heavily on it as the foremost tool of engagement abroad produces more conflict and at tremendous cost usually borne much more heavily by local, Indigenous populations. Rather than confronting this reality, foreign challengers have too often been repurposed to fulfill political ends, whip up xenophobia, or justify incursions overseas. This well-worn utility explains why conflicts like the GWOT are not unique to twenty-first-century America.

Notes

Introduction

1. George W. Bush, "Remarks to Employees in the Pentagon and an Exchange with Reporters in Arlington, Virginia," September 17, 2001, American Presidency Project, University of California, Santa Barbara, www.presidency.ucsb.edu/node/211537.
2. Hobsbawm, *Bandits*, 7.
3. B. Bowden, *Empire of Civilization*; Jacobson, *Barbarian Virtues*; Bederman, *Manliness and Civilization*.
4. Joes, *Guerrilla Warfare*, 3–7.
5. Scholarly analyses about the concept and definition of "terrorism" are voluminous. Some good starting points include Hoffman, *Inside Terrorism*; Laqueur, *History of Terrorism*; Law, *Terrorism*; Townshend, *Terrorism*; Stampnitzky, *Disciplining Terror*.
6. Some relevant classic works about the impulses spurring American imperialism at the turn of the twentieth century include Hoganson, *Fighting for American Manhood*; Hunt, *Ideology and U.S. Foreign Policy*; LaFeber, *New Empire*; Rosenberg, *Spreading the American Dream*; Williams, *Tragedy of American Diplomacy*.
7. Grandin, *Empire's Workshop*.
8. See Neagle, "Bandit Worth Hunting," www.tandfonline.com.
9. "Human Costs," August 2023, https://watson.brown.edu/costsofwar/costs/human; and "Estimate of U.S. Post-9/11 War Spending, in $ Billions FY2001–FY2022," September 1, 2021, https://watson.brown.edu/costsofwar/figures/2021/Budgetary Costs, both from Costs of War Project, Watson Institute for International and Public Affairs, Brown University.

Chapter One

1. US Department of War, *Annual Reports*, 9:629–31; Jones, *Honor in the Dust*, 220–36; Welch, "American Atrocities."
2. Jones, *Honor in the Dust*, 282–316; Linn, *Philippine War*, 313–18; Boot, *Savage Wars of Peace*, 120–23.
3. Jones, *Honor in the Dust*, 155.
4. Linn, *U.S. Army and Counterinsurgency*, 2–3; S. Harris, *God's Arbiters*, 12.
5. Jones, *Honor in the Dust*, 43–44; Linn, *U.S. Army and Counterinsurgency*, 5.
6. Wildman, *Aguinaldo*, 155; Boot, *Savage Wars of Peace*, 103; S. Harris, *God's Arbiters*, 186; Linn, *Philippine War*, 19–20.
7. Aguinaldo, "True Version of the Philippine Revolution," 4–6; S. Harris, *God's Arbiters*, 10; Jones, *Honor in the Dust*, 44.
8. Aguinaldo, "True Version of the Philippine Revolution," 6.

9. Zimmermann, *First Great Triumph*, 268–70, 300–309; Aguinaldo, "True Version of the Philippine Revolution," 18; US Senate, *Affairs in the Philippine Islands*, 2928.

10. "Gen. Emilio Aguinaldo," *Minneapolis Journal*, May 6, 1898; "Smallest Fighting Machine in the World," *Philadelphia Inquirer*, September 4, 1898; "Our Relations to the Philippines," *Springfield (MA) Daily Republican*, July 29, 1898.

11. Zimmermann, *First Great Triumph*, 307; Aguinaldo, "True Version of the Philippine Revolution," 40, 42; Jones, *Honor in the Dust*, 88.

12. Linn, *Philippine War*, 26; Jones, *Honor in the Dust*, 98.

13. Jones, *Honor in the Dust*, 110.

14. Aguinaldo, "True Version of the Philippine Revolution," 54; Linn, *Philippine War*, 52–64.

15. Kramer, *Blood of Government*, 111–12; Poplin, "Letters of W. Thomas Osborne," 162.

16. US Senate, *Affairs in the Philippine Islands*, 70.

17. US Senate, *Affairs in the Philippine Islands*, 70; Boot, *Savage Wars of Peace*, 113; Poultney Bigelow, "How to Convert a White Man into a Savage," *Independent*, May 1902, 1160; Gatewood, *Black Americans*, 269.

18. Jones, *Honor in the Dust*, 147; Worcester, *Philippines Past and Present*, 384.

19. Linn, *U.S. Army and Counterinsurgency*, 133.

20. Crandall, *America's Dirty Wars*, 79; Jones, *Honor in the Dust*, 142, 205; Linn, *U.S. Army and Counterinsurgency*, 38, 57.

21. Esty, *American Press on the Philippines*, 7; Kramer, *Blood of Government*, 130.

22. Callwell, *Small Wars*; Fellman, *In the Name of God and Country*, 186–89; Walter Williams, "United States Indian Policy," 826–28.

23. Storey and Codman, *Secretary Root's Record*, 54; Kramer, *Blood of Government*, 90.

24. Storey and Codman, *Secretary Root's Record*, 10; Welch, "American Atrocities in the Philippines," 241.

25. Anonymous to *Wisconsin Weekly Advocate*, May 17, 1900, 280, and Patrick Mason to *Gazette* (Cleveland), September 29, 1900, 257, both in Gatewood, "Smoked Yankees."

26. "General Orders No. 100: The Lieber Code," April 24, 1863, Avalon Project, https://avalon.law.yale.edu/19th_century/lieber.asp; Witt, *Lincoln's Code*, 2–4.

27. Welch, "American Atrocities in the Philippines," 235; Paul Kramer, "The Water Cure," *New Yorker*, February 25, 2008.

28. Worcester, *Philippines Past and Present*, 281; Witt, *Lincoln's Code*, 359–63.

29. Boot, *Savage Wars of Peace*, 123–24.

30. Kramer, *Blood of Government*, 148; Storey and Codman, *Secretary Root's Record*, 45. See also Jones, *Honor in the Dust*, 274.

31. US Senate, *Affairs in the Philippine Islands*, 558–63.

32. "After Aguinaldo, What?," *Los Angeles Times*, March 29, 1901; "Aguinaldo," *New York Tribune*, March 29, 1901; "The Mighty Aguinaldo," *Boston Daily Globe*, March 27, 1901; "Aguinaldo Now Counted as Dead," *Chicago Daily Tribune*, March 1, 1901.

33. Gatewood, *Black Americans*, 273; Boot, *Savage Wars of Peace*, 117–18.

34. Jones, *Honor in the Dust*, 216–17; Boot, *Savage Wars of Peace*, 118–19; "How Funston Did It," *New York Times*, March 29, 1901; Aguinaldo, with Pacis, *Second Look at America*, 122, 128.

35. "After Aguinaldo, What?," *Los Angeles Times*, March 29, 1901; "Aguinaldo," *New*

York Tribune, March 29, 1901; "Dewey Talks of Funston's Feat," Chicago Daily Tribune, March 29, 1901; "Otis Thinks Aguinaldo Honest," New York Tribune, March 29, 1901.

36. Wildman, Aguinaldo, 363, 365–67; "Aguinaldo on Captor," Washington Post, March 31, 1901; "Aguinaldo Has Sworn Fealty," Chicago Daily Tribune, April 3, 1901.

37. Roosevelt, "Proclamation 483—Granting Pardon and Amnesty to Participants in Insurrection in the Philippines," July 4, 1902, American Presidency Project, University of California, Santa Barbara, www.presidency.ucsb.edu/node/207304.

38. Kramer, Blood of Government, 33.

39. Arnold, Moro War, 6–9; Hawkins, Making Moros, 9–10.

40. Arnold, Moro War, 15–16, 85–88.

41. Dphrepaulezz, "'Right Sort of White Men,'" 16, 110; Arnold, Moro War, 105.

42. Arnold, Moro War, 27–39; "Moro Fort Is Taken After a Severe Battle," Chicago Tribune, May 5, 1902.

43. Arnold, Moro War, 104; Kramer, Blood of Government, 155; Cullinane, "Bringing in the Brigands," 55–60.

44. Robert Lee Bullard, "Preparing Our Moros for Government," Atlantic, March 1906, 385–94; Lieut. L. B., "The Regular and the Savage: A Flash-Light View of War in the Philippines," Lippincott's Monthly Magazine, December 1904, 731; Hawkins, Making Moros, 58.

45. Hawkins, Making Moros, 35.

46. Arnold, Moro War, 118; Hawkins, Making Moros, 117; Dphrepaulezz, "'Right Sort of White Men,'" 146.

47. Edgerton, American Datu, 149; Dphrepaulezz, "'Right Sort of White Men,'" 127–31.

48. Arnold, Moro War, 100–103.

49. Arnold, Moro War, 132–33; Edgerton, American Datu, 110–14.

50. Arnold, Moro War, 134–36; Edgerton, American Datu, 115–16.

51. Arnold, Moro War, 136–37; "Ali Meets His Fate," Washington Post, December 13, 1905.

52. Edgerton, American Datu, 97, 161–67; Arnold, Moro War, 139–77; Dphrepaulezz, "'Right Sort of White Men,'" 144–79.

53. Edgerton, American Datu, 220–25.

54. Edgerton, American Datu, 228–29, 240.

55. Boot, Savage Wars of Peace, 125; US Department of State, Office of the Historian, "The Philippine-American War, 1899–1902," accessed December 18, 2024, https://history.state.gov/milestones/1899–1913/war (no longer available).

56. Margaret Parton, "The Red, White, Blue, and Gold: Philippine Republic's Flag Rises," New York Herald Tribune, July 5, 1946; Aguinaldo, with Pacis, Second Look at America, 66, 247.

57. "Aguinaldo, 94, Dies; Led Filipino Revolts," New York Times, February 6, 1964.

Chapter Two

1. Tompkins, Chasing Villa, 137–44; "Attack on Our Cavalry at Parral," 249–53; Thomas and Allen, Mexican Punitive Expedition, chap. 4, 2–5.

2. "Pancho Villa, Professional Murderer," *El Paso Herald*, April 1, 1916, https://texas history.unt.edu/ark:/67531/metapth137565/; "Villa Alive or Dead," reprinted in *New York Times*, March 10, 1916; "Reward for Villa Planned," *New York Times*, March 13, 1916.

3. "What If It Had Been Whole Army of Plunderers?," *Tacoma Times*, March 13, 1916; "Lodge Assails Wilson," *New York Times*, March 16, 1916.

4. Tumulty, *Woodrow Wilson*, 157–58 (emphasis in original).

5. Frank Polk to Woodrow Wilson, March 21, 1916, in Link, *Papers of Woodrow Wilson*, 36:351; Katz, *Life and Times*, 571; "Wilson Warns against 'Unscrupulous Influences' Inspiring Mexican Rumors to Cause Intervention," *New York Times*, March 26, 1916.

6. Katz, *Life and Times*, 1–8; "Villa, Bandit and Brute, May Be Mexican President," *New York Times*, December 14, 1913.

7. Theodore Roosevelt to James Creelman, March 7, 1908, Theodore Roosevelt Papers, Library of Congress Manuscript Division, www.theodorerooseveltcenter.org/Research/Digital-Library/Record/ImageViewer?libID=o201906.

8. "Mining Decree Issued by Francisco Villa at Monterey, March 19, 1915," 894–95; Secretary of State to Special Agent Carothers, April 7, 1915, 895–96; Acting Secretary of State to Special Agent Carothers, April 10, 1915, 896; Vice Consul Coen to the Secretary of State, April 11, 1915, 896–99; Special Agent Carothers to the Secretary of State, April 12, 1915, 899; Secretary of State to Special Agent Carothers, April 15, 1915, 899; Special Agent Carothers to the Secretary of State, April 15, 1915, 901; Mine and Smelter Operators et al. to Special Agent Canova, April 21, 1916, 903–9; Secretary of State to Special Agent Carothers, April 22, 1915, 909; Special Agent Carothers to the Secretary of State, April 22, 1915, 909; Special Agent Carothers to the Secretary of State, April 26, 1915, 910; Acting Secretary of State to Vice Consul Coen, April 29, 1915, 910; Sierra Consolidated Mines Company to the Secretary of State, May 8, 1915, 910–11; Vice Consul Coen to the Secretary of State, May 15, 1915, 911–15; Special Agent Carothers to the Secretary of State, May 21, 1915, 917; Mine and Smelter Operators' Association to the Secretary of State, August 6, 1915, 933; Secretary of State to the Mine and Smelter Operators' Association, August 6, 1915, 933–34; Special Agent Carothers to the Secretary of State, August 10, 1915, 934; General Scott to the Secretary of State, August 10, 1915, 935; Special Agent Carothers to the Secretary of State, August 12, 1915, 935, all in Fuller, *Papers Relating to the Foreign Relations . . . 1915*; Katz, "Pancho Villa and the Attack," 103–4; Meyers, "Pancho Villa and the Multinationals," 342–48.

9. "Warm Welcome by General Pershing for Villa and Obregon in El Paso," *El Paso Times*, August 27, 1914, www.elpasotimes.com/story/news/history/blogs/tales-from-the-morgue/2014/08/26/1914-warm-welcome-by-general-pershing-for-villa-and-obregon-in-el-paso/31490807/; Katz, *Life and Times*, 318.

10. E. Alexander Powell, "A Visit to the Bandit-General Pancho Villa," *New York Times*, March 29, 1914; "A Romantic Side to General 'Pancho' Villa, One-Time Bandit," *Albuquerque Journal*, May 8, 1914; H. L. Wilson to Secretary of State, January 11, 1913, in Fuller, *Papers Relating to the Foreign Relations . . . 1913*, 693; "Story of the Remarkable Career of Villa, Bandit and General," *Wilkes-Barre Times Leader*, April 28, 1914; "Meteoric Rise of General Villa from Bandit to Hero of Country," *Kalamazoo Gazette*, April 19, 1914.

11. Powell, "Visit to the Bandit-General"; "Small Loss to US in Mexican Wars," *New York Times*, May 27, 1914; William Jennings Bryan to Woodrow Wilson, August 3, 1914, in Link, *Papers of Woodrow Wilson*, 30:340.

12. Schmutz to Secretary of State, June 15, 1915, in Fuller, *Papers Relating to the Foreign Relations . . . 1915*, 710.

13. Cobb to Secretary of State, October 16, 1915, in Fuller, *Papers Relating to the Foreign Relations . . . 1915*, 769.

14. Hart, *Empire and Revolution*, 305–12, 321–26; Wilson to Water Hines Page, June 1, 1914, in Link, *Papers of Woodrow Wilson*, 30:131.

15. S. A. Milliken, "Name of Pancho Villa Will Go Down as That of One Unique in History of World," *Albuquerque Journal*, May 30, 1914.

16. John Lind to William Jennings Bryan, December 5, 1913, in Link, *Papers of Woodrow Wilson*, 29:14.

17. Tompkins, *Chasing Villa*, 50; Welsome, *General and the Jaguar*, 81, 83.

18. Welsome, *General and the Jaguar*, 110–27; Boot, *Savage Wars of Peace*, 182–85; Katz, "Pancho Villa and the Attack," 101; George Carothers to Secretary of State, Cobb to Secretary of State, and General Pershing to General Funston, all dated March 9, 1916, in Fuller, *Papers Relating to the Foreign Relations . . . 1916*, 480, 481; Link, *Wilson*, 205; Crandall, *America's Dirty Wars*, 89.

19. Braddy, *Paradox of Pancho Villa*, 54; Katz, *Life and Times*, 566; Boot, *Savage Wars of Peace*, 185; Crandall, *America's Dirty Wars*, 91.

20. "Troopers Itching to Go after Villa," *New York Times*, March 10, 1916; Welsome, *General and the Jaguar*, 143.

21. Welsome, *General and the Jaguar*, 66–68; Katz, *Life and Times*, 558–59; Cobb to Secretary of State, January 12, 1916, in Fuller, *Papers Relating to the Foreign Relations . . . 1916*, 652; Pershing, *My Life*, 335.

22. Katz, "Pancho Villa and the Attack," 116; Lansing to Silliman, January 12, 1916, in Fuller, *Papers Relating to the Foreign Relations . . . 1916*, 653; "Lopez Tells of Villa's Motives," *Hartford Herald*, May 31, 1916; Katz, *Life and Times*, 576–77.

23. "Miles Keen for Action," *New York Times*, March 10, 1916; "The Only Solution," *Olympia (WA) Daily Recorder*, November 13, 1916; Lansing to Silliman and Belt, March 9, 1916, in Fuller, *Papers Relating to the Foreign Relations . . . 1916*, 481.

24. Letcher to Secretary of State, February 9, 1916, in Fuller, *Papers Relating to the Foreign Relations . . . 1916*, 468; Katz, *Life and Times*, 613.

25. "Taft Favors Pursuit," *New York Times*, March 11, 1916; "Pershing Reserves Anxious to Fight," *New York Times*, March 31, 1916.

26. White, "Muddied Waters of Columbus," 81–92; Katz, *Life and Times*, 551–57; Braddy, *Paradox of Pancho Villa*, 49–51.

27. Katz, *Life and Times*, 529–30.

28. Katz, *Life and Times*, 528, 552–53; Welsome, *General and the Jaguar*, 61.

29. "Lopez Tells of Villa's Motives," *Hartford Herald*, May 31, 1916; Welsome, *General and the Jaguar*, 110; Pershing to Funston, March 9, 1916, in Fuller, *Papers Relating to the Foreign Relations . . . 1916*, 481; Katz, *Life and Times*, 564.

30. Katz, *Life and Times*, 532, 557.

31. Adjutant General McCain to Funston, March 10, 1916, in Fuller, *Papers Relating to the Foreign Relations . . . 1916*, 483; McCain to Funston, March 10, 1916, in John J. Pershing, *Punitive Expedition Report*, October 10, 1916, www.paperlessarchives.com/FreeTitles/PanchoVillaCaptureExpeditionPershingReport.pdf; Congressional Resolution of March 17, 1916, in Fuller, *Papers Relating to the Foreign Relations . . . 1916*, 491–92.

32. Pershing to Funston, April 14, 1916, in Link, *Papers of Woodrow Wilson*, 36:589.

33. Pershing, *My Life*, 344, 345, 347; Tompkins, *Chasing Villa*, 130, 138.

34. Frank B. Elser, "Army Hunting Villa Struck by Storm; Aviators Risk Death in 60-Mile Gale," *New York Times*, March 26, 1916; "6 Aeroplanes Lost in Mexico Campaign," *New York Times*, April 23, 1916; Prieto, *Mexican Expedition*, 52–57.

35. Tompkins, *Chasing Villa*, 147; Katz, *Life and Times*, 606.

36. Katz, *Life and Times*, 609; Welsome, *General and the Jaguar*, 291, 296; Knott, *Secret and Sanctioned*, 155, 171. Knott asserts that Pershing covered up the assassination attempt, which did not become known publicly for decades, and that President Wilson had no knowledge of it.

37. Carranza to Mexican Ambassador to the United States Eliseo Arredondo, March 11, 1916, 486; Lansing to Silliman, March 13, 1916, 486–87; Arredondo to Frank L. Polk, March 19, 1916, 495–96; all in Fuller, *Papers Relating to the Foreign Relations . . . 1916*.

38. Prieto, *Mexican Expedition*, 43–48; Welsome, *General and the Jaguar*, 270–86; Funston to Pershing, May 4, 1916, in Fuller, *Papers Relating to the Foreign Relations . . . 1916*, 539.

39. Pershing to Funston, April 14, 1916, in Link, *Papers of Woodrow Wilson*, 36:589; Tompkins, *Chasing Villa*, 199; Patton quoted in Katz, *Life and Times*, 605.

40. "Report of the Secretary of War," November 20, 1917, in US Department of War, *War Department: Annual Reports*, 1917, 10; Pershing, *My Life*, 362.

41. Sandos, "Pancho Villa and American Security," 303; Funston to Baker, May 26, 1916, in Fuller, *Papers Relating to the Foreign Relations . . . 1916*, 564; Katz, *Life and Times*, 575–76; Boot, *Savage Wars of Peace*, 193.

42. Katz, *Life and Times*, 606–8; "Villa Raiders Sentenced," *New York Times*, August 28, 1917; "16 Villa Men in New Mexico Are Pardoned by Governor," *New York Times*, November 23, 1920; William Q. Sabatini, "Luna County Courthouse—Deming, N.M.," *New Mexico Architecture*, November–December 1986), https://digitalrepository.unm.edu/cgi/viewcontent.cgi?article=2345&context=nma; Morgan, *Raid and Reconciliation*, 169–70.

43. Sandos, "Pancho Villa and American Security," 310; Thomas and Allen, *Mexican Punitive Expedition*, chap. 5, 1.

44. Dow to Acting Secretary of State, June 16, 1919, 2:558; and J. B. Stewart to Acting Secretary of State, February 8, 1919, 2:565–69, both in Fuller, *Papers Relating to the Foreign Relations . . . 1919*; "Hugo Says Villa Treated Him Well," *New York Times*, December 17, 1919.

45. "The Return of Villa," *New York Times*, June 29, 1917.

46. "Noble and Patriotic Villa," *Fort-Worth Star Telegram*, November 19, 1917; "A Reformed Bandit," *Oregonian*, June 27, 1922.

47. Katz, *Life and Times*, 719–29, 761–82.
48. "Pancho Villa and Mexico," *Washington Post*, July 21, 1923; Timothy G. Turner, "Pancho Villa—Caveman," *Los Angeles Times*, July 23, 1923.
49. "Villa," *Hartford Courant*, July 22, 1923; "Francisco Villa," *New York Times*, July 23, 1923.
50. "Mexico's No. 1 Bandit—Pancho Villa, 1950," *It's Steve Lopez's Big Blog O'Fun!!!* (blog), February 8, 2013, https://fourcolorglasses.wordpress.com/2013/02/08/mexicos-no-1-bandit-pancho-villa-1950; "Pancho Villa 'Tiger of the North,'" *Western Comics Adventures* (blog), June 18, 2012, http://westerncomicsadventures.blogspot.com/2012/06/pancho-villa-tiger-of-north.html.
51. Morgan, *Raid and Reconciliation*, 1–4; John V. Young, "A Park for Pancho Villa," *New York Times*, February 20, 1966.

Chapter Three

1. Macaulay, *Sandino Affair*, 71, 72.
2. Sheesley, *Sandino in the Streets*, 38, 40–41; Ramírez and Conrad, *Sandino*, 81.
3. Macaulay, *Sandino Affair*, 76–82; Cummins, *Quijote on a Burro*, 53–55; Eberhardt to Secretary of State, July 17, 1927, in Fuller, *Papers Relating to the Foreign Relations . . . 1927*, 3:440.
4. Stimson, *Henry L. Stimson's American Policy*, 39–40.
5. McPherson, *Invaded*, 14, 75; Macaulay, *Sandino Affair*, 23–25, 34.
6. Eberhardt to Secretary of State, May 12, 1927, in Fuller, *Papers Relating to the Foreign Relations . . . 1927*, 3:347.
7. Navarro-Genie, *Augusto "Cesar" Sandino*, 3–7.
8. Navarro-Genie, *Augusto "Cesar" Sandino*, 9–14.
9. Sheesley, *Sandino in the Streets*, 26–27.
10. Navarro-Genie, *Augusto "Cesar" Sandino*, 104.
11. "The Return to Nicaragua, 1926," 41; Sandino to Froylán Turcios, September 20, 1927, 106; and "Manifesto to the Nicaraguan People concerning the Elections," October 6, 1927, 111, all in Navarro-Genie, *Augusto "Cesar" Sandino*.
12. "Manifesto," July 1, 1927, in Navarro-Genie, *Augusto "Cesar" Sandino*, 76; Stimson, *Henry L. Stimson's American Policy*, 35; Edward T. Folliard, "Department of State Denounces Sandino As Ruthless Bandit," *Washington Post*, April 19, 1931.
13. "Manifesto," 76; Sandino to D. F. Sellers, February 3, 1928, in Fuller, *Papers Relating to the Foreign Relations . . . 1928*, 3:569.
14. Eberhardt to Secretary of State, June 30, 1927, in Fuller, *Papers Relating to the Foreign Relations . . . 1927*, 3:439–40; Sheesley, *Sandino in the Streets*, 53–55 (emphasis in original).
15. Letter to Colonel Félix Pedro Zeledón, October 21, 1927, in Navarro-Genie, *Augusto "Cesar" Sandino*, 116.
16. "El Chipoton, or the Siege of El Chipote, 1927–1928," in Navarro-Genie, *Augusto "Cesar" Sandino*, 164; Macaulay, *Sandino Affair*, 147, 212–13; Sheesley, *Sandino in the Streets*, 82; Boot, *Savage Wars of Peace*, 247; McPherson, *Invaded*, 89.

17. "Kellogg Justifies Defense," *New York Times*, July 19, 1927; Munro to Secretary of State, January 11, 1928, and Kellogg to Munro, January 13, 1928, in Fuller, *Papers Relating to the Foreign Relations . . . 1928*, 3:560–61.

18. Bhatia, "Fighting Words," 14.

19. Richard Grossman, "'The Blood of the People': The Guardia Nacional's Fifty-Year War against the People of Nicaragua," in Menjívar and Rodríguez, *When States Kill*, 69; Convention (IV) respecting the Laws and Customs of War on Land and Its Annex: Regulations concerning the Laws and Customs of War on Land, The Hague, October 18, 1907, https://ihl-databases.icrc.org/applic/ihl/ihl.nsf/0/1d1726425f6955aec125641e0038bfd6; R. H. Dunlap, Area Commander, to Commanding General, 2nd Brigade, December 27, 1928, Record Group 127, entry 206, box 2—Nicaragua: 2nd Brigade, 1927–1932, Miscellaneous Correspondence, Bandits, National Archives, College Park, MD.

20. "The Destruction of Quilalí," January 4, 1928, in Navarro-Genie, *Augusto "Cesar" Sandino*, 154–55.

21. "Resolution Number 20: Confiscation of North American Properties," January 6, 1928, in Navarro-Genie, *Augusto "Cesar" Sandino*, 156.

22. Carleton Beals, "On the Sandino Front," *Nation*, February 29, 1928, 233; Beals, "Sandino—Bandit or Patriot?," *Nation*, March 28, 1928, 341; Beals, "This Is War, Gentlemen!," *Nation*, April 11, 1928, 404–6.

23. Tierney, "United States and Nicaragua," 113; Eberhardt to Secretary of State, September 20, 1928, in Fuller, *Papers Relating to the Foreign Relations . . . 1928*, 3:588–89.

24. Macaulay, *Sandino Affair*, 108, 211; Fletcher to Eberhardt, May 26, 1928, in Fuller, *Papers Relating to the Foreign Relations . . . 1928*, 3:574–75.

25. Bacevich, "American Electoral Mission," 258; "The United States and Nicaragua: A Survey of Relations from 1909–1932," Department of State, Latin American Series, no. 6, 1932, in Stimson, *Henry L. Stimson's American Policy*, 239; Sheesley, *Sandino in the Streets*, 77.

26. Gobat, *Confronting the American Dream*, 236–37; Michael J. Schroeder, "The Sandino Rebellion Revisited: Civil War, Imperialism, Popular Nationalism, and State Formation Muddied Up Together in the Segovias of Nicaragua, 1926–1934," in Joseph, LeGrand, and Salvatore, *Close Encounters of Empire*, 232–36; Open Letter from J. M. Moncada, July 2, 1927, Record Group 127, entry 43A, box 29, GN 2—Sandino letters, originals, and copies, 9 Nov 16–22 Jul 28, National Archives.

27. Eberhardt to Secretary of State, March 16, 1929, in Fuller, *Papers Relating to the Foreign Relations . . . 1929*, 3:554.

28. McPherson, *Invaded*, 226; Clark Memorandum of Conversation with Mexican Ambassador, May 17, 1929, in Fuller, *Papers Relating to the Foreign Relations . . . 1929*, 3:587.

29. McPherson, *Invaded*, 227.

30. McPherson, *Invaded*, 88; Eberhardt to Secretary of State, May 16, 1929, in Fuller, *Papers Relating to the Foreign Relations . . . 1929*, 3:554.

31. Tierney, "United States and Nicaragua," 214–21; Crandall, *America's Dirty Wars*, 145.

32. "The President's News Conference," April 17, 1931, American Presidency Project, University of California, Santa Barbara, www.presidency.ucsb.edu/node/212203.

33. Stimson to Moncada, November 24, 1930, in Fuller, *Papers Relating to the Foreign Relations . . . 1930*, 3:684.
34. Stimson, *Henry L. Stimson's American Policy*, 237. See also Stimson to Hanna, April 20, 1931, in Fuller, *Papers Relating to the Foreign Relations . . . 1931*, 2:815.
35. Sheesley, *Sandino in the Streets*, 91–92.
36. *Boston Globe*, December 3, 1933; *Chicago Tribune*, February 23, 1934; Dennis, "Nicaragua," 499; Grossman, "Solidarity with Sandino," 71–72.
37. Tierney, "United States and Nicaragua," 231; Langley, *Banana Wars*, 215; Macaulay, *Sandino Affair*, 145; Cummins, *Quijote in a Burro*, 121–22.
38. Sheesley, *Sandino in the Streets*, 46–51; Beals, "Sandino—Bandit or Patriot?," 341; Letter to Colonel Félix Pedro Zeledón, November 26, 1927, in Navarro-Genie, *Augusto "Cesar" Sandino*, 128; Carleton Beals, "To the Nicaraguan Border," *Nation*, February 22, 1928, 204.
39. Crandall, *America's Dirty Wars*, 148; Macaulay, *Sandino Affair*, 225.
40. Macaulay, *Sandino Affair*, 239; Cummins, *Quijote on a Burro*, 98, 137.
41. Gobat, *Confronting the American Dream*, 216.
42. Macaulay, *Sandino Affair*, 254–56.
43. Macaulay, *Sandino Affair*, 253; Lane to Secretary of State, February 23, 1934, in Farrar and McCornack, *Foreign Relations . . . 1934*, 5:535.

Chapter Four

1. "At the United Nations," December 11, 1964, in Deutschmann, *Che Guevara*, 334.
2. Guevara, *Guerrilla Warfare*, 3–4.
3. Jules Dubois, "Plans for 'Red Empire' in South America Told," *Chicago Tribune*, October 2, 1961; Peter Grothe, "An Interview with Guevara," *Washington Post*, November 28, 1960.
4. Anderson, *Che Guevara*, 593–94.
5. A sampling of this speculation includes "Lesser Job Hinted for Maj. Guevara," *New York Times*, June 14, 1965; Seymour Freidin, "Communists Puzzled as Much as West Is Over Mystery of Guevara," *Boston Globe*, October 7, 1965; "Guevara Reported Seized in Peru," *New York Times*, October 9, 1965; "Cuba: Rebel without a Pause," *Newsweek*, October 18, 1965; "Donde Esta? Whatever Became of Che," *New York Times*, April 10, 1966; "Che Directing Reds in Peru, Newsman Says," *Chicago Tribune*, May 6, 1966; "Red Mystery Leader Guevara Reported Seen in Argentina," *Atlanta Constitution*, July 7, 1966; Deutschmann, *Che*, 30.
6. One biographer claims Guevara's birth certificate was fudged to conceal the fact that he was conceived before his parents were married and that he was really born on May 14, 1928. Anderson, *Che Guevara*, 3–4, 21–22.
7. Castañeda, *Compañero*, 71.
8. Castañeda, *Compañero*, 76–91; R. Harris, *Death of a Revolutionary*; Anderson, *Che Guevara*, 124.
9. Anderson, *Che Guevara*, 167–72, 187–96.
10. Castañeda, *Compañero*, 105–17; "Despatch from the Consulate at Santiago de Cuba to the Department of State," February 21, 1958, in Glennon, *Foreign Relations*

. . . 1958–1960, 6:35, https://history.state.gov/historicaldocuments/frus1958-60v06/d18.

11. Castañeda, *Compañero*, 143–44; Anderson, *Che Guevara*, 370–73; "Castro's Brain," *Time*, August 8, 1960.

12. Norman Gall, "The Legacy of Che Guevara," *Commentary*, December 1967, 36; Castañeda, *Compañero*, 235–36.

13. "Political Sovereignty and Economic Independence," March 20, 1960, in Deutschmann, *Che Guevara*, 99; Jules Dubois, "Guevara Irks Delegates to Latin Parley," *Chicago Tribune*, August 7, 1961.

14. Guevara, *Guerrilla Warfare*, 5, 7.

15. Guevara, *Guerrilla Warfare*, 17, 56.

16. 106 Cong. Rec. H586–87 (January 14, 1960) (Extension of remarks of Hon. H. Allen Smith), www.congress.gov/bound-congressional-record/1960/01/14/extensions-of-remarks-section; 109 Cong. Rec. S2068–69 (February 7, 1963) (Extension of remarks of Hon. William G. Bray), www.congress.gov/bound-congressional-record/1963/02/07/extensions-of-remarks-section.

17. Tad Szulc, "Shadowy Power behind Castro," *New York Times Magazine*, June 19, 1960.

18. Laura Bergquist Knebel, interview by Nelson Aldrich, December 8, 1965, pp. 12, 15–16, JFKOH-LK-01, John F. Kennedy Oral History Collection, John F. Kennedy Presidential Library and Museum, www.jfklibrary.org/asset-viewer/archives/jfkoh-lk-01.

19. James, *Che Guevara*, 145; "Memorandum for the President [Goodwin to Kennedy], Subject: Conversation with Commandante [sic] Ernesto Guevara of Cuba," August 22, 1961, Papers of John F. Kennedy, Presidential Papers, President's Office Files, Countries, Cuba: Security, 1961, JFKPOF-115-003, John F. Kennedy Presidential Library and Museum, www.jfklibrary.org/asset-viewer/archives/JFKPOF/115/JFKPOF-115-003.

20. Castañeda, *Compañero*, 208; Cong. Rec. H1242 (January 28, 1963) (Remarks of Don L. Short); "Memorandum for the President [Goodwin to Kennedy] . . .," August 22, 1961.

21. "To Fidel Castro," April 1, 1965, in Deutschmann, *Che Guevara*, 374; Castro quoted in Deutschmann, *Che Guevara*, 30.

22. Anderson, *Che Guevara*, 595–97; Castañeda, *Compañero*, 306.

23. Guevara, *Congo Diary*, 15; Anderson, *Che Guevara*, 615; Richard Gott, "The Year Che Went Missing," *Guardian*, November 30, 1996.

24. Castañeda, *Compañero*, 316, 326.

25. Central Intelligence Agency, Office of Current Intelligence, Weekly Summary, October 8, 1965, p. 28, General CIA Records, Freedom of Information Act Electronic Reading Room, CIA.gov, www.cia.gov/readingroom/docs/CIA-RDP79-00927A005000090001-9.pdf; Bamford, *Body of Secrets*, 181; Tim Elfrink, "He Buried Che," *Miami New Times*, August 6, 2009, www.miaminewtimes.com/news/he-buried-che-6365574.

26. Hawes and Koenig, *Cold War Navy Seal*, 163–67.

27. Anderson, *Che Guevara*, 641–43; Castañeda, *Compañero*, 327.

28. Guevara, *Congo Diary*, 229.

29. "Message to the Tricontinental," April 16, 1967, in Deutschmann, *Che Guevara*, 356.

30. James, *Complete Bolivian Diaries of Che Guevara*, 17–18; Bell, *Myth of the Guerrilla*, 221.

31. Anderson, *Che Guevara*, 658, 666. Guevara's eldest child, Hildita, then ten years old, was not present for fear that she would see through his cover.

32. James, *Che Guevara*, 215–16; Harris, *Death of a Revolutionary*, 159; Taibo, *Guevara*, 479–80; Anderson, *Che Guevara*, 674; James, *Diaries of Che Guevara*, 237.

33. Anderson, *Che Guevara*, 678–79; Bell, *Myth of the Guerrilla*, 227; James, *Diaries of Che Guevara*, 242.

34. Sheer, *Diary of Che Guevara*.

35. Weiss and Maurer, *Hunting Che*, 17.

36. Douglas Henderson, interview by Sheldon Stern, August 30, 1978, 122, 130, JFKOH-DH-01, John F. Kennedy Oral History Collection, John F. Kennedy Presidential Library and Museum, https://www.jfklibrary.org/asset-viewer/archives/jfkoh-dh-01; State Department Cable, La Paz 2697, "Guerrilla Situation—Bolivia," April 22, 1967, Presidential Papers, National Security File: Latin America Country Files, box 8, folder "Bolivia v. 4 (1/66–12/68)," LBJ Presidential Library, accessed via the National Security Archive, https://nsarchive.gwu.edu/document/24580-document-1-state-department-cable-la-paz-2697-guerrilla-situation-bolivia-april-22; James, *Che Guevara*, 280.

37. Prado, *Defeat of Che Guevara*, 86; Weiss and Maurer, *Hunting Che*, 83–84, 104–5; Ryan, *Fall of Che Guevara*, 89–92.

38. "Report Cuba's Guevara Leads Bolivia Rebels," *Chicago Tribune*, March 29, 1967; "Bolivians Pressing Drive on Guerrillas," *New York Times*, March 30, 1967; "Bolivian Troops Fight Guerrillas," *New York Times*, March 31, 1967; Herbert Matthews, "Latin America: Guerrillas at Large," *New York Times*, April 10, 1967; NSC Memorandum, Walt Rostow to President Johnson, May 11, 1967, Presidential Papers, National Security File: Latin America Country Files, box 8, folder "Bolivia v. 4 (1/66–12/68) 3 of 3," LBJ Presidential Library, accessed via National Security Archive, https://nsarchive.gwu.edu/document/24583-document-4-nsc-memorandum-walt-rostow-president-johnson-may-11-1967-declassified (emphasis in original).

39. CIA Memorandum, Latin America Division to the Deputy Inspector General, "Statement by Benton H. Mizones [Félix Rodríguez] concerning His Assignment in Bolivia in 1967," June 3, 1975, record number 104-10103-10219, file number 80T01357A, JFK Assassination Records, National Security Archive, https://nsarchive.gwu.edu/document/24608-document-29-cia-memorandum-latin-america-division-deputy-inspector-general-statement; Rodríguez and Weisman, *Shadow Warrior*, 128–29; Elfrink, "He Buried Che."

40. Sheer, *Diary of Che Guevara*, 113, 164–65, 173.

41. Taibo, *Guevara*, 518; Moreno, "Che Guevara on Guerrilla Warfare," 126; Ryan, *Fall of Che Guevara*, 104–6; James, *Diaries of Che Guevara*, 47.

42. McCormick and Berger, "Ernesto (Che) Guevara," 351; NSC Memorandum, William Bowdler to Walt Rostow, September 6, 1967, Presidential Papers, National Security File: Latin America Country Files, box 8, folder "Bolivia v. 4 (1/66–12/68) 2 of 3," LBJ Presidential Library, accessed via National Security Archive, https://nsarchive.gwu.edu/document/24594-document-15-nsc-memorandum-william-bowdler-walt-rostow-conveying-cia-battle-accounts.

43. CIA Memorandum, "Statement by Benton H. Mizones [Félix Rodríguez]"; Rodríguez and Weisman, *Shadow Warrior*, 143–51.

44. "Reward Offered for Guevara," *New York Times*, September 16, 1967; "OAS Views Photos Said to Show Guevara," *New York Times*, September 23, 1967.

45. Anderson, *Che Guevara*, 696–97; Sheer, *Diary of Che Guevara*, 190.

46. Anderson, *Che Guevara*, 702; Castañeda, *Compañero*, 399.

47. Prado, *Defeat of Che Guevara*, 246–49; Rodríguez and Weisman, *Shadow Warrior*, 165.

48. Rodríguez and Weisman, *Shadow Warrior*, 161–62; Anderson, *Che Guevara*, 703–5; Taibo, *Guevara, Also Known as Che*, 557.

49. Rodríguez and Weisman, *Shadow Warrior*, 166; Weiss and Maurer, *Hunting Che*, 208.

50. Rodríguez and Weisman, *Shadow Warrior*, 12–14. One Guevara biographer states that a Bolivian officer, Lt. Col. Andrés Selich, was present during the discussion, but Rodríguez does not mention that in his memoir. According to Selich's notes, their talk addressed "diverse themes of the Bolivian Revolution as well as the Cuban Revolution," but he provides no other detail. Anderson, *Che Guevara*, 705–6.

51. Prado, *Defeat of Che Guevara*, 182; Weiss and Maurer, *Hunting Che*, 230. There are conflicting accounts as to precisely when other captured guerrillas were executed. Willy and another fighter, a Peruvian named Juan Pablo Chang (code name: El Chino) may have been killed at the same time as Guevara or earlier while he was talking with Rodríguez. Anderson, *Che Guevara*, 707.

52. Rodríguez and Weisman, *Shadow Warrior*, 15, 164–65, 169.

53. Rodríguez and Weisman, *Shadow Warrior*, 16; Anderson, *Che Guevara*, 709–10; Taibo, *Guevara, Also Known as Che*, 561.

54. Taibo, *Guevara, Also Known as Che*, 564, 566; Anderson, *Che Guevara*, 712–13; Jon Lee Anderson, "Bones Now Seem to Prove That Che Is Dead," *New York Times*, July 5, 1997; Larry Rohter, "Cuba Buries Che, the Man, but Keeps the Myth Alive," *New York Times*, October 18, 1997.

55. "Medical Report Indicates Delay in Guevara's Death," *New York Times*, October 12, 1967; Juan de Onís, "Guevara's Execution in a Schoolhouse Recounted," *New York Times*, December 4, 1967; Anderson, *Che Guevara*, 712–13; Rostow to Johnson, "Death of 'Che' Guevara," October 11, 1967, Presidential Papers, National Security File: Latin America Country Files, box 8, folder "Bolivia v. 4 (1/66–12/68) 3 of 3," LBJ Presidential Library, accessed via National Security Archive, https://nsarchive.gwu.edu/document/24604-document-25-nsc-memo-rostow-lbj-death-che-guevara-october-11-1967-declassified.

56. James A. Wechsler, "Will There Be Other Guevaras . . . ?," *Boston Globe*, October 14, 1967; Bernard Brennan, "'Che' Peddled Violence," *Hartford Courant*, October 15, 1967; "Che's Legacy," *Washington Post*, October 13, 1967. See also Gall, "Legacy of Che Guevara"; Paul Hoffman, "Che Guevara: Latin-American Political Adventurer," *New York Times*, October 11, 1967; "Guevara: Man and Myth," *New York Times*, October 12, 1967; and "Death of a Professional Rebel," *Los Angeles Times*, October 12, 1967.

57. Lewis H. Diubuid, "Guevara: A True Revolutionary," *Washington Post*, October 11, 1967; Charles P. Howard, "Freedom Fighter Che Guevara Was Martyr to the Poor," *Philadelphia Tribune*, October 28, 1967; Ryan, *Fall of Che Guevara*, 162.

58. C. L. Sulzberger, "Foreign Affairs: The One Who Got Away?," *New York Times*, October 8, 1967.

59. Ryan, *Fall of Che Guevara*, 143–46; Jay Nordlinger, "The Anti-Che," *National Review*, August 7, 2013, www.nationalreview.com/magazine/2013/08/05/anti-che/.

60. Anderson, *Che Guevara*, 720–22; Andreas Freund, "Envoy in Bolivia Is Slain in Paris," *New York Times*, May 12, 1976; Jens Glüsing, "The Curse of Che Guevara," *Spiegel International*, October 8, 2007, www.spiegel.de/international/world/santo-ernesto-the-curse-of-che-guevara-a-510155.html.

61. Debate between the President and Former Vice President Walter F. Mondale in Kansas City, Missouri, October 21, 1984, American Presidency Project, University of California, Santa Barbara, www.presidency.ucsb.edu/node/217277; Remarks at a Reagan-Bush Rally in Glen Ellyn, Illinois, October 16, 1984, American Presidency Project, University of California, Santa Barbara, www.presidency.ucsb.edu/node/260837.

62. Cong. Rec. H1509, (March 22, 2016) (Che Guevara Poster), www.congress.gov/114/crec/2016/03/22/CREC-2016-03-22-pt1-PgH1509.pdf; Captive Nations Week, Cong. Rec., H5923 (July 18, 2017), www.congress.gov/115/crec/2017/07/18/CREC-2017-07-18-pt1-PgH5923.pdf.

63. Anthony Faiola, "Come to Che World!," *Washington Post*, August 18, 1997; Ruta Verde, "The Che Route (Ruta del Che)," accessed December 18, 2024, www.rutaverdebolivia.com/tour/che-guevara-tour/; McCormick and Berger, "Ernesto (Che) Guevara," 356.

64. Juan de Onís, "Guevara Messages Show Castro Led Bolivian Drive," *New York Times*, July 1, 1968.

65. "To His Children," 1965, in Deutschmann, *Che Guevara*, 371.

Chapter Five

1. US House of Representatives Subcommittee on Western Hemisphere Affairs, *Future of the Andean War on Drugs*, 1.

2. M. Bowden, *Killing Pablo*, 110–11; Murphy and Peña, *Manhunters*, 201; James Brooke, "How Escobar, a Rare Jailbird, Lined His Nest," *New York Times*, August 5, 1992; R. Escobar, *Escobar*, 205.

3. US House of Representatives, *Future of the Andean War on Drugs*, 2.

4. "No Deals for Pablo Escobar," *Washington Post*, December 10, 1992.

5. Randall, *Colombia and the United States*.

6. Richard Nixon, "Remarks about an Intensified Program for Drug Abuse Prevention and Control," June 17, 1971, American Presidency Project, University of California, Santa Barbara, www.presidency.ucsb.edu/node/240238.

7. National Security Decision Directive Number 221, April 8, 1986, https://irp.fas.org/offdocs/nsdd/nsdd-221.pdf; Ronald Reagan, "Remarks at a White House Briefing for Service Organization Representatives on Drug Abuse," July 30, 1986, American

Presidency Project, University of California, Santa Barbara, www.presidency.ucsb.edu/node/259325; "The Fight against Drug Trafficking: Setting Priorities," *New York Times*, April 10, 1988.

8. Gootenberg, *Andean Cocaine*, 16–17, 312; US House of Representatives, *Future of the Andean War on Drugs*, 34; M. Bowden, *Killing Pablo*, 64.

9. "ABC News Close-Up: The Cocaine Cartel," August 20, 1983, Paley Center for Media, www.paleycenter.org/collection/item/?q=&p=1&item=T:06630.

10. M. Bowden, *Killing Pablo*, 64; Ruiz, "The Problem of Popularity," 1076; R. Escobar, *Escobar*, 1, 19.

11. Gugliotta and Leen, *Kings of Cocaine*, 24; J. P. Escobar, *Pablo Escobar*, 36, 41–42; R. Escobar, *Escobar*, 140; M. Bowden, *Killing Pablo*, 24.

12. J. P. Escobar, *Pablo Escobar*, 34–35; Gugliotta and Leen, *Kings of Cocaine*, 25; M. Bowden, *Killing Pablo*, 19–20.

13. Gootenberg, *Andean Cocaine*, 297–302.

14. Gugliotta and Leen, *Kings of Cocaine*, 25; M. Bowden, *Killing Pablo*, 24.

15. R. Escobar, *Escobar*, 50, 76; Gugliotta and Leen, *Kings of Cocaine*, 18–19.

16. Cran, "Godfather of Cocaine," *Frontline*; J. P. Escobar, *Pablo Escobar*, 73–93; R. Escobar, *Escobar*, 81; Gugliotta and Leen, *Kings of Cocaine*, 112.

17. M. Bowden, *Killing Pablo*, 29; Thompson, "Pablo Escobar, Drug Baron," 56; Steven Gutkin, "Drug Kingpin a Hero to Thousands," Associated Press, June 11, 1991.

18. R. Escobar, *Escobar*, 17; M. Bowden, *Killing Pablo*, 31, 51; Crandall, *Driven by Drugs*, 28–29; J. P. Escobar, *Pablo Escobar*, 113.

19. R. Escobar, *Escobar*, 87; J. P. Escobar, *Pablo Escobar*, photo insert.

20. M. Bowden, *Killing Pablo*, 34–41.

21. Gugliotta and Leen, *Kings of Cocaine*, 129–37.

22. Gugliotta and Leen, *Kings of Cocaine*, 146–63; Jon Nordheimer, "US Details Workings of Vast Drug Ring," *New York Times*, November 19, 1986; Joseph B. Treaster, "Drug Baron Gives Up in Colombia as End to Extradition Is Approved," *New York Times*, June 20, 1991.

23. Cran, "Godfather of Cocaine," *Frontline*; "Statement of Thomas G. Byrne, Deputy Assistant Administrator for Intelligence, Drug Enforcement Administration, on Nicaraguan Government Participation in Drug Trafficking before the Committee on Foreign Affairs Task Force on International Narcotics Control," US House of Representatives, March 11, 1986, collection Roberts, John G.: Files, folder "JGR/Contra Aid (2 of 5)," box 11, Ronald Reagan Presidential Library and Museum, www.reaganlibrary.gov/public/digitallibrary/smof/counsel/roberts/box-011/40-485-6908381-011-025-2017.pdf; Murphy and Peña, *Manhunters*, 117–18; Robert Moss, "Drugs & Blood: The Cuban Connection," *New York Post*, October 18, 1985; Julia Preston, "Cuba Details Drug Deals," *Washington Post*, June 23, 1989; Gugliotta and Leen, *Kings of Cocaine*, 94; J. P. Escobar, *Pablo Escobar*, 137–40.

24. Gugliotta and Leen, *Kings of Cocaine*, 141–43, 208, 236.

25. "¡NARCOGUERRILLA!," *Semana*, October 23, 1994, www.semana.com/nacion/articulo/narcoguerrilla/23840-3/.

26. Central Intelligence Agency, Directorate of Intelligence, "Terrorism Review," July 26, 1984, p. 12, General CIA Records, Freedom of Information Act Electronic

Reading Room, CIA.gov, www.cia.gov/readingroom/docs/CIA-RDP85-01095R000100090002-4.pdf; Charles Anthony Gillespie Jr., oral history interview by Charles Stuart Kennedy, October 28, 1996, 624, Foreign Affairs Oral History Collection of the Association for Diplomatic Studies and Training, Manuscript Division, Library of Congress, https://loc.gov/item/mfdipbib000420.

27. R. Escobar, *Escobar*, 17; Boykin and Vincent, *Never Surrender*, 226; M. Bowden, *Killing Pablo*, 48.

28. Jack Anderson and Joseph Spear, "When Americans Buy, Colombians Pay," *Washington Post*, December 13, 1988; Robert D. McFadden, "Drug Trafficker Convicted of Blowing Up Jetliner," *New York Times*, December 20, 1994; "For Medellín Assassin, 10 Life Sentences," *New York Times*, May 6, 1995.

29. Peter DeShazo, oral history interview by Charles Stuart Kennedy, August 14, 2013, 29, Association for Diplomatic Studies and Training, Foreign Affairs Oral History Project, https://adst.org/OH%20TOCs/DeShazo-Peter.pdf; Murphy and Peña, *Manhunters*, 117–18; Gillespie, oral history interview, 626; Gugliotta and Leen, *Kings of Cocaine*, 184.

30. "The US Should Help Colombia," *Hartford Courant*, August 22, 1989; "Memorandum of Telephone Conversation," President George H. W. Bush and Virgilio Barco Vargas, president of Colombia, August 21, 1989, Memoranda of Meetings and Telephone Conversations (Memcons/Telcons), George H. W. Bush Presidential Library and Museum, https://bush41library.tamu.edu/files/memcons-telcons/1989-08-21—Barco.pdf.

31. Murphy and Peña, *Manhunters*, 180; M. Bowden, *Killing Pablo*, 70–78.

32. Leslie Wirpsa, "US-Trained Drug Commandoes Set to Hunt Colombian Rebels," *National Catholic Reporter*, January 1994; M. Bowden, *Killing Pablo*, 90; Smith, *Killer Elite*, 166.

33. Clawson and Lee, *Andean Cocaine Industry*, 52; Steven Gutkin, "Escobar's Surrender: Government Victory or Appeasement," Associated Press, June 19, 1991; Jon Lee Anderson, "The Afterlife of Pablo Escobar," *New Yorker*, March 5, 2018.

34. William R. Long, "Drug Lord Evades Capture as He Terrorizes Colombia," *Los Angeles Times*, May 27, 1990; Cecilia Rodríguez, "Colombians Forced to Bargain with the Devil," *Wall Street Journal*, February 1, 1991.

35. Gillespie, oral history interview, 622; Anderson and Spear, "When Americans Buy, Colombians Pay," *Washington Post*, December 13, 1988; "Memorandum of Conversation," President George H. W. Bush and Alfredo Cristiani, president of El Salvador, June 12, 1991, Memoranda of Meetings and Telephone Conversations (Memcons/Telcons), George H. W. Bush Presidential Library and Museum, https://bush41library.tamu.edu/files/memcons-telcons/1991-06-12—Cristiani%20[1].pdf; US House of Representatives Subcommittee on Western Hemisphere Affairs, *Future of the Andean War on Drugs*, 34–35.

36. M. Bowden, *Killing Pablo*, 94–95.

37. M. Bowden, *Killing Pablo*, 101–3.

38. Boykin and Vincent, *Never Surrender*, 221; "The Escobar Deal: How Helpful?," *Los Angeles Times*, June 21, 1991; Murphy and Peña, *Manhunters*, 201; Peter B. Bensinger, "Escobar's Gilded Cage," *New York Times*, June 24, 1991.

39. César Gaviria, "We Didn't Surrender to Escobar," *Washington Post*, June 30, 1991; "The Mote in Colombia's Eye," *Hartford Courant*, July 4, 1991.

40. "Memorandum of Telephone Conversation," President George H. W. Bush and César Gaviria Trujillo, president of Colombia, June 20, 1991, Memoranda of Meetings and Telephone Conversations (Memcons/Telcons), George H. W. Bush Presidential Library and Museum, https://bush41library.tamu.edu/files/memcons-telcons/1991-06-20—Gaviria%20Trujillio.pdf.

41. Douglas Farah and Don Podesta, "Jailed Drug Lord Said to Order Killings," *Washington Post*, July 20, 1992; Murphy and Peña, *Manhunters*, 215–18.

42. Douglas Farah, "The Crackup," *Washington Post*, July 21, 1996; M. Bowden, *Killing Pablo*, 118–33; J. P. Escobar, *Pablo Escobar*, 237; R. Escobar, *Escobar*, 213; "Army Says Fleeing Escobar Likely Dressed as Woman," *Los Angeles Times*, July 27, 1992.

43. Statement by Press Secretary Fitzwater on the Escape of Pablo Escobar, July 23, 1992, American Presidency Project, University of California, Santa Barbara, www.presidency.ucsb.edu/node/267868; "Bring Him In—Dead or Alive," *Hartford Courant*, July 24, 1992.

44. Murphy and Peña, *Manhunters*, 156; M. Bowden, *Killing Pablo*, 145; Boykin and Vincent, *Never Surrender*, 230.

45. Thompson, "Pablo Escobar, Drug Baron," 91; Ruth Marcus, "Kidnapping Outside US Is Upheld," *Washington Post*, June 16, 1992; James Brooke, "US Military Planes Join Search for Escaped Colombia Drug Lord," *New York Times*, July 31, 1992; M. Bowden, *Killing Pablo*, 140, 145.

46. M. Bowden, *Killing Pablo*, 141, 154; Boykin and Vincent, *Never Surrender*, 236; Brooke, "US Military Planes Join Search."

47. Russell Watson and Peter Katel, "Death on the Spot," *Newsweek*, December 13, 1993; M. Bowden, *Killing Pablo*, 145.

48. Murphy and Peña, *Manhunters*, 248; US Defense Intelligence Agency, "Information Paper on 'Los Pepes,'" undated, https://nsarchive2.gwu.edu/NSAEBB/NSAEBB243/19930400-dia.pdf; and memo from the American embassy in Bogota to the Secretary of State, document 1993BOGOTA01634, February 1, 1993, https://nsarchive2.gwu.edu/NSAEBB/NSAEBB243/19930201.pdf, both in "Colombian Paramilitaries and the United States: 'Unraveling the Pepes Tangled Web,'" Electronic Briefing Book No. 243, National Security Archive; James Brooke, "Old Drug Allies Terrorizing Escobar," *New York Times*, March 4, 1993.

49. Murphy and Peña, *Manhunters*, 259; "Unraveling the Pepes Tangled Web," US Embassy Bogotá cable, August 6, 1993, National Security Archive, https://nsarchive2.gwu.edu/NSAEBB/NSAEBB243/19930806.pdf; J. P. Escobar, *Pablo Escobar*, 262.

50. M. Bowden, *Killing Pablo*, 189–90, 231–36.

51. M. Bowden, *Killing Pablo*, 218, 229–31.

52. Murphy and Peña, *Manhunters*, 290–91; M. Bowden, *Killing Pablo*, 239–47.

53. M. Bowden, *Killing Pablo*, 248–49.

54. Boykin and Vincent, *Never Surrender*, 292; M. Bowden, *Killing Pablo*, 253–60; J. P. Escobar, *Pablo Escobar*, 286; R. Escobar, *Escobar*, 250–51.

55. Murphy and Peña, *Manhunters*, 303.

56. William J. Clinton, "Message to President Cesar Gaviria of Colombia on the Death of Pablo Escobar," December 2, 1993, American Presidency Project, University of California, Santa Barbara, www.presidency.ucsb.edu/node/218810; "If Only Killing Escobar Were Enough," *Chicago Tribune*, December 5, 1993; Murphy and Peña, *Manhunters*, 324.

57. James Brooke, "Drug Lord Is Buried," *New York Times*, December 4, 1993; Humberto de la Calle, "Battle to the Death," *Washington Post*, December 24, 1993; Murphy and Peña, *Manhunters*, 324.

58. Pobutsky, *Pablo Escobar and Colombian Narcoculture*, 243.

59. Ruiz, "Problem of Popularity," 1073.

60. Ruiz, "Problem of Popularity," 1079–80; Pobutsky, *Pablo Escobar and Colombian Narcoculture*, 241.

61. Pobutsky, *Pablo Escobar and Colombian Narcoculture*, 41–45; Naef, "'Narco-Heritage,'" 492; Henry Alford, "I Just Got Back from Medellín!," *New York Times*, January 20, 2013.

62. Naef, "'Narco-Heritage,'" 494–95; Anderson, "Afterlife of Pablo Escobar"; Pobutsky, *Pablo Escobar and Colombian Narcoculture*, 66; Rothbart, "Latin America," *Dark Tourist*.

63. Megan Specia, "Pablo Escobar's Home Is Demolished in Colombia, Along with a Painful Legacy," *New York Times*, February 22, 2019; Jeff Campagna, "Pablo Escobar's Private Prison Is Now Run by Monks for Senior Citizens," *Daily Beast*, June 7, 2014, www.thedailybeast.com/pablo-escobars-private-prison-is-now-run-by-monks-for-senior-citizens?ref=scroll; Anderson, "Afterlife of Pablo Escobar"; Jesse Katz, "Pablo Escobar Will Never Die," *GQ*, September 1, 2015.

64. "If Only Killing Escobar Were Enough"; "One Drug Lord Dies," *New York Times*, December 4, 1993; Anderson, "Afterlife of Pablo Escobar."

65. Crandall, *Driven by Drugs*, 1, 7; Farber, *War on Drugs*, 1.

66. George H. W. Bush, "Joint News Conference following the Drug Summit in Cartagena, Colombia," February 15, 1990, American Presidency Project, University of California, Santa Barbara, www.presidency.ucsb.edu/node/264183; George W. Bush, "The President's News Conference with President Álvaro Uribe Vélez of Colombia in Cartagena, Colombia," November 22, 2004, American Presidency Project, University of California, Santa Barbara, www.presidency.ucsb.edu/node/213561.

Chapter Six

1. Fury, *Kill bin Laden*, xx, 74, 75.

2. US Senate Committee on Foreign Relations, *Tora Bora Revisited*, 11; Fury, *Kill bin Laden*, 209.

3. Fury, *Kill bin Laden*, 150, 151, 233–34; Berntsen and Pezzullo, *Jawbreaker*, 274–75.

4. Berntsen and Pezzullo, *Jawbreaker*, 290; Bergen, *Longest War*, 76–77, 81.

5. Fury, *Kill bin Laden*, 277–78; Bergen, *Rise and Fall*, 175–77.

6. Blaine Harden, "For Many, Sorrow Turns to Anger and Talk of Vengeance," *New York Times*, September 14, 2001.

7. "Estimate of US Post-9/11 War Spending," September 1, 2021, https://watson.brown.edu/costsofwar/figures/2021/BudgetaryCosts; and "Human Costs of Post-9/11

Wars," August 2023, https://watson.brown.edu/costsofwar/figures/2021/WarDeath Toll, both from Costs of War Project, Watson Institute for International and Public Affairs, Brown University.

8. Jimmy Carter, "State of the Union Address Delivered before a Joint Session of the Congress," January 23, 1980, American Presidency Project, University of California, Santa Barbara, www.presidency.ucsb.edu/node/249681; Robert Pear, "Arming Afghan Guerillas: A Huge Effort Led by US," *New York Times*, April 18, 1988.

9. Bergen, *Rise and Fall*, 9.

10. Bergen, *Rise and Fall*, 11, 18, 89; Wright, *Looming Tower*, 87.

11. Bergen, *Rise and Fall*, 23–44; Wright, *Looming Tower*, 127–38.

12. Bergen, *Rise and Fall*, 44; Bergen, *Osama bin Laden*, 81; Gerges, *Far Enemy*, 1; Robinson, *Global Jihad*, 5.

13. Bergen, *Longest War*, 26.

14. Coll, *Ghost Wars*, 222.

15. Wright, *Looming Tower*, 238–39.

16. Sageman, *Understanding Terror Networks*, 39; Bergen, *Rise and Fall*, 62–64.

17. Bennett, "Wandering Mujahadin," 2; Wright, *Looming Tower*, 225; Bergen, *Rise and Fall*, 71–72, 107; Clarke, *Against All Enemies*, 141.

18. Rashid, *Taliban*; Dam, *Looking for the Enemy*, 154–56; Alex Strick van Linschoten, "Taliban Public Punishments, 1996–2001," accessed December 18, 2024, www.alexstrick.com/talibanexecutions.

19. Robinson, *Global Jihad*, 72; Lawrence, *Messages to the World*, 24–41.

20. Tenet and Harlow, *At the Center of the Storm*, 113; Clarke, *Against All Enemies*, 149; Coll, *Ghost Wars*, 391.

21. Lawrence, *Messages to the World*, 51, 58–62; "Osama Bin Laden," *Nightline*.

22. Bergen, *Osama bin Laden*, xxix, 181, 214, 215. In another outlet, Miller wrote that bin Laden had a "firm handshake" and spoke in a "raspy" voice, depictions that differ from the account he gave to Bergen. See John Miller, "Greetings America, My Name Is Osama bin Laden," *Esquire*, February 1999.

23. Philip Shenon, "US Pressing Kabul to Oust Saudi Linked to Bombings," *New York Times*, August 19, 1998; "In Self-Defense," *Washington Post*, August 21, 1998; Edward G. Shirley, "The Etiquette of Killing bin Laden," *Wall Street Journal*, August 27, 1998.

24. William Claiborne, "Targets Described as Primitive Camps," *Washington Post*, August 22, 1998.

25. Thomas L. Friedman, "Angry, Wired and Deadly," *New York Times*, August 22, 1998; Jim Hoagland, "One Raid in the Long War," *Washington Post*, August 23, 1998; "'Wag the Dog' Back in Spotlight," CNN.com, August 21, 1998, https://edition.cnn.com/ALLPOLITICS/1998/08/21/wag.the.dog/.

26. Clinton, *My Life*, 804; Clarke, *Against All Enemies*, 199–200; Coll, *Ghost Wars*, 446–49; Wright, *Looming Tower*, 329–30.

27. Wright, *Looming Tower*, 360–61.

28. Richard A. Clarke to Condoleezza Rice, January 25, 2001, in "Bush Administration's First Memo on al-Qaeda Declassified," Electronic Briefing Book No. 147, National Security Archive, https://nsarchive2.gwu.edu/NSAEBB/NSAEBB147/clarke%20memo.pdf; Rice, *No Higher Honor*, 65.

29. National Commission, *9/11 Commission Report*, 259; CIA, "Bin Laden Determined to Strike in US," August 6, 2001, in "The President's Daily Brief," April 12, 2004, Electronic Briefing Book No. 116, National Security Archive, https://nsarchive2.gwu.edu/NSAEBB/NSAEBB116/pdb8-6-2001.pdf; Rice, *No Higher Honor*, xvi; George W. Bush, "Remarks and an Exchange with Reporters at Fort Hood, Texas," April 11, 2004, American Presidency Project, University of California, Santa Barbara, www.presidency.ucsb.edu/node/213103.

30. Clarke, *Against All Enemies*, 2; Lawrence, *Messages to the World*, 104, 107, 119, 242.

31. Lahoud, *Bin Laden Papers*, 15, 26; Bergen, *Rise and Fall*, 159–61; Gerges, *Far Enemy*, 186–92, 284–86.

32. Charles Krauthammer, "To War, Not to Court," *Washington Post*, September 12, 2001; Thomas L. Friedman, "World War III," *New York Times*, September 13, 2001.

33. George W. Bush, "Address before a Joint Session of the Congress on the United States Response to the Terrorist Attacks of September 11," September 20, 2001, American Presidency Project, University of California, Santa Barbara, www.presidency.ucsb.edu/node/213749; Bush, *Decision Points*, 154.

34. Bergen, *Rise and Fall*, 163–64; Gopal, *No Good Men*, 13.

35. Schroen, *First In*, 34, 35; Coll, *Ghost Wars*, 271.

36. George W. Bush, "Remarks Prior to Discussions with Muslim Community Leaders and an Exchange with Reporters," September 26, 2001, American Presidency Project, University of California, Santa Barbara, www.presidency.ucsb.edu/node/214419.

37. George W. Bush, "The President's News Conference," October 11, 2001, American Presidency Project, University of California, Santa Barbara, www.presidency.ucsb.edu/node/216279; George W. Bush, "Remarks on Lighting the Hanukkah Menorah and an Exchange with Reporters," December 10, 2001, American Presidency Project, University of California, Santa Barbara, www.presidency.ucsb.edu/node/212900; David Ignatius, "The Psyche of a Bin Laden," *Washington Post*, October 28, 2001.

38. Bush, *Decision Points*, 128, 140; George W. Bush, "Remarks to Employees in the Pentagon and an Exchange with Reporters in Arlington, Virginia," September 17, 2001, American Presidency Project, University of California, Santa Barbara, www.presidency.ucsb.edu/node/211537; Woodward, *Bush at War*, 101; George W. Bush, "Remarks on Arrival at the White House and an Exchange with Reporters," September 16, 2001, American Presidency Project, University of California, Santa Barbara, www.presidency.ucsb.edu/node/213051; Bernard Lewis, "Jihad vs. Crusade," *Wall Street Journal*, September 27, 2001; "Press Briefing by Ari Fleischer," September 18, 2001, American Presidency Project, University of California, Santa Barbara, www.presidency.ucsb.edu/node/271697.

39. Blaine Harden, "For Many, Sorrow Turns to Anger and Talk of Vengeance," *New York Times*, September 14, 2001; John Tierney, "Fantasies of Vengeance, Fed by Fury," *New York Times*, September 18, 2001.

40. Kevin Merida, "Osama Bin Laden, Capitalist Tool," *Washington Post*, October 6, 2001; Stacy Wong, "Flushed with Contempt," *Hartford Courant*, October 18, 2001; "Osama bin Laden Has Farty Pants," *South Park*.

41. George W. Bush, "The President's News Conference," March 13, 2002, American Presidency Project, University of California, Santa Barbara, www.presidency.ucsb

.edu/node/212036; Maureen Dowd, "Is Osama Pea-Green?," *New York Times*, November 20, 2002.

42. Bergen, *Manhunt*, 53.

43. "The Real Agenda," *New York Times*, July 16, 2006.

44. Obama, *A Promised Land*, 677; Bergen, *Manhunt*, 92.

45. Bergen, *Rise and Fall*, 196–98; McRaven, *Sea Stories*, 275–76; Owen and Maurer, *No Easy Day*, 172.

46. Bergen, *Rise and Fall*, xx, 209, 210; Lahoud, *Bin Laden Papers*, 205; Bergen, *Manhunt*, 13.

47. Lahoud, *Bin Laden Papers*, 130–40, 261; Bergen, *Rise and Fall*, 217.

48. Obama, *Promised Land*, 679–83; McRaven, *Sea Stories*, 280–96.

49. Owen and Maurer, *No Easy Day*, 218–33; O'Neill, *Operator*, 308–9.

50. McRaven, *Sea Stories*, 320; O'Neill, *Operator*, 309–10.

51. O'Neill, *Operator*, 310.

52. Owen and Maurer, *No Easy Day*, 236.

53. O'Neill, *Operator*, 312; Bergen, *Rise and Fall*, 225.

54. O'Neill, *Operator*, 316, 319; Soufan, *Anatomy of Terror*, 39; Owen and Maurer, *No Easy Day*, 249.

55. "No Escape This Time," *Hartford Courant*, May 3, 2011; Alexandra Petri, "Osama's Dead—Party On!," *Washington Post*, May 7, 2011; Jonathan Haidt, "Why We Celebrate a Killing," *New York Times*, May 8, 2011.

56. Barack Obama, "Remarks on the Death of Al Qaeda Terrorist Organization Leader Usama bin Laden," May 1, 2011, American Presidency Project, University of California, Santa Barbara, www.presidency.ucsb.edu/node/289988; Obama, "Obama on Bin Laden"; Maureen Dowd, "Killing Evil Doesn't Make Us Evil," *New York Times*, May 8, 2011; Charles Krauthammer, "Evil Does Not Die of Natural Causes," *Washington Post*, May 6, 2011.

57. Rhodes, *World as It Is*, 140.

58. "Human and Budgetary Costs to Date of the US War in Afghanistan, 2001–2022," August 2021, https://watson.brown.edu/costsofwar/figures/2021/human-and-budgetary-costs-date-us-war-afghanistan-2001-2022; and "Blood and Treasure: United States Budgetary Costs and Human Costs of 20 Years of War in Iraq and Syria, 2003–2023," March 15, 2023, https://watson.brown.edu/costsofwar/papers/2023/IraqSyria20, both from Costs of War Project, Watson Institute for International and Public Affairs, Brown University.

59. Stephanie Savell and 5W Infographics, "This Map Shows Where in the World the US Military Is Combatting Terrorism," *Smithsonian Magazine*, January 2019, www.smithsonianmag.com/history/map-shows-places-world-where-us-military-operates-180970997/; Bob Woodward, "CIA Told to Do 'Whatever Necessary' to Kill bin Laden," *Washington Post*, October 21, 2001.

Conclusion

1. Eric Schmitt, "Two Decades after 9/11, Militants Have Only Multiplied," *New York Times*, November 20, 2018.

2. Rukmini Callimachi and Andrew Rossback, "Extreme Brutality and Detailed Record-Keeping," *New York Times*, April 4, 2018; McCants, *ISIS Apocalypse*, 93.

3. McCants, *ISIS Apocalypse*, 74.

4. Warrick, *Black Flags*, 255–57; McCants, *ISIS Apocalypse*, 75.

5. Seth G. Jones, James Dobbins, Daniel Byman, Christopher S. Chivvis, Ben Connable, Jeffrey Martini, Eric Robertson, and Nathan Chandler, "Rolling Back the Islamic State," RAND Corporation, April 20, 2017, www.rand.org/pubs/research_reports/RR1912.html; Patricia Zengerle and Jonathan Landay, "CIA Director Says Islamic State Still Serious Threat," Reuters, June 15, 2016, www.reuters.com/article/us-mideast-crisis-fighters/cia-director-says-islamic-state-still-serious-threat-idUSKCN0Z21ST.

6. Peter Baker, "Obama, with Reluctance, Returns to Action in Iraq," *New York Times*, August 7, 2014; "The Fundamental Horror of ISIS," *New York Times*, October 2, 2014.

7. Karen DeYoung, "Reward for Information on ISIS Leader Increased to $25 Million," *Washington Post*, December 16, 2016; Rukmini Callimachi, "ISIS Releases a Recording It Says Was Made by Its Leader," *New York Times*, May 14, 2015; Joshua Jamerson, "ISIS Leader Pulls from bin Laden Playbook in New Message," *Wall Street Journal*, September 29, 2017.

8. Niall McCarthy, "The Rise and Fall of ISIS," Statista, December 10, 2019, www.statista.com/chart/20255/the-rise-and-fall-of-isis/; Rukmini Callimachi and Falih Hassan, "Abu Bakr al-Baghdadi, ISIS Leader Known for His Brutality, Is Dead at 48," *New York Times*, October 27, 2019; Rukmini Callimachi, "ISIS Held Kayla Mueller, US Aid Worker, as Sex Slave before Fatal Airstrike," *New York Times*, August 14, 2015; Adam Goldman and Rukmini Callimachi, "ISIS Leader al-Baghdadi May Have Had US Hostage Executed, Witness Says," *New York Times*, November 12, 2019.

9. Donald J. Trump, "Statement on the Death of Islamic State of Iraq and Syria (ISIS) Terrorist Organization Leader Abu Bakr al-Baghdadi," October 27, 2019, American Presidency Project, University of California, Santa Barbara, www.presidency.ucsb.edu/node/334993.

10. Peter Baker, Eric Schmitt, and Helene Cooper, "ISIS Leader al-Baghdadi Is Dead, Trump Says," *New York Times*, October 27, 2019; Ben Hubbard and Eric Schmitt, "As Kurds Tracked ISIS Leader, US Withdrawal Threw Raid into Turmoil," *New York Times*, October 28, 2019; Julian E. Barnes and Eric Schmitt, "Intelligence from al-Baghdadi Raid, including 2 Prisoners, Could Reveal Trove of ISIS Clues," *New York Times*, October 28, 2019.

11. Eric Schmitt, Helene Cooper, and Julian E. Barnes, "Trump's Syria Troop Withdrawal Complicated Plans for al-Baghdadi Raid," *New York Times*, October 27, 2019; Michael Crowley, "How Commandos Could Quickly Confirm They Got Their Target," *New York Times*, October 27, 2019; Jim Garamone, US Department of Defense, "Central Command Chief Gives Details on Baghdadi Raid," October 30, 2019, www.defense.gov/News/News-Stories/Article/Article/2003960/central-command-chief-gives-details-on-baghdadi-raid/.

12. Donald J. Trump, "Remarks on the Death of Islamic State of Iraq and Syria (ISIS) Terrorist Organization Leader Abu Bakr al-Baghdadi and an Exchange with Reporters," October 27, 2019, American Presidency Project, University of California, Santa

Barbara, www.presidency.ucsb.edu/node/334992; Peter Baker and Eric Schmitt, "The 'Whimpering' Terrorist Only Trump Seems to Have Heard," *New York Times*, November 1, 2019.

13. Donald J. Trump, Tweets of October 9, 2019, American Presidency Project, University of California, Santa Barbara, www.presidency.ucsb.edu/node/341191.

14. Trump, "Remarks on the Death," October 27, 2019; Donald J. Trump, "Remarks on Signing an Executive Order on the Commission on Law Enforcement and the Administration of Justice at the International Association of Chiefs of Police Annual Conference and Exposition in Chicago, Illinois," October 28, 2019, American Presidency Project, University of California, Santa Barbara, www.presidency.ucsb.edu/node/334995.

15. George W. Bush, "The President's News Conference," April 13, 2004, American Presidency Project, University of California, Santa Barbara, www.presidency.ucsb.edu/node/211840.

Bibliography

Primary Sources

Archives and Manuscript Collections

Library of Congress, Washington, DC
   Manuscript Division
      David Foote Sellers Papers
      Robert Patterson Hughes Papers
      Rounsevelle Wildman and Edwin Wildman Papers
      Theodore Roosevelt Papers
National Archives, College Park, MD
   Record Group 127 — Records of the US Marine Corps
   Record Group 350 — Records of the Bureau of Insular Affairs

Newspapers and Periodicals

Albuquerque Journal	Hartford Herald	New York Tribune
Associated Press	Kalamazoo Gazette	Olympia Daily Recorder
Atlanta Journal Constitution	Lippincott's Monthly	Oregonian
Atlantic Monthly	Magazine	Outlook
Baltimore Sun	Los Angeles Sentinel	Philadelphia Inquirer
Boston Globe	Los Angeles Times	Philadelphia Tribune
Chicago Tribune	Miami New Times	Pittsburgh Courier
Daily Beast	Minneapolis Journal	Semana
Economist	Nation	Smithsonian Magazine
El Paso Herald	New Mexico Architecture	Springfield Daily
El Paso Times	New Statesman	Republican
Esquire	Newsweek	Tacoma Times
Fort-Worth Star Telegram	New Yorker	Time
GQ	New York Post	Wall Street Journal
Guardian	New York Times	Washington Post
Hartford Courant	New York Times Magazine	Wilkes-Barre Times Leader

Published Reports and Documentary Collections

Bennett, Gina. "The Wandering Mujahadin: Armed and Dangerous." US Department of State, Bureau of Intelligence and Research, Weekend Edition, August 21–22, 1993. https://archive.blogs.harvard.edu/mesh/files/2008/03/wandering_mujahidin.pdf.

Farrar, Victor J., and Richard P. McCornack, eds. *Foreign Relations of the United States: Diplomatic Papers, 1934*. Vol. 5, *The American Republics*. Washington, DC: Government Printing Office, 1952.
Fuller, Joseph V., ed. *Papers Relating to the Foreign Relations of the United States, 1919*. Vol. 2. Washington, DC: Government Printing Office, 1934.
———, ed. *Papers Relating to the Foreign Relations of the United States, 1927*. Vol. 3. Washington, DC: Government Printing Office, 1942.
———, ed. *Papers Relating to the Foreign Relations of the United States, 1928*. Vol. 3. Washington, DC: Government Printing Office, 1943.
———, ed. *Papers Relating to the Foreign Relations of the United States, 1929*. Vol. 3. Washington, DC: Government Printing Office, 1946.
———. *Papers Relating to the Foreign Relations of the United States, 1931*. Vol. 2. Washington, DC: Government Printing Office, 1944.
———, ed. *Papers Relating to the Foreign Relations of the United States, with the Address of the President to Congress December 2, 1913*. Washington, DC: Government Printing Office, 1920.
———, ed. *Papers Relating to the Foreign Relations of the United States, with the Address of the President to Congress December 7, 1915*. Washington, DC: Government Printing Office, 1924.
———, ed. *Papers Relating to the Foreign Relations of the United States, with the Address of the President to Congress December 5, 1916*. Washington, DC: Government Printing Office, 1925.
Gatewood, Willard, ed. *"Smoked Yankees" and the Struggle for Empire: Letters from Negro Soldiers, 1898-1902*. Urbana: University of Illinois Press, 1971.
Glennon, John P., ed. *Foreign Relations of the United States, 1958-1960*. Vol. 6, *Cuba*. Washington, DC: Government Printing Office, 1991.
Lawrence, Bruce, ed. *Messages to the World: The Statements of Osama bin Laden*. London: Verso, 2005.
Link, Arthur S., ed. *The Papers of Woodrow Wilson*. Vol. 29, *1913-1914*. Princeton, NJ: Princeton University Press, 1979.
———, ed. *The Papers of Woodrow Wilson*. Vol. 30, *May-September 1914*. Princeton, NJ: Princeton University Press, 1979.
———, ed. *The Papers of Woodrow Wilson*. Vol. 36, *January-May 1916*. Princeton, NJ: Princeton University Press, 1981.
May, Ernest R., ed. *The 9/11 Commission Report with Related Documents*. Boston: Bedford/St. Martin's, 2007.
National Commission on Terrorist Attacks upon the United States. *The 9/11 Commission Report: Final Report of the National Commission on Terrorist Attacks upon the United States*. Washington, DC: Government Printing Office, 2004. www.9-11commission.gov/report/911Report.pdf.
Ramírez, Sergio, and Robert Edgar Conrad, eds. *Sandino: The Testimony of a Nicaraguan Patriot, 1921-1934*. Princeton, NJ: Princeton University Press, 1990.
US Department of War. *Annual Reports of the War Department for the Fiscal Year Ended June 30, 1902*. Vol. 9, *Report of the Lieutenant-General Commanding the Army and Department Commanders*. Washington, DC: Government Printing Office, 1902.

———. *War Department: Annual Reports, 1917.* Vol. 1. Washington, DC: Government Printing Office, 1918.
US House of Representatives. *Future of the Andean War on Drugs after the Escape of Pablo Escobar: Joint Hearing before the Subcommittee on Western Hemisphere Affairs and Task Force on International Narcotics Control of the Committee on Foreign Affairs.* 102nd Cong., 2nd sess., July 29, 1992. Washington, DC: Government Printing Office, 1993.
US Senate. *Affairs in the Philippine Islands. Hearing Before the Committee on the Philippines of the United States Senate.* 57th Cong., 1st sess., 1902. S. Doc 331 (3 parts). Washington, DC: Government Printing Office, 1902.
———. *Tora Bora Revisited: How We Failed to Get bin Laden and Why It Matters Today.* 111th Cong., 1st sess., November 30, 2009. Washington, DC: Government Printing Office, 2009.

Speeches, Addresses, and Memoirs

Aguinaldo, Emilio. *True Version of the Philippine Revolution.* Tarlak, Philippines, September 1899.
Aguinaldo, Emilio, with Vicente Albano Pacis. *A Second Look at America.* New York: Robert Speller & Sons, 1957.
Berntsen, Gary, and Ralph Pezzullo. *Jawbreaker: The Attack on bin Laden and Al-Qaeda: A Personal Account by the CIA's Key Field Commander.* New York: Crown, 2005.
Boykin, William G., and Lynn Vincent. *Never Surrender: A Soldier's Journey to the Crossroads of Faith and Freedom.* New York: FaithWords, 2011.
Brennan, John O. *Undaunted: My Fight against America's Enemies at Home and Abroad.* New York: Celadon, 2020.
Bush, George W. *Decision Points.* New York: Crown, 2010.
Clarke, Richard A. *Against All Enemies: Inside America's War on Terror.* New York: Free Press, 2004.
Clinton, Bill. *My Life.* New York: Vintage, 2005.
Deutschmann, David, ed. *Che: A Memoir by Fidel Castro.* 2nd ed. New York: Ocean Press, 2006.
———, ed. *Che Guevara and the Cuban Revolution: Writing and Speeches of Ernesto Che Guevara.* Sydney: Pathfinder, 1987.
Escobar, Juan Pablo. *Pablo Escobar: My Father.* Translated by Andrea Rosenberg. New York: St. Martin's, 2016.
Escobar, Roberto. *Escobar: The Inside Story of Pablo Escobar, the World's Most Powerful Criminal.* London: Hodder, 2010.
Fury, Dalton. *Kill Bin Laden: A Delta Force Commander's Account of the Hunt for the World's Most Wanted Man.* New York: St. Martin's Griffin, 2008.
Guevara, Ernesto. *Congo Diary: Episodes of the Revolutionary War in the Congo.* Melbourne: Ocean Press, 2011.
Hawes, James M., and Mary Ann Koenig. *Cold War Navy Seal: My Story of Che Guevara, War in the Congo, and the Communist Threat in Africa.* New York: Skyhorse, 2018.
James, Daniel, ed. *The Complete Bolivian Diaries of Che Guevara and Other Captured Documents.* New York: Stein and Day, 1968.

McRaven, William H. *Sea Stories: My Life in Special Operations*. New York: Grand Central Publishing, 2019.
Murphy, Steve, and Javier F. Peña. *Manhunters: How We Took Down Pablo Escobar*. New York: St. Martin's, 2019.
Obama, Barack. *A Promised Land*. New York: Crown, 2020.
O'Neill, Robert. *The Operator: Firing the Shots That Killed Osama bin Laden and My Years as a SEAL Team Warrior*. New York: Scribner, 2017.
Owen, Mark, and Kevin Maurer. *No Easy Day: The Firsthand Account of the Mission That Killed Osama bin Laden*. New York: Dutton, 2016.
Pershing, John J. *My Life before the World War, 1860-1917: A Memoir*. Edited by John T. Greenwood. Lexington: University Press of Kentucky, 2013.
Prado Salmón, Gary. *The Defeat of Che Guevara: Military Response to Guerrilla Challenge in Bolivia*. Translated by John Deredita. Westport, CT: Praeger, 1990.
Rhodes, Ben. *The World as It Is: A Memoir of the Obama White House*. New York: Random House, 2018.
Rice, Condoleezza. *No Higher Honor: A Memoir of My Years in Washington*. New York: Crown, 2011.
Rodríguez, Félix, and John Weisman. *Shadow Warrior: The CIA Hero of a Hundred Unknown Battles*. New York: Simon & Schuster, 1989.
Schroen, Gary C. *First In: An Insider's Account of How the CIA Spearheaded the War on Terror in Afghanistan*. New York: Presidio, 2005.
Sheer, Robert, ed. *The Diary of Che Guevara: Bolivia, November 7, 1966-October 7, 1967*. New York: Bantam, 1968.
Stimson, Henry L. *Henry L. Stimson's American Policy in Nicaragua: The Lasting Legacy*. New York: Markus Wiener, 1991.
Tenet, George, and Bill Harlow. *At the Center of the Storm: My Years at the CIA*. New York: HarperCollins, 2007.
Tumulty, Joseph P. *Woodrow Wilson as I Know Him*. Garden City, NY: Doubleday, Page, 1921.

Secondary Sources

Books

Anderson, Jon Lee. *Che Guevara: A Revolutionary Life*. Rev. ed. New York: Grove, 2010.
Arnold, James R. *The Moro War: How America Battled a Muslim Insurgency in the Philippine Jungle, 1902-1913*. New York: Bloomsbury, 2011.
Bamford, James. *Body of Secrets: Anatomy of the Ultra-Secret National Security Agency*. New York: Anchor, 2002.
Bederman, Gail. *Manliness and Civilization: A Cultural History of Gender and Race in the United States, 1880-1917*. Chicago: University of Chicago Press, 1995.
Bell, J. Boyer. *The Myth of the Guerrilla: Revolutionary Theory and Malpractice*. New York: Alfred A. Knopf, 1971.
Bergen, Peter. *The Longest War: The Enduring Conflict between America and al-Qaeda*. New York: Free Press, 2011.

———. *Manhunt: The Ten-Year Search for bin Laden from 9/11 to Abbottabad.* New York: Crown, 2012.
———. *The Osama bin Laden I Know: An Oral History of al Qaeda's Leader.* New York: Free Press, 2006.
———. *The Rise and Fall of Osama bin Laden.* New York: Simon & Schuster, 2021.
Boot, Max. *The Savage Wars of Peace: Small Wars and the Rise of American Power.* New York: Basic Books, 2003.
Bowden, Brett. *The Empire of Civilization: The Evolution of an Imperial Idea.* Chicago: University of Chicago Press, 2009.
Bowden, Mark. *The Finish: The Killing of Osama bin Laden.* New York: Atlantic Monthly Press, 2012.
———. *Killing Pablo: The Hunt for the World's Greatest Outlaw.* New York: Penguin, 2001.
Braddy, Haldeen. *The Paradox of Pancho Villa.* El Paso: Texas Western College Press, 1978.
Brody, David. *Visualizing American Empire: Orientalism and Imperialism in the Philippines.* Chicago: University of Chicago Press, 2010.
Brunk, Samuel, and Ben Fallaw, eds. *Heroes and Hero Cults in Latin America.* Austin: University of Texas Press, 2006.
Callwell, C. E. *Small Wars: Their Principles and Practice.* Lincoln University of Nebraska Press, 1996.
Carr, Matthew. *The Infernal Machine: A History of Terrorism.* New York: New Press, 2006.
Castañeda, Jorge G. *Compañero: The Life and Death of Che Guevara.* New York: Knopf, 1998.
Chailand, Gerard, and Arnaud Blin. *The History of Terrorism: From Antiquity to al Qaeda.* Berkeley: University of California Press, 2007.
Clawson, Patrick L., and Rensselear W. Lee III. *The Andean Cocaine Industry.* New York: St. Martin's, 1998.
Coll, Steve. *Ghost Wars: The Secret History of the CIA, Afghanistan, and bin Laden from the Soviet Invasion to September 10, 2001.* New York: Penguin, 2005.
Crandall, Russell. *America's Dirty Wars: Irregular Warfare from 1776 to the War on Terror.* New York: Cambridge University Press, 2014.
———. *Driven by Drugs: U.S. Policy toward Colombia.* Boulder, CO: Lynne Reinner, 2002.
Cummins, Lejeune. *Quijote on a Burro: Sandino and the Marines, a Study in the Formulation of Foreign Policy.* Mexico City: La Impresora Azeteca, 1958.
Dam, Bette. *Looking for the Enemy: Mullah Omar and the Unknown Taliban.* Noida, India: HarperCollins, 2021.
Edgerton, Ronald K. *American Datu: John J. Pershing and Counterinsurgency Warfare in the Muslim Philippines, 1899–1913.* Lexington: University Press of Kentucky, 2020.
Esty, Thomas Bruce, ed. *Views of the American Press on the Philippines.* New York: Esty & Esty, 1899.
Farber, David, ed. *The War on Drugs: A History.* New York: New York University Press, 2022.

Fellman, Michael. *In the Name of God and Country: Reconsidering Terrorism in American History*. New Haven, CT: Yale University Press, 2010.
Gatewood, Willard B. *Black Americans and the White Man's Burden, 1898–1903*. Urbana: University of Illinois Press, 1975.
Gerges, Fawaz A. *The Far Enemy: Why Jihad Went Global*. New ed. New York: Cambridge University Press, 2009.
———. *The Rise and Fall of al-Qaeda*. New York: Oxford University Press, 2011.
Gobat, Michel. *Confronting the American Dream: Nicaragua under U.S. Imperial Rule*. Durham, NC: Duke University Press, 2005.
Gootenberg, Paul. *Andean Cocaine: The Making of a Global Drug*. Chapel Hill: University of North Carolina Press, 1994.
Gopal, Anand. *No Good Men among the Living: America, the Taliban, and the War through Afghan Eyes*. New York: Picador, 2014.
Grandin, Greg. *Empire's Workshop: Latin America, the United States, and the Rise of the New Imperialism*. New York: Henry Holt, 2006.
Guevara, Ernesto. *Guerrilla Warfare*. New York: Praeger, 1961.
Gugliotta, Guy, and Jeff Leen. *Kings of Cocaine: Inside the Medellin Cartel*. New York: Simon & Schuster, 1989.
Haley, P. Edward. *Revolution and Intervention: The Diplomacy of Taft and Wilson with Mexico, 1910–1917*. Cambridge, MA: MIT Press, 1970.
Harris, Richard. *The Death of a Revolutionary: Che Guevara's Last Mission*. New York: Collier, 1970.
Harris, Susan K. *God's Arbiters: Americans and the Philippines, 1898–1902*. New York: Oxford University Press, 2011.
Hart, John Mason. *Empire and Revolution: The Americans in Mexico since the Civil War*. Berkeley: University of California Press, 2002.
Hawkins, Michael. *Making Moros: Imperial Historicism and American Military Rule in the Philippines' Muslim South*. Dekalb: Northern Illinois University Press, 2013.
Hobsbawm, Eric. *Bandits*. New York: New Press, 2000.
Hoffman, Bruce. *Inside Terrorism*. 3rd ed. New York: Columbia University Press, 2017.
Hoganson, Kristin L. *Fighting for American Manhood: How Gender Politics Provoked the Spanish-American and Philippine-American Wars*. New Haven, CT: Yale University Press, 1998.
Hunt, Michael H. *Ideology and U.S. Foreign Policy*. New Haven, CT: Yale University Press, 1997.
Immerwahr, Daniel. *How to Hide an Empire: A History of the Greater United States*. New York: Farrar, Straus and Giroux, 2019.
Jacobson, Matthew Frye. *Barbarian Virtues: The United States Encounters Foreign Peoples at Home and Abroad, 1876–1917*. New York: Hill and Wang, 2000.
James, Daniel. *Che Guevara: A Biography*. New York: Stein and Day, 1969.
Joes, Anthony James. *Guerrilla Warfare: A Historical, Biographical, and Bibliographical Sourcebook*. Westport: Greenwood, 1996.
Jones, Gregg. *Honor in the Dust: Theodore Roosevelt, War in the Philippines, and the Rise and Fall of America's Imperial Dream*. New York: New American Library, 2012.

Joseph, Gilbert M., Catherine C. LeGrand, and Ricardo D. Salvatore, eds. *Close Encounters of Empire: Writing the Cultural History of U.S.-Latin American Relations.* Durham, NC: Duke University Press, 1998.

Kamman, William. *A Search for Stability: United States Diplomacy toward Nicaragua, 1925-1933.* Notre Dame, IN: University of Notre Dame Press, 1968.

Katz, Friedrich. *The Life and Times of Pancho Villa.* Stanford, CA: Stanford University Press, 1998.

Keesing, Felix Maxwell, and Marie Martin Keesing. *Taming Philippine Headhunters: A Study of Government and of Cultural Change in Northern Luzon.* Stanford, CA: Stanford University Press, 1934.

Knott, Stephen F. *Secret and Sanctioned: Covert Operations and the American Presidency.* New York: Oxford University Press, 1996.

Kramer, Paul. *The Blood of Government: Race, Empire, the United States, and the Philippines.* Chapel Hill: University of North Carolina Press, 2006.

LaFeber, Walter. *The New Empire: An Interpretation of American Expansion, 1860-1898.* 35th anniversary ed. Ithaca, NY Cornell University Press, 1998.

Lahoud, Nelly. *The Bin Laden Papers: How the Abbottabad Raid Revealed the Truth about Al-Qaeda, Its Leader and His Family.* New Haven, CT: Yale University Press, 2022.

Langley, Lester. *The Banana Wars: United States Intervention in the Caribbean, 1898-1934.* Lanham: Rowman & Littlefield, 2002.

Laqueur, Walter. *A History of Terrorism.* New York: Routledge, 2017.

Law, Randall D. *Terrorism: A History.* 2nd ed. Malden, MA: Polity, 2016.

Law, Randall D., ed. *The Routledge History of Terrorism.* New York: Routledge, 2015.

Lee, Wayne E. *Barbarians and Brothers: Anglo-American Warfare, 1500-1865.* New York: Oxford University Press, 2011.

Link, Arthur S. *Wilson: Confusions and Crises, 1915-1916.* Princeton, NJ: Princeton University Press, 1964.

Linn, Brian McAllister. *The Philippine War: 1899-1902.* Lawrence: University Press of Kansas, 2000.

———. *The U.S. Army and Counterinsurgency in the Philippine War, 1899-1902.* Chapel Hill: University of North Carolina Press, 1989.

Macaulay, Neill. *The Sandino Affair.* Chicago: Quadrangle, 1967.

Mackay, Joseph. *The Counterinsurgent Imagination: A New Intellectual History.* New York: Cambridge University Press, 2023.

McCants, William. *The ISIS Apocalypse: The History, Strategy, and Doomsday Vision of the Islamic State.* New York: St. Martin's, 2015.

McPherson, Alan. *The Invaded: How Latin Americans and Their Allies Fought and Ended U.S. Occupations.* New York: Oxford University Press, 2014.

Menjívar, Cecilia, and Néstor Rodríguez, eds. *When States Kill: Latin America, the U.S., and Technologies of Terror.* Austin: University of Texas Press, 2005.

Morgan, Brandon. *Raid and Reconciliation: Pancho Villa, Modernization, and Violence in the U.S.-Mexico Borderlands.* Linccln: University of Nebraska Press, 2024.

Naftali, Timothy. *Blind Spot: The Secret History of American Counterterrorism.* New York: Basic Books, 2005.

Navarro-Genie, Marco A. *Augusto "Cesar" Sandino: Messiah of Light and Truth.* Syracuse: Syracuse University Press, 2002.

Pobutsky, Aldona Bialowas. *Pablo Escobar and Colombian Narcoculture.* Gainesville: University Press of Florida, 2020.

Prieto, Julie Irene. *The Mexican Expedition, 1916–1917.* Washington, DC: Center of Military History, 2016.

Randall, Stephen J. *Colombia and the United States: Hegemony and Interdependence.* Athens: University of Georgia Press, 1992.

Rashid, Ahmed. *Taliban: Militant Islam, Oil, and Fundamentalism in Central Asia.* New Haven, CT: Yale University Press, 2000.

Robinson, Glenn E. *Global Jihad: A Brief History.* Stanford, CA: Stanford University Press, 2020.

Rosenberg, Emily S. *Spreading the American Dream: American Economic and Cultural Expansion, 1890–1945.* New York: Hill and Wang, 1982.

Runkle, Benjamin. *Wanted Dead or Alive: Manhunts from Geronimo to Bin Laden.* New York: St. Martin's, 2011.

Ryan, Henry Butterfield. *The Fall of Che Guevara: A Story of Soldiers, Spies, and Diplomats.* New York: Oxford University Press, 1998.

Sageman, Marc. *Understanding Terror Networks.* Philadelphia: University of Pennsylvania Press, 2004.

Sauvage, Léo. *Che Guevara: The Failure of a Revolutionary.* Translated by Raoul Frémont. Englewood Cliffs, NJ: Prentice-Hall, 1973.

Scheuer, Michael. *Osama bin Laden.* New York: Oxford University Press, 2011.

Schmitt, Eric, and Thom Shanker. *Counterstrike: The Untold Story of America's Secret Campaign against Al Qaeda.* New York: Times Books, 2011.

Sheesley, Joel C. *Sandino in the Streets.* Translated and edited by Wayne G. Bragg. Bloomington: Indiana University Press, 1991.

Smith, Michael. *Killer Elite: The Inside Story of America's Most Secret Special Operations Team.* New York: St. Martin's, 2007.

Soufan, Ali. *Anatomy of Terror: From the Death of bin Laden to the Rise of the Islamic State.* New York: Norton, 2017.

Stampnitzky, Lisa. *Disciplining Terror: How Experts Invented "Terrorism."* New York: Cambridge University Press, 2013.

Storey, Moorfield, and Julian Codman. *Secretary Root's Record: "Marked Severities" in Philippine Warfare: An Analysis of the Law and Facts Bearing on the Action and Utterances of President Roosevelt and Secretary Root.* Boston: G. H. Ellis, 1902.

Taibo, Paco Ignacio. *Guevara, Also Known as Che.* Translated by Martin Michael Roberts. New York: St. Martin's, 1997.

Thomas, Robert S., and Inez V. Allen. *The Mexican Punitive Expedition under Brigadier General John J. Pershing, United States Army, 1916–1917.* Washington, DC: Department of the Army, Office of the Chief of Military History, War Histories Division, 1954.

Tierney, John J., Jr. *Chasing Ghosts: Unconventional Warfare in American History.* Washington, DC: Potomac, 2006.

Tompkins, Frank. *Chasing Villa: The Story behind the Story of Pershing's Expedition into Mexico.* Harrisburg, PA: Military Service Publishing, 1934.

Townshend, Charles. *Terrorism: A Very Short Introduction*. 3rd ed. New York: Oxford University Press, 2002.

Warrick, Joby. *Black Flags: The Rise of ISIS*. New York: Anchor, 2016.

Weiss, Mitch, and Kevin Maurer. *Hunting Che: How a U.S. Special Forces Team Helped Capture the World's Most Famous Revolutionary*. New York: Berkley Caliber, 2013.

Welsome, Eileen. *The General and the Jaguar: Pershing's Hunt for Pancho Villa, A True Story of Revolution and Revenge*. New York: Little, Brown, 2006.

Wildman, Edwin. *Aguinaldo: A Narrative of Filipino Ambitions*. Boston: Lothrup, 1901.

Williams, William Appleman. *The Tragedy of American Diplomacy*. 2nd ed. New York: Dell, 1972.

Witt, John Fabian. *Lincoln's Code: The Laws of War in American History*. New York: Free Press, 2012.

Woodward, Bob. *Bush at War*. New York: Simon & Schuster, 2002.

———. *Obama's Wars*. New York: Simon & Schuster, 2010.

———. *State of Denial: Bush at War, Part III*. New York: Simon & Schuster, 2006.

Worcester, Dean. *The Philippines Past and Present*. Vol. 1. New York: Macmillan, 1914.

Wright, Lawrence. *The Looming Tower: Al Qaeda and the Road to 9/11*. New York: Alfred A. Knopf, 2006.

Zimmermann, Warren. *First Great Triumph: How Five Americans Made Their Country a World Power*. New York: Farrar, Straus and Giroux, 2002.

Articles

"The Attack on Our Cavalry at Parral." *Journal of the US Cavalry Association* 27 (July 1916–June 1917): 249–53.

Bacevich, Andrew J. "The American Electoral Mission in Nicaragua, 1927–1928." *Diplomatic History* 4 (Summer 1980): 241–61.

Baylen, Joseph O. "Sandino: Patriot or Bandit?" *Hispanic American Historical Review* 31 (August 1951): 394–419.

Bhatia, Michael V. "Fighting Words: Naming Terrorists, Bandits, Rebels and Other Violent Actors." *Third World Quarterly* 26 (2005): 5–22.

Byler, Charles. "Pacifying the Moros: American Military Government in the Southern Philippines, 1899–1913." *Military Review* 85 (May–June 2005): 41–45.

Cabanas, Miguel A. "A Trauma's History: Pablo Escobar as Ghostly Myth and the Neoliberal Social Contract." *Revista de Estudios Hispánicos* 53 (March 2019): 165–85.

Chapman, Gregory Dean. "Taking up the White Man's Burden: Tennesseans in the Philippine Insurrection, 1899." *Tennessee Historical Quarterly* 47 (Spring 1988): 27–40.

Chiesa, Luis E., and Alexander K. A. Greenawalt. "Beyond War: Bin Laden, Escobar, and the Justification of Targeted Killing." *Washington and Lee Law Review* 69 (Summer 2012): 1371–1470.

Chipman, Don D. "Osama bin Laden and Guerrilla Warfare." *Studies in Conflict & Terrorism* 26 (2003): 163–70.

Cullinane, Michael. "Bringing in the Brigands: The Politics of Pacification in the Colonial Philippines, 1902–1907." *Philippine Studies* 57 (March 2009): 55–60.

Dennis, Lawrence. "Nicaragua: In Again, Out Again." *Foreign Affairs* 9 (April 1931): 496–500.
Dumouchel, Paul. "Revenge or Justice? Obama Gets Osama." *Contagion: Journal of Violence, Mimesis, and Culture* 19 (2012): 9–17.
Er, Mevliyar. "Abd-el-Krim al-Khattabi: The Unknown Mentor of Che Guevara." *Terrorism and Political Violence* 29 (2017): 137–59.
Flanigan, Shawn Teresa. "Terrorists Next Door? A Comparison of Mexican Drug Cartels and Middle Eastern Terrorist Organizations." *Terrorism and Political Violence* 24 (2012): 279–94.
Grossman, Richard. "Solidarity with Sandino: The Anti-Intervention and Solidarity Movements in the United States, 1927–1933." *Latin American Perspectives* 36 (November 2009): 67–79.
Hasian, Marouf, Jr. "American Exceptionalism and the bin Laden Raid." *Third World Quarterly* 33 (2012): 1803–20.
Heilbrunn, Jacob. "Bin Laden's Demise: Death of a Salesman." *World Affairs* 174 (July/August 2011): 7–12.
Joseph, Gilbert M. "On the Trail of Latin American Bandits: A Reexamination of Peasant Resistance." *Latin American Research Review* 25 (1990): 7–53.
Katz, Friedrich. "Pancho Villa and the Attack on Columbus, New Mexico." *American Historical Review* 83 (February 1978): 101–30.
Kuder, Edward M. "The Moros in the Philippines." *Far Eastern Quarterly* 4 (1945): 119–26.
McCants, William. "The Believer: How an Introvert with a Passion for Religion and Soccer Became Abu Bakr al-Baghdadi, Leader of the Islamic State." DGO-Digital original. Brookings Institution, 2015. http://www.jstor.org/stable/10.7864/j.ctt1729vp6.
McCormick, Gordon H., and Mark T. Berger. "Ernesto (Che) Guevara: The Last 'Heroic' Guerrilla." *Studies in Conflict and Terrorism* 42 (2019): 336–62.
Mégret, Frédéric. "Bin Laden: Tale of a Death Foretold." *Journal of Genocide Research* 20 (2018): 290–304.
Meyers, William K. "Pancho Villa and the Multinationals: United States Mining Interests in Villista, Mexico, 1913–1915." *Journal of Latin American Studies* 23 (May 1991): 339–63.
Moreno, José A. "Che Guevara on Guerrilla Warfare: Doctrine, Practice, and Evaluation." *Comparative Studies in Society and History* 12 (April 1970): 114–33.
Naef, Patrick James. "'Narco-Heritage' and the Touristification of the Drug Lord Pablo Escobar in Medellin, Colombia." *Journal of Anthropological Research* 74 (Winter 2018): 485–502.
Neagle, Michael E. "A Bandit Worth Hunting: Pancho Villa and America's War on Terror in Mexico, 1916–1917." *Terrorism and Political Violence* 33 (October 2021): 1492–1510. www.tandfonline.com.
Perla, Hector, Jr. "Heirs of Sandino: The Nicaraguan Revolution and the U.S.-Nicaragua Solidarity Movement." *Latin American Perspectives* 36 (November 2009): 80–100.

Poplin, Richard R. "The Letters of W. Thomas Osborne: A Spanish-American War Soldier of Bedford County." *Tennessee Historical Quarterly* 22 (June 1963): 152–69.

Ruiz, Jason. "The Problem of Popularity: Transforming Pablo Escobar in U.S. Media." *Journal of Popular Culture* 53 (October 2020): 1066–85.

Runkle, Benjamin. "Tora Bora Reconsidered: Lessons from 125 Years of Strategic Manhunts." *Joint Force Quarterly* 70 (July 2013): 40–46.

Sandos, James A. "Pancho Villa and American Security: Woodrow Wilson's Mexican Diplomacy Reconsidered." *Journal of Latin American Studies* 13 (November 1981): 293–311.

Schroeder, Michael J. "Bandits and Blanket Thieves, Communists and Terrorists: The Politics of Naming Sandinistas in Nicaragua, 1927–36 and 1979–90." *Third World Quarterly* 26 (2005): 67–86.

Tate, Michael L. "Pershing's Punitive Expedition: Pursuer of Bandits or Presidential Panacea." *Americas* 32 (July 1975): 46–71.

Thompson, David P. "Pablo Escobar, Drug Baron: His Surrender, Imprisonment, and Escape." *Studies in Conflict and Terrorism* 19 (1996): 55–91.

Welch, Richard E. "American Atrocities in the Philippines: The Indictment and the Response." *Pacific Historical Review* 43 (May 1974): 233–53.

White, E. Bruce. "The Muddied Waters of Columbus, New Mexico." *Americas* 32 (July 1975): 72–91.

Williams, Walter L. "United States Indian Policy and the Debate over Philippine Annexation: Implications for the Origins of American Imperialism." *Journal of American History* 66 (March 1980): 810–31.

Theses and Dissertations

Bowley, Jenna L. "Robin Hood or Villain: The Social Constructions of Pablo Escobar." Honors thesis, University of Maine, 2013.

Dietz, Rebekah K. "Illicit Networks: Targeting the Nexus between Terrorists, Proliferators, and Narcotraffickers." Master's thesis, Naval Postgraduate School, 2010.

Dphrepaulezz, Omar. "'The Right Sort of White Men': General Leonard Wood and the U.S. Army in the Southern Philippines." PhD diss., University of Connecticut, 2013.

Paulet, Anne. "The Only Good Indian Is a Dead Indian: The Use of United States Indian Policy as a Guide for the Conquest and Occupation of the Philippines, 1898–1905." PhD diss., Rutgers University, 1995.

Tierney, John J., Jr. "The United States and Nicaragua, 1927–1932: Decisions for De-Escalation and Withdrawal." PhD diss., University of Pennsylvania, 1969.

Videos

Cran, William, dir. *Frontline*. Season 13, episode 7, "The Godfather of Cocaine." Aired March 25, 1997, on PBS.

Miller, John, reporter. "Osama bin Laden: The Most Dangerous Man You've Never Heard Of." *Nightline*. Aired June 10, 1998, on ABC. https://youtu.be/zDq9tMu1Jm0.

Obama, Barack. "Obama on bin Laden: The Full *60 Minutes* Interview." Interview by Steve Kroft, *60 Minutes*. Aired May 15, 2011, on CBS. www.cbsnews.com/news/obama-on-bin-laden-the-full-60-minutes-interview/.

Parker, Trey, dir. *South Park*. Season 5, episode 9, "Osama bin Laden Has Farty Pants." Aired November 7, 2001, on Comedy Central.

Rothbart, Colin, dir. *Dark Tourist*. Season 1, episode 1, "Latin America." Aired July 20, 2018, on Netflix.

Index

Page numbers in italics indicate illustrations.

Abbottabad, 144; bin Laden compound in, 144–45, 146
ABC News, 105, 136
Abu Ghraib, 144
Abu Nidal, 5
Achuapa, 70
Aden, 138
Afghanistan, 1, 145, 148, 154; civil war in, 133; post-Soviet war conditions in, 133; Soviet invasion of, 129–31, 132, 133; US aid to, 130, 131, 133, 143; US bombing of in 1998, 137; US war in, 7, 49, 127–29, 140, 143, 149, 158
Africa, 78, 82, 85, 86, 95, 131, 144
Agua Prieta, 46, 47
Aguinaldo, Emilio, 5, 26, 28, 29, 128, 156; alliance with United States, 13–14, 32; American depictions of, 10, 14, 17, 19; background of, 12; as bandit, 32; capture of, 23–25, 30, 35, 157; death of, 32; in hiding, 23; as rebel leader, 12; rebellion against Spain, 12–14; tactics against US forces, 15–17, 19–20
aircraft: in hunt for Escobar, 113, 118; in hunt for Sandino, 57, 66, 67; in hunt for Villa, 48–49; in hunt for Zarqawi, 151
Alarcón Ramírez, Dariel, 98
al-Badri, Ibrahim Awwad Ibrahim. *See* al-Baghdadi, Abu Bakr
al-Baghdadi, Abu Bakr, 156; background of, 152; death of, 154–55; as ISIS emir, 152–53; as jihadist, 152; US pursuit of, 153–55; violence of, 154–55
Albright, Madeline, 136
Albuquerque Journal, 41

Alec Station, 133. *See also* Central Intelligence Agency
al-Fadl, Jamal, 133
Ali, Datu, 29–30
al Jazeera, 139
al-Kuwaiti, Abrar, 146
al-Kuwaiti, Abu Ahmed, 144–45, 146
al-Qaeda, 1, 132, 138; affiliation with al Qaeda in Iraq, 151; alliance with Taliban, 134, 141; attack on US embassies in Africa, 136; attack on USS *Cole*, 138; diminishment of, 129, 143–44, 145, 149, 151; and global war on terror, 140, 149; initial operations of, 132–33; and ISIS, 153–54; mission of, 131, 132, 136; and 9/11 attacks, 138–39; origins of, 131; at Tora Bora, 127–28; US operations against, 137–138, 140–41, 158
al-Qaeda in Iraq (AQI), 144, 151, 152. *See also* ISIS
Altamirano, Pedro, 70
al-Zarqawi, Abu Musab, 151
al-Zawahiri, Ayman, 128, 136; and ISIS, 152
American exceptionalism, 157
American Express, 110
American Federation of Labor, 64
American Indians, 2, 19, 39, 71
americanistas, 18
American Samoa, 11
Amil, Datu, 31
Anglo-Saxon, 52, 59
anti-Americanism, 54, 110, 136; in Mexico, 40, 44, 47
anticapitalism, 6–7, 78, 157
anticommunism, 6, 77, 90, 91–92, 104, 157

193

anti-imperialism, 16, 64, 69–70, 74, 83
Antioquia, 105
Arabian Sea, 148
Arabs, 130–131
Arab Spring, 145
Arango Arámbula, José Doroteo.
　See Villa, Pancho
Arbenz, Jacobo, 79
Argentina, 78, 80, 92, 157; as Guevara
　native homeland, 6, 77, 79, 80, 88
Arlington, 139
Asia, 11
assassins, 107, 111, 114, 141; as epithet, 35,
　57, 71, 72, 82. See also *sicarios*
assassinations, 21, 98, 118; attempt
　on Villa, 49, 164n36; of Lara, 111; of
　Lumumba, 86; of Madero, 38
Associated Press, 44, 47, 109, 114
Atlanta, 123
Atlantic, 28
atomic bomb, 134
Avianca Flight 203, 112
Avon Comics, 54

Baghdad, 153
Baker, Newton, 51
Balangiga massacre, 9–10, 25, 28, 157
Baldwin, Frank D., 27
banditry, 2, 19, 28, 36, 70, 72
bandits, 1, 7, 19, 36, 44, 51, 70, 128, 151,
　156–57; Aguinaldo as, 32; al-Qaeda
　as, 137; American military as, 66, 73;
　Baghdadi as, 154; Escobar as, 119; Sandinistas as, 65, 68, 72, 74; Sandino as,
　6, 58, 64–65, 71–73; utility of term, 2–4,
　64–65, 71; Villa as, 36, 39, 41, 47, 52–54
barbarism, 41, 157; and bin Laden, 141;
　and Moros, 5; and Sandino, 71; and
　Villistas, 44
Barco Vargas, Virgilio, 113, 114
Bardem, Javier, 123
Barrientos, René, 90, 91, 98
Bates Agreement, 26, 27
Batista, Fulgencio, 80
Bay of Pigs invasion, 81

Bayang, 27
Beals, Carleton, 66–67, 72–73
Belgium, 86
Bell, J. Franklin, 22
Benítez, Ramón, 86. See also Guevara,
　Ernesto "Che"
Bensinger, Peter, 115
Bergen, Peter, 130, 136
Berntsen, Gary, 128
Bhatia, Michael, 65
bin Laden, Amal, 148
bin Laden, Khalid, 147
bin Laden, Mohammad, 130
bin Laden, Osama, 1, 5, 7, 125, 156;
　American conceptions of, 129, 141–42;
　American reactions to death of, 148–
　49; animosity toward United States,
　131–32, 134–36; and attack on USS *Cole*,
　138; background of, 130; barbarism of,
　141; and George W. Bush, 129, 141–42,
　143; and CIA, 133–35, 144; comparison
　to Baghdadi, 153–54; compound in Abbottabad, 144–45; death of, 145–49, 151,
　154, 158; as emir of al-Qaeda, 131–32,
　143–44, 145; fatwa of, 135–36; and FBI,
　137; fight against Soviet Union, 130–31;
　in hiding, 128–29, 143–45; historical
　comparison to Crusades, 132, 142;
　and ISIS, 144, 149; masculinity of, 136;
　mission of, 131, 152; and 9/11 attacks,
　7, 127, 129, 138, 139–40, 143, 145, 148;
　origins of jihadism, 130–31; personal
　aesthetic of, 131–32, 145; in Pakistan,
　128, 143, 144; proposed defense of
　Kuwait, 132; relationship with Omar,
　134, 140; sanctuary in Afghanistan,
　133–38; sanctuary in Sudan, 132–33;
　as terrorist, 7, 127, 129, 139, 143; at Tora
　Bora, 127–29, 150; US pursuit of, after
　9/11, 141–49; US pursuit of, before 9/11,
　133–35, 137–38; views on Israel, 131, 134
Bissonnette, Matt, 147–48
Black, Cofer, 141
"Black Hawk Down" incident, 133
Black Hawk helicopters, 145

Bloque de Busqueda. *See* Search Bloc
Bogotá, 113, 117
Bolivia, 1, 94, 96, 97, 98; Guevara mission in, 7, 88–96, 99–100, 156; military capability, 90–92, 93, 100; partnership with United States, 91–92, 93, 100; peasants in, 91, 93, 94; political conditions in, 88, 90
Bolivian Communist Party (PCB), 90, 91, 93
Bolivian Liberation Army, 93, 98
bolo, 9, 27, 31
Bolshevism, 59, 73. *See also* socialism
Bonaparte, Napoleon, 2
Bonifacio, Andrés, 12
Boston, 11
Boston Globe, 72, 97
Bowden, Mark, 107, 112, 118, 121
Boykin, William G. "Jerry," 112, 115, 117, 118, 121
Bray, William G., 82
Brigade 2506, 92, 95
Brigandage Act, 27
Bryan, William Jennings, 39
Bryan-Chamorro Treaty (1916), 58
Bud Bagsak, 29, 31
Bud Dajo, 31
Bullard, Robert L., 28
Busby, Morris, 119, 120
Bush, George H. W., 113, 114, 116, 118, 125; administration of, 117
Bush, George W., 1, 7, 125, 138; administration of, 6, 66, 127, 128, 138, 140, 143, 144, 157; and bin Laden, 129, 141–42, 143; on empire, 156; and global war on terror, 140, 144; and President's Daily Brief, 138–39
Bush, Laura, 142
Bustos, Ciro, 92
Butters, Charles, 63

Cabot Lodge, Henry, 22, 35
Calderón, Margarita, 60
Cali cartel, 119, 124
caliphate, 131, 152, 153, 155. *See also* ISIS

Calle, Humberto de la, 122–23
Cambodia, 153
Camp Bucca, 152
campesinos, 61, 67
Camp Furlong, 42, 54
Canal Zone (Panama), 58
capitalism, 77, 88, 142. *See also* anticapitalism
Caribbean Sea, 4, 53
Carlos the Jackal, 5
Carnegie, Andrew, 16
Carothers, George, 45
Carrancista, 44, 46, 47, 48, 50, 51
Carranza, Venustiano, 38, 40, 44, 46, 47, 50, 51
Carrizal, 50, 51
Cartagena, 125
Carter, Jimmy, 129
Castaño, Carlos, 119
Castaño, Fidel, 119
Castillo Chávez, José, 93–94
Castro, Fidel, 81, 98, 99; and Bolivia mission, 88; and Congo mission, 86; and Guevara, 78, 80, 82, 85, 87, 90, 95, 96, 97; and war on drugs, 111
Castro, Raúl, 80, 81, 99
Catholic, 25, 79
Cavite, 12
CBS News, 139, 148
Central America, 4, 6, 58, 62, 63
Central Intelligence Agency (CIA), 7, 77, 95, 98, 134, 153; and coup in Guatemala, 79; and narcoterrorism, 111; operatives in Afghanistan, 127, 140–41; search for bin Laden, 133–35, 144; search for Escobar in Colombia, 103; search for Guevara in Bolivia, 92, 94, 96–97; search for Guevara in the Congo, 86–87; at Tora Bora, 127. *See also* Bay of Pigs invasion
Centra Spike, 113, 117, 118, 120
Cervantes, Candelario, 51
Chang, Juan Pablo, 170n51
Che Guevara International Brigade, 98
Cheney, Dick, 150

Chicago, 70
Chicago Tribune, 23, 27, 72; on Escobar, 122, 124
Chihuahua, 48, 49, 50, 51
Chile, 98, 107, 157
China, 81, 138
Christian, 132, 134
Ciudad Juárez, 52
civil war: in Afghanistan, 133; in Colombia, 104; in Guatemala, 79; in Iraq, 151; in Nicaragua, 59, 60; in Syria, 151; in United States, 20, 21, 44
Clark, J. Reuben, 69
Clarke, Richard, 135, 137–38; and September 11, 2001, attacks, 139; outreach to Rice, 138
Cleveland Gazette, 20
Clinton, Bill, 121–22, 135, 138; administration of, 133, 134, 137; 1998 strikes on al-Qaeda, 137, 139
CNN, 135–36
Coahuila, 52
Cobb, Zachary, 40
Coca-Cola, 105
cocaine, 107, 115, 124; origins and popular use of, 105
Cochise, 19
Cold War, 2, 4, 76, 82, 90; and Afghanistan, 133; and Colombia, 103–4; effect on US foreign policy, 85, 100; and global war on terror, 150; and Guevara, 6, 77, 83, 99
Colombia, 1, 7, 78, 102, 158; antinarcotics efforts, 110, 116; extradition treaty with United States, 109, 112, 115; importance in drug trade, 105, 124–25; political conditions in, 104, 107, 111–12; support for United States, 104; and US aid, 104, 113, 117, 118, 125; US criticism of, 103, 114, 115, 118, 121; violence in, 113–16
Colossus of the North, 54, 69
Columbus, NM, 36, 41, 45, 54; attack on, 6, 33, 35, 42, 44, 46–48, 50–51, 52, 53
Columbus Courier, 42
Commercial Hotel, 42, 45

communism, 81, 87, 97–98, 104. *See also* anticommunism; socialism
Communist Party (Mexico), 69
communists, 76, 129, 130; in Bolivia, 91, 93; Guevara as, 77, 83; Lumumba as, 86; and Sandino, 72. *See also* Bolivian Communist Party; Communist Party (Mexico)
Company C, Ninth Regiment, 9
concentration camp, 22
Congo, 85; Guevara mission in, 7, 85–88
Conservative Party (Colombia), 104
Conservative Party (Nicaragua), 59, 61
constabulary: in Philippines, 30; in Mexico, 49
Constitutionalists, 38
Coolidge, Calvin, 57, 59, 67, 68, 73
Cotabato Valley, 30
cotta, 30, 31
counterterrorism, 7, 129, 133, 135, 138, 139, 140, 141, 149
Crocker, Ryan, 153
crusade, 142
Crusaders, 132
Cuba, 78, 80, 82, 85, 95, 98, 99, 100, 144; exiles of, 80, 81, 86, 87, 92; Guevara burial in, 96; and Guevara mission in Bolivia, 91, 92; and Guevara mission in the Congo, 86, 87–88; Obama's trip to, 99; rebellion against Spain, 12, 19, 24; relations with Soviet Union, 78, 85; US interventions in, 11, 13, 26, 58, 77, 81; and war on drugs, 111. *See also* Cuban Revolution
Cuba, Simón, 94, 95
Cuban Missile Crisis, 85, 104
Cuban National Bank, 78, 81
Cuban Revolution, 76, 77, 88, 170n50; Guevara's participation in, 6, 80–81; resistance to United States, 81–82
Czechoslovakia, 87

Dar es Salaam, 136
Dark Tourist (TV series), 124
Debray, Régis, 92

dehumanization: of Baghdadi, 155;
    of Escobar, 114, 115; utility of, 4, 157;
    of Villa, 6, 45, 53
Delta Force, 112, 113, 117, 118, 121; and
    Baghdadi raid, 154-55; at Tora Bora,
    127-28
del Toro, Benicio, 123
Desert Storm, 132
Dewey, George, 13, 14
Díaz, Adolfo, 59
Díaz, Porfirio, 36-37
Disney World, 110
Dominican Republic, 49, 58, 77, 78
Dowd, Maureen, 143, 149
Drug Enforcement Administration
    (DEA), 7, 103, 110, 113-23 passim
Dunlap, R. H., 65
Durango, 36, 45, 53

Eberhardt, Charles C., 57, 59-60, 67, 69, 70
Egypt, 125, 132, 154
Egyptian Islamic Jihad, 136
Ejército Defensor de la Soberanía
    Nacional de Nicaragua. See
    Sandinistas
El Chipote, 63, 66
El Espectador, 110
El Paso, 38, 40, 43, 50
El Paso Herald, 35
El Salvador, 70, 101, 157
empire, 7; and military interventions,
    58, 151; resistance abroad to, 4, 69; US
    development of, 3-4, 11, 58, 156. *See
    also* imperialism
enhanced interrogation techniques, 144.
    See also torture
Erbil, 154
Eritrea, 133
Escobar, Abel, 105
Escobar, Hermila, 105
Escobar, Juan Pablo, 106, 109, 114, 117, 119,
    120, 121
Escobar, Manuela, 106, 120
Escobar, Pablo, 7, 101, 128, 156; American depictions of, 103, 112, 113-17;
    background of, 105-6; as bandit, 119;
    charity of, 109, 112, 122; concern for
    family, 119-20; death impact in war on
    drugs, 124-25; death of, 120-21, 158;
    dehumanization of, 114, 115; escape
    from La Catedral, 102, 112, 117; evasion
    of authorities, 113, 115, 118, 120; fear of
    US extradition, 7, 102, 109, 115, 117-18;
    as head of Medellín cartel, 105, 107;
    image in US popular culture, 123-24;
    lifestyle of, 109-10; and Los Pepes,
    119; as outlaw, 107; as petty criminal,
    106-7; plea bargain of, 115; political
    ambitions of, 109, 112; political career
    of, 109-10; public reactions to death
    of, 121-23; use of violence, 103, 107,
    111-12, 114, 116; US indictments of, 110,
    112. *See also* narcoterrorism
Escobar, Roberto, 102, 105, 107, 112, 117,
    121, 124
Espinosa, José María, 49
Europe, 2, 16, 32, 45, 58, 59, 82; and
    imperialism, 11, 142
Extraditables, 109, 118. *See also* Escobar,
    Pablo; Medellín cartel
ExxonMobil, 155

Fagan, Richard, 72
Fahd (king), 132
Farabundo Martí National Liberation
    Front (FMLN), 101
far enemy, 131, 134, 140. *See also* al-Qaeda
Federal Bureau of Investigation (FBI),
    110, 133, 138; bin Laden on Ten Most
    Wanted list, 137
Feland, Logan, 72
First Nebraska volunteers, 15
First Tennessee Cavalry, 16
fisabil, 26
Fitzwater, Marlin, 117
5 Commando, 86, 87
Fleischer, Ari, 142
Florida, 77, 99, 105, 153
foco, 88, 91
Forbes, 105

Index 197

Foreign Affairs, 72
Fort Bliss, 38
Fort Bragg, 146
Fort Worth Star-Telegram, 52
France, 2, 19, 65, 86, 92, 98, 115
Franks, Tommy, 128
French Revolution, 3
Frente Sandinista de Liberación Nacional (FSLN), 101, 111. *See also* Sandinistas
Friedman, Thomas L., 140
Funston, Frederick, 24; and capture of Aguinaldo, 24, 30; and Punitive Expedition, 35, 48, 50
Fury, Dalton, 127. *See also* Greer, Thomas

Gable, Clark, 54
Gadea, Hilda, 79, 81
Gadhafi, Moammar, 113
Galán, Luis, 112, 113
Galeano, Fernando, 116
gangster, 71
Gaviria, César, 112, 115–16, 117, 119, 121; administration of, 118
Gaviria, Gustavo, 113, 115
Germany, 3, 32, 35, 45, 67, 76, 120
Geronimo, 48; as code name for bin Laden, 147
Ghanem, Alia, 130
Gillespie, Charles, Jr., 112, 113, 114
Glenn, Edwin F., 21
global war on terror (GWOT), 1, 5, 125, 127, 128, 136–37, 156; alliance with Pakistan, 143; comparisons in Mexico, 48; comparisons in Nicaragua, 6, 58, 66; cost of, 129, 149–50; as crusade, 142; endurance of, 5, 158; expansive mission of, 144, 150, 151; launch of, 7, 140; prisoner treatment in, 6, 157
Gompers, Samuel, 16
González, Adolfo Mena. *See* Guevara, Ernesto "Che"
Goodwin, Richard, 83, 85
Graceland, 110
Granma (yacht), 80

Great Britain, 19, 32, 127
Great Depression, 71
Green, William, 64
Greer, Thomas, 127–28
Grenada, 113
Griffith, Samuel, 72
gringos, 43, 46, 47
Guam, 3, 11
Guantánamo Bay Naval Base, 144
Guardia Nacional (GN), 57, 69; and death of Sandino, 75; origins of, 59; political influence of, 74; and US Marines, 63–64, 66, 68, 70, 74
Guatemala, 157; Guevara in, 79; Sandino in, 60
Guerrero, Mexico, 51
guerrillas, 1, 72, 86, 88, 156; Bolivian rebels as, 90–95, 100; Colombian groups as, 104, 111; Cuban rebels as, 80; Filipino rebels as, 10, 16, 19–23, 30; Guevara as, 6, 78; Sandinistas as, 6, 63; utility of term, 2
guerrilla warfare, 72, 82, 85–86, 100; Filipino rebels' use of, 19–20, 28; Guevara's theories about, 77–78, 82, 100
Guevara, Aleida, 81, 87, 96
Guevara, Ernesto "Che," 6, 76, 128, 156, 157; in American political discourse, 99; background of, 78–79, 167n6; body of, 96–97, 97; as bureaucrat in Cuba, 77–78, 81, 85; capture of, 94–95, 170n50; and Fidel Castro, 78, 80, 81, 85, 87, 88, 90, 95, 97; considerations of Latin America, 77, 86; creation of *Motorcycle Diaries*, 79; as critic of US foreign policy, 76, 77, 81–85; and Escobar, 123; execution of, 95–96, 170n51; as head of Cuban National Bank, 78, 81; health problems, 78–79, 93; as inspiration in Latin America, 76, 101, 157; meeting with Goodwin, 83, 85; in Mexico, 79–80; as minister of industries, 78, 81; mission in Bolivia, 88–96, 100; mission in Congo, 85–88, 100; as part of Cuban Revolution, 80–81;

public disappearance of, 77–78, 85, 92; resignation from Cuban government, 85; and socialism, 77, 80, 88, 99, 100; and Soviet Union, 77–78, 82, 85; theories about guerrilla warfare, 77–78, 82, 100; US depictions of, 77–78, 81–83; US reactions about death of, 93
Guevara, Hilda (Hildita), 79
Guevara, Moisés, 93
Guevara Lynch, Ernesto, 79
Gulf War, 150. *See also* Desert Storm

Hacienda Napoles, 109, 110, 124
hadith, 131
Hague, The, 65
Haiti, 58, 77
Hartford Courant: on bin Laden, 148; on Escobar, 113, 116, 117; on Guevara, 97–98; on Villa, 53
Hassan, Panglima, 29
Hatfield, G. D., 55, 57
Havana, 88, 93, 99
Hawai'i, 3, 11
Hawes, James, 87
Henao, Maria Victoria, 106, 120
Henderson, Douglas, 91–92, 93
hippopotamuses, 109, 124
Hitler, Adolf, 5
Hobsbawm, Eric, 2, 47
Holmes, Thomas B., 43
Holocaust, 153
Holy Land, 132
Honduras, 55, 60, 70
Hong Kong, 12, 13, 23
Hoover, Herbert, 6, 57, 68, 71–72; administration of, 70, 74
Huerta, Victoriano, 38, 41, 46
Hughes, Robert P., 23
Hugo, Frank, 52
Humboldt, IA, 35
Humphrey, Hubert H., 77
Hussein, Saddam, 5, 132, 143

Idlib Province, 154
Ignatius, David, 141

ilustrados, 12
imperialism, 77, 83, 88, 156; and terrorism, 156; and United States, 6, 32, 76, 83, 134, 159n6. *See also* anti-imperialism; empire; Europe
Indiana, 142
Indian Wars. *See* American Indians
infidel, 132
insurgents, 2, 31, 49; in Bolivia, 90, 156; in Colombia, 111; in Iraq, 151, 152; in Nicaragua, 65; in Philippines, 5, 9–10, 12, 14, 15–16, 18–19, 22–25, 27, 29, 30–31, 157
insurrectos, 9, 10, 22
Iran, 129, 151
Iran-Contra Scandal, 98
Iraq, 49, 134, 138, 144; and Desert Storm, 132; and ISIS, 151–55; as part of global war on terror, 129; US military in, 7, 143, 149–50, 151–56
Ireland, 25
ISIS, 149, 158; affiliates of, 154, 158; expansion of, 152; origins of, 151; violence of, 151–54; *See also* al Qaeda in Iraq; caliphate
Islam, 26, 130, 131, 132, 139; and Taliban, 133
Islamists, 7, 131, 140, 153. *See also* jihadists
Israel, 125, 151; bin Laden's views of, 131, 134; murder of 1972 Olympic team, 3

Jackson, Jesse, 99
Jaji, 131
Jalalabad, 145
Japan, 31, 32, 49, 76
JAWBREAKER, 140–41. *See also* Central Intelligence Agency
Jesús, Alvaro de, 120
jihad, 132, 133; bin Laden's declaration of, 134; in Philippines, 26
jihadists, 131, 132, 133, 134, 139; in ISIS, 151–53
Jim Crow, 19, 39, 59
Johnson, Lyndon B., 32, 92, 97
Jolo, 28, 31

Index 199

Jouvenal, Peter, 136
juramentado, 28

Kabila, Laurent, 86
Kabul, 134
Kaczynski, Theodore, 7
Kandahar, 133, 135
Katipunan, 12
Katz, Friedrich, 44, 46, 47, 49
Kellogg, Frank, 64, 68
Kennedy, John F., 82, 85; administration of, 81, 83, 85; impressions of Guevara, 83
Kenya, 136
Khost, 137
Khrushchev, Nikita, 81
King Abdulaziz University, 130
Kipling, Rudyard, 11
Knebel, Laura Bergquist, 83
Korean War, 92, 104
Kramer, Paul, 20
Krauthammer, Charles, 140, 149
Ku Klux Klan, 7
Kunar province, 128, 143
Kurds, 153, 154
Kuwait, 132

La Catedral, 112, 115, 118, 120, 124; conditions in, 102, 116; raid on, 117. *See also* Escobar, Pablo
La Esperanza, 92
La Higuera, 94–95
Lake Lanao, 27
Lake Tanganyika, 87
Lane, Arthur Bliss, 75
Lansing, Robert, 44–45, 50
La Paz, 88
Lara Bonilla, Rodrigo, 110, 111
Las Vegas, 110
Latin America, 62, 74, 75, 82, 87, 98, 104; Guevara as inspiration in, 76, 101, 157; Guevara's considerations of, 77, 86; Sandino as inspiration in, 69, 75; US interventions in, 3–4, 54, 77, 79, 92; and war on drugs, 103, 110

La Violencia, 104, 107
Lehder, Carlos, 107
Lewis, Bernard, 142
Liberal Party (Colombia), 104
Liberal Party (Nicaragua), 59, 60, 61, 67, 68
Libya, 113, 154
Lieber Code, 21
Lil Wayne, 123
Lincoln Memorial, 98
Lind, John, 41
Linn, Brian, 15, 18, 19
Little Big Horn, 9
Look Magazine, 83
Looney Tunes, 142
López, Nico, 80
López, Pablo, 44, 47
Los Angeles Times: on Aguinaldo, 24; on Escobar, 114, 115; on Villa, 53
Los Olivos, 120
Los Pepes, 119
Lozano, Ismael, 33
Lozano, José Salomón, 118
Lumumba, Patrice, 86
Luzon, 10, 12, 18, 19, 22, 23, 24, 25, 28, 29

Macabebe Scouts, 21, 23, 24
MacArthur, Arthur, 19, 24–25, 32
MacArthur, Douglas, 32
Macaulay, Neill, 63, 74
Madero, Francisco, 37–38
Malabang, 27
Managua, 68
Manila, 10, 12, 13, 14, 15, 20, 25; Battle of, 15–16
Manila Bay, 13
Martí, Farabundo, 70
Martínez, Hugo, Jr., 120
Marxism, 70, 113
Mason, Patrick, 20
Matagalpa, Nicaragua, 72
McCoy, Frank, 30
McFarland, Howard, 20
McKinley, William, 11, 13; administration of, 13, 14

McRaven, William, 146–47
McVeigh, Timothy, 7
Medal of Honor, 24, 27
Medellín, 102, 105, 107, 109, 118, 120, 122, 124; Barrio Pablo Escobar, 109; US consulate in, 103, 113; violent conditions in, 113–14
Medellín cartel, 7, 113, 119, 123, 124; operations of, 105, 107, 110, 114; plea bargains of, 115; and US extradition, 109; violence of, 111
Meese, Edwin, 114
Mérida, 69
Meridan (CT) Morning Record, 19
Mexican Revolution, 6, 36–40, 46, 52
Mexico, 1, 31, 32, 43, 44, 49, 157, 158; Guevara in, 78, 79–80; political conditions in, 36–38, 46; relations with United States, 6, 37–38, 46, 50, 54; and Rodríguez Gacha, 107; Sandino in, 60, 62, 69–70; US interventions in, 35, 37, 40, 52, 58, 69, 77; US officials in, 40–41, 45; Villa operations in, 38–41, 46–47, 52–53. *See also* Mexican Revolution; Punitive Expedition
Mexico City, 69
Miami, 109
Middle East, 5, 7, 129, 134, 138, 139, 142, 144, 156; autocrats in, 131, 132, 151
Miles, Nelson, 24, 44–45
Miller, Charles D., 51
Miller, John, 136, 176n22
Mindanao, 25, 27, 29–30
Minh, Ho Chi, 83
Ministry of Industries (Cuba), 78
Minneapolis Journal, 14
Miro, Doug, 123
Mohammad (Prophet), 29, 130, 131, 153
Monaco building, 124
Moncada, Gerardo, 116
Moncada, José María, 60–61, 67, 68, 70, 72
Mondale, Walter, 99
Monje, Mario, 90
Monsen, Frederick L., 39
Moro Province, 5, 26, 27, 29, 31

Moros, 10, 39, 48, 157; American depiction of, 28; and barbarism, 5; and Philippine-American War, 25–31; as savage, 26–28
Moro Scouts, 31
Mosul, 153
Mueller, Kayla, 154
mujahideen, 129, 130
Munich, 3
Muñoz-Mosquera, Dandeny, 112
Munro, Dana, 64
Murphy, Steve, 113, 117, 118, 119, 121, 122, 123
Muslims, 129, 131, 132, 141; bin Laden appeal to, 134, 135, 139, 145; ISIS appeal to, 153; opposition to Soviet war in Afghanistan, 130; in Philippines, 5, 10, 26, 27

Nairobi, 136
Namiquipa, Mexico, 49, 51
Ñancahuazú, 90
narcocracy, 112
narcoculture, 123
Narcos (TV series), 123
narcoterrorism, 7, 103, 112, 113, 123, 125; CIA definition of, 111
narcotourism, 123–24
narcotrafficking, 111, 113, 114, 115, 125
Nation (magazine), 66
National Liberation Army (ELN), 104
National Security Agency, 87
National Security Decision Directive Number 221, 104
Navy SEALs, 87, 145–49
near enemy, 131, 132, 134. *See also* al-Qaeda
Netflix, 123, 124
New York, 58, 138, 139
New York Times, 42; on bin Laden, 129, 142, 143, 149; on Escobar, 115, 119, 124; on global war on terror, 140, 144; on Guevara, 83, 98; on ISIS, 153; on Sandino, 64; on Villa, 36, 39, 44, 52, 53, 54

Index 201

New York Tribune, 24
New York World, 35
Nicaragua, 1, 6, 49, 54, 63, 65, 66, 67, 71, 72, 73, 157; civil war in, 59, 60; elections in, 62, 67, 68, 71, 74; peasants in, 57, 61; popular views about Sandino, 68, 74; and socialism, 111; US intervention in, 55, 58–59, 62–64, 68–70, 77; and war on drugs, 111
Nicaraguan National Guard. *See* Guardia Nacional (GN)
Nigeria, 154
Nightline (TV series), 136
19th of April Movement (M-19), 104; raid on Palace of Justice, 111
Niquinohomo, Nicaragua, 60
Nixon, Richard, 104
nonstate actors, 1, 156, 157
Noriega, Manuel, 111
North Carolina, 146
Northern Alliance, 134; and United States, 140, 143
Nueva Segovia, 55, 64. *See also* Segovias

Obama, Barack, 99, 149; administration of, 145, 149; and bin Laden, 144, 145, 148; considerations in Abbottabad mission, 145–46
Obregón, Álvaro, 50, 53
Ochoa, Fabio, 107, 115
Ochoa, Jorge Luis, 107, 115
Ochoa, Juan David, 107, 115
Ocotal, 55, 63, 67, 70
oil, 132, 145; in Mexico, 37, 60; in Syria, 155–56; and US Middle East policy, 129
Old West, 117, 142
Olympia Daily Recorder, 44
Omar, Mullah Mohammad, 133; relationship with bin Laden, 134, 140
O'Neill, Robert, 147–48
Operation Enduring Freedom, 141
Operation Inherent Resolve, 153
Operation Neptune's Spear, 146–49. *See also* bin Laden, Osama; Obama, Barack
Oregonian, 53

Organization of American States (OAS), 81, 88, 90
Orlando, 153
Osborne, Thomas, 16
Otis, Elwell, 24
Ottoman Empire, 152
outlaw, 2, 30; Escobar as, 107; Sandino as, 57, 64, 69, 71; Villa as, 6, 32, 36, 53
Ovando, Alfredo, 97, 100

Pact of Biak-na-Bato, 12
Pakistan, 127, 129, 130, 140, 145, 148; bin Laden hiding in, 128, 143, 144
Palanan, 23
Palestine, 134, 139, 151
Panama, 58, 77, 96; and war on drugs, 111
Pancho Villa State Park, 54
Paris, 98
Parra, Guido, 119
Parral, 33, 36, 48, 50, 53
paternalism, 59
Patton, George S., 50
peasants, 2; in Bolivia, 91, 93, 94; in Nicaragua, 57, 61
Peña, Javier, 115, 117, 118, 122, 123
Pennsylvania, 139
Pentagon, 139
Perseguidos por Pablo Escobar. *See* Los Pepes
Pershing, John "Black Jack," 38, 44, 45, 47; in Philippines, 31, 48; and Punitive Expedition, 35, 48–51
Persian Gulf, 129
Peru, 78, 79, 91; and international drug trade, 107
Petri, Alexandra, 148
Philadelphia Inquirer, 14
Philadelphia Tribune, 98
Philippine-American War, 9–10, 15–31, 32, 35, 39, 48, 157; Black soldier perspectives of, 20–21; brutality of conflict, 16, 17–18, 21–23; death toll, 31; and Moro War, 25–31; torture in, 10, 15, 21, 22

Philippine Commission, 27
Philippines, 1, 5; independence, 31; rebellion against Spain, 11–14; US acquisition of, 3, 10, 11, 12–15, 31–32. *See also* Philippine-American War
Phoenix Program, 98
Piang, Datu, 29–30
Pinochet, Augusto, 107
Powell, E. Alexander, 39
Prado Salmón, Gary, 94–95, 98
President's Daily Brief (PDB), 138–39
prisoners, 21, 144, 157; of ISIS, 152; in Mexico, 39, 47; in Nicaragua, 5, 64–66, 75; in Philippines, 5, 15, 21, 27, 28
Puerto Rico, 3, 11, 95
Puller, Lewis "Chesty," 64
Punitive Expedition, 33–36, 47–51, 52, 53; in Philippines, 27
Punta del Este, 83
puritans, 157

Quezon, Manuel, 32
Quilalí, Nicaragua, 66
Qur'an, 131

race, 2, 3, 4, 62; American conceptions in Nicaragua, 58–59; American conceptions in Philippines, 11, 19–21; and Villa, 39, 41
Rangers (Bolivia), 92, 94–95
Rangers (US Army), 128
Ravel, Sam, 45
Reagan, Nancy, 104
Reagan, Ronald, 99; administration of, 105, 111; and war on drugs, 104–5
resacas, 93
Revolutionary Armed Forces of Colombia (FARC), 101, 104; cooperation with narcotraffickers, 111
Revolutionary Nationalist Movement (MNR), 88, 90
Rhodes, Ben, 149
Rhodesia, 86
Rice, Condoleezza, 138–39
Rivas, Dagoberto, 60

Rodríguez, Félix, 92–93, 94, 98; interrogation of Guevara, 95–96
Rodríguez Gacha, José Gonzalo, 107
Rollins, Joseph, 23
Rome, 65
Roosevelt, Franklin D., 75
Roosevelt, Theodore, 26, 37; and Moro War, 25, 27; and Philippine-American War, 13, 19
Roosevelt Corollary, 65
Root, Elihu, 20, 23
Rosario, Argentina, 79
Ros-Lehtinen, Ileana, 99
Rostow, Walt, 92, 97
Russia, 138, 151
Rwanda, 153

Sacasa, Juan Batista, 74–75; government of, 74
Salafism, 131
Samaipata, Bolivia, 93
Samar, 9–10
San Albino, 63
San Bernardino, 153
Sandinistas, 6, 66, 68, 69; as bandits, 65, 68, 72, 74; end and rebirth of movement, 75, 101, 111; engagements against United States, 57, 67, 70, 74; as guerrillas, 6, 63; origin of, 61; tactics of, 63–64
Sandino, Augusto, 6, 54, 128, 137, 156, 157; agreement to end rebellion, 74; background of, 60–61; barbarism of, 71; and battle at Ocotal, 55, 57; comparisons to Villa, 61–62; death of, 75; journey to Mexico, 69–70; opposition to Tipitapa Agreement, 59–60, 62; opposition to US imperialism, 64, 76; as outlaw, 57, 64, 69, 71; physical appearance of, 55, 61; rebellion against United States, 61–74; rhetorical flair of, 55, 57, 61, 63, 66–68, 71–72; tactics of, 63–64. *See also* Guardia Nacional; Nicaragua
Sandino, Gregorio, 60, 75

Index 203

Sandino, Sócrates, 75
San Francisco, 58
San Pedro de la Cueva, 47
Santa Cruz de Villegas, 33
Santa Isabel, 42–44, 45, 46
Santiago, Cuba, 80
Saudi Arabia, 130, 133, 134; US military presence in, 132
savagery, 10, 21, 28, 41, 66
savages, 1, 156; and Aguinaldo, 5; and Filipinos, 11, 20–21; and Moros, 26–28, 31; utility of term, 2; and Villa, 6, 41
Schmutz, Gaston, 40
Schroen, Gary, 140–41
Scott, Hugh, 28, 29, 38–39, 50
Seal, Barry, 110–11
Search Bloc, 113–14, 118; discovery and killing of Escobar, 120–21; and Los Pepes, 119
Segovia, Lázaro, 24
Segovias (Nicaragua), 61, 68, 69, 71
Selich, Andrés, 170n50
September 11, 2001, attacks, 1, 125, 149, 151; and bin Laden, 7, 127, 129, 138, 139, 143, 145, 148; and Columbus, NM, 6, 35; details of, 139; popular reaction to, 140–42; reflections on fifth anniversary of, 144; Taliban reaction to, 140
Serna, Celia de la, 79
Seventeenth Infantry, 30
Shelton, Ralph "Pappy," 92
Shias, 151. *See also* Muslims
sicarios, 114, 116. *See also* assassins
Sierra Maestra mountains, 80
Simbas, 86, 87
Sinatra, Frank, 110
Singapore, 23
Sitting Bull, 19
60 Minutes, 148
Smith, H. Allen, 82
Smith, Jacob H., 10
socialism, 79, 82; and Colombia, 104; and Cuba, 78, 81, 95; and Guevara, 77, 80, 88, 99, 100; and Nicaragua, 111. *See also* communism

Somalia, 129, 133
Somoza, Anastasio, 74–75
South Africa, 19, 86
South America, 77, 91; Guevara and, 79, 88, 92; in war on drugs, 105
South Park, 142
Soviet Union, 2, 59, 76, 81, 104, 131; Guevara and, 77–78, 82, 85; war in Afghanistan, 129–31, 132, 133, 143
Spain, 5, 19, 23, 25–26, 38, 105. *See also* Cuba; Philippines; War of 1898
Special Forces, 7; in Afghanistan, 141, 143; search for Escobar, 103. *See also* Navy SEALs
Spencer, Bunk, 47
Springfield (MA) Daily Republican, 14
Stalin, Joseph, 5
Stewart, William, 19
Stimson, Henry, 59, 70, 71–72
Sudan, 132–33, 137
Sultan of Sulu, 27, 29
Sulzberger, C. L., 98
Sunnis, 131, 151. *See also* Muslims
Swahili, 86
Syria, 129; ISIS in 151–55; US forces in, 154–56
Szulc, Tad, 83

Tacoma Times, 35
Taft, William Howard, 16, 27, 45
Tagalog, 12, 25
Taliban, 141; alliance with al-Qaeda, 134, 140; origins of, 133–34; pre-9/11 US pressure on, 137, 140; rule over Afghanistan, 134; war with United States, 141, 143, 149
Tal Placido, Hilario, 24
Tania, 93
Tanzania, 86, 87, 136
Tarnak Farm, 135
Tawhid wal Jihad. *See* ISIS
Tecumseh, 19
Téllez, Manuel C., 69
Tenet, George, 134, 138
Terán, Mario, 96, 98

204   Index

terrorism, 112, 139; 149; and Bush administration, 138–44; and Clinton administration, 136–38; in Colombia, 116, 119, 122; contested definitions of, 3, 159n5; and criminal justice, 140, 149; distinction from guerrilla warfare, 82; distinction from narcoterrorism, 111–12; and empire, 7, 156; in Nicaragua, 67; in Philippines, 16, 19. *See also* counterterrorism; global war on terror; terrorists

terrorists, 1, 5, 129, 135–141, 156–157; Baghdadi as, 154; bin Laden as, 7, 127, 129, 139, 143; domestic, 7; Escobar as, 112, 115, 123; and Guevara, 87; in Philippines, 18; United States as, 135–36; utility of term, 1, 2–3, 4, 7, 157; and war on drugs, 104. *See also* global war on terror; terrorism

Thirteenth Cavalry, 33, 38, 41

Time magazine, 81

Tipitapa Agreement, 59, 60, 62

Toft, Joe, 116

Tomahawk missiles, 137

Tompkins, Frank, 33, 36, 48, 49, 50

Tora Bora, 127–29, 131, 143, 150

Torreón, 45

Torricelli, Robert, 102–3, 117

torture, 94; in global war on terror, 144, 157; in Nicaragua, 63–64; in Philippine-American War, 10, 15, 21, 22

Tranquilandia, 110

Treaty of Paris, 15

Trump, Donald J., 154–56; and Baghdadi, 154–55

Tshombe, Moïse, 86

Tumulty, Joseph, 35

Tunisia, 19

Turkey, 154

Twain, Mark, 5, 16

Twenty-Second Infantry, 30

26th of July Movement, 80. *See also* Cuban Revolution

2 Chainz, 123

United Arab Emirates, 138

United Fruit Company, 60, 63, 79

United Nations, 77, 78

unlawful enemy combatants, 66, 144

Uruguay, 83, 88

US Air Force, 127

US Capitol, 61, 102, 117, 139

US Central Command (CENTCOM), 128

US Congress, 144; criticism of Nicaragua mission, 70–71; and Guevara, 82, 99; and Villa, 48; and War of 1898, 13

US Defense Intelligence Agency, 119

US Department of State, 39, 64, 113

US Department of War, 27, 51

US embassy: in Colombia, 103, 113, 118, 119; in Eritrea, 133; in Kenya, 136; in Tanzania, 136

US Green Berets, 92, 127

US House of Representatives, 99, 102

US Marines, 6, 58, 59, 62, 65, 67, 72, 73, 73; drawdown in Nicaragua, 68, 70–71, 74; and Guardia Nacional, 63–64, 66, 68, 70, 74; in Ocotal, 55, 57; Sandino depiction of, 61, 64, 66

US Senate, 15, 85, 127; criticism of Nicaragua mission, 70–71; testimony to regarding US mission in Philippines, 13, 16, 23

USA PATRIOT Act, 144

USS *Carl Vinson*, 148

USS *Cole*, 138

Vallegrande, 96

Velásquez, Jhon Jairo, 124

Venezuela, 78

Vera Cruz, 40

Vietnam, 78, 98

Vietnam War, 88, 100, 130

Villa, Pancho, 6, 32, 37, 61, 128, 137, 156, 157; American depictions of, 36, 39–41, 52; and American reactions to Columbus, NM, attack, 44–45; American reactions to death of, 53–54; assassination attempt on, 49; and attack on Columbus, NM, 42, 45–47;

Index   205

Villa, Pancho (continued)
and attack on Santa Isabel, 42–44; background of, 36; as bandit, 36, 39, 41, 47, 52–54; death of, 53; dehumanization of, 6, 45, 53; operations of during Mexican Revolution, 36, 38–41; as outlaw, 6, 32, 36, 53; pre-1916 relationship with United States, 38–39, 40–41; and race, 39, 41; as savage, 6, 41; US pursuit of, 43, 47–51. See also Mexico
Villistas, 45, 46, 49, 50, 52; and attack on Columbus, NM, 42, 47, 51; and attack on Santa Isabel, 42–44; and barbarism, 44
Villoldo, Gustavo, 87, 92
Virginia, 139, 153

Wag the Dog (movie), 137
Walker, John Walton, 42
Waller, Littleton "Tony," 10, 28
Wall Street, 57, 72
Wall Street Journal, 114, 136–37
warlords, 127, 133
War of 1812, 35
War of 1898 (Spanish-American War), 3, 11, 12–15, 44, 58
war on drugs, 102, 124–25, 158; modern origins of, 104; as US national security threat, 103, 104–5
war on terror. See global war on terror
Washington, George, 39, 73
Washington Post, 115–16, 136, 137; on bin Laden, 141, 148, 149; on Escobar, 103, 114, 122–23; on Guevara, 98; on Moro War, 30; on 9/11, 140; on Sandino, 72; on Villa, 53
water cure, 5, 21, 22
Wells, H. L., 20
West, Kanye, 123
Wheeler, Burton, 70
White House, 35, 61, 72, 104, 110, 137, 138, 139, 147
"white man's burden," 11
Wilson, Henry Lane, 38
Wilson, Woodrow, 46; administration of, 35–36, 38, 39, 40, 46, 47, 50; alliance with Villa, 38–41; and Punitive Expedition, 35–36, 51
Wood, Leonard, 26, 28, 29–31
Worcester, Dean, 18, 21
Worker's Party of America, 72
World's Fair (1904), 30
World Trade Center: 1993 attack on, 120, 133; 2001 attack on, 139
World War I, 31, 35, 46, 51, 67, 152
World War II, 31, 32, 50, 76, 134, 139
Wyoming, 142

Yankee, 71, 75, 83
Yazidis, 153
Yemen, 129, 132, 138
Yucatán Peninsula, 69

Zapata, Emiliano, 38, 46
Zedong, Mao, 81
Zenteno Anaya, Joaquín, 95, 96, 98

www.ingramcontent.com/pod-product-compliance
Lightning Source LLC
Chambersburg PA
CBHW021855230426
43671CB00006B/404